THE THEATRE
OF MARTIN M

M000285228

Patrick Lonergan is a lecturer in English at National University of Ireland, Galway. His first book, *Theatre and Globalization: Irish Drama in the Celtic Tiger Era*, won the 2008 Theatre Book Prize and a 2010 book award from the European Society for the Study of English. He is director of the Synge Summer School for Irish Drama, and has published and lectured widely on Irish theatre.

THE THEATRE AND FILMS OF MARTIN McDONAGH

Patrick Lonergan

Methuen Drama

Methuen Drama

Methuen Drama, an imprint of Bloomsbury Publishing Plc

1 3 5 7 9 10 8 6 4 2

First published in Great Britain in 2012 by Methuen Drama

Methuen Drama
Bloomsbury Publishing Plc
50 Bedford Square
London WC1B 3DP
www.methuendrama.com

ISBN 9781408136119 (paperback)
ISBN 9781408160596 (hardback)

A CIP catalogue record for this book is available from the British Library

Available in the USA from Bloomsbury Academic & Professional,
175 Fifth Avenue /3rd Floor, New York, NY10010.
www.BloomsburyAcademicUSA.com

Typeset by Country Setting, Kingsdown, Kent
Printed and bound in Great Britain by the MPG Books Group

For my mother Madeleine and in memory of my father Paddy

CONTENTS

5 Performance and critical perspectives

ACKNOWLEDGEMENTS

I wish to express my thanks to my home university, National University of Ireland, Galway, which granted me a period of sabbatical leave to allow me to complete this book. I am also grateful to the staff of the university's Hardiman Library, which holds the Druid Theatre Archive. And I must thank the staff of the Shakespeare Library in Stratford-upon-Avon, who provided very useful information about the premiere production of *The Lieutenant of Inishmore*. I am also very appreciative of the support of Druid Theatre company, especially from Thomas Conway, Garry Hynes, Rory Lorton and Sinead McPhillips.

Some of the research that this book draws on was completed as part of a research project on the internationalisation of Irish drama, which was funded by the Irish Research Council for the Humanities and Social Sciences. I gratefully acknowledge the Council's support.

Many of the ideas presented here were developed and clarified during conversations (often very heated ones) with colleagues and friends, especially Joan Dean, Karen Fricker, Nicholas Grene, Werner Huber, Eamonn Jordan, José Lanters, Martin Middeke, Karen O'Brien, Riana O'Dwyer, Shaun Richards, Tony Roche and Shelley Troupe. I also have to thank those people who have published some of my earlier work on McDonagh, especially Richard Rankin Russell and the editors of *Irish Studies Review*. And I am glad to be able to thank Jill Dolan, Stacy Wolf and the participants in Princeton's 2011 Global Irish Seminar for allowing me to discuss some of these ideas at a crucial stage in the book's composition.

My thanks to Mark Dudgeon at Methuen Drama for commissioning this work, and for supporting it (and me) at all stages during its preparation. Thanks also to Ross Fulton and Neil Dowden for their work on bringing the book to publication. I also wish to thank Martin McDonagh for permission to quote from *The Pillowman*, *In Bruges* and *A Behanding in Spokane*, and am also grateful to Charlotte Knight of Knight Hall Agency.

As ever, my family provided essential encouragement and much practical help, and I hope that my wife Therese and daughter Saoirse know how grateful I am. This book is dedicated to my parents: to my mother Madeleine, who did so much to foster and then share my love of theatre, and to the memory of my father, who passed away shortly before this book was completed. Many of Martin McDonagh's plays show that our parents' influence is inescapable; but unlike most of McDonagh's characters, that is an inevitability for which I'm very grateful.

ABBREVIATIONS

Quotations from the plays and screenplays of McDonagh are indicated by the following abbreviations, which correspond to the editions specified below.

BQ   *The Beauty Queen of Leenane* (London: Methuen Drama, 1996)

SC   *A Skull in Connemara* (London: Methuen Drama, 1997)

LW   *The Lonesome West* (London: Methuen Drama, 1997)

CI   *The Cripple of Inishmaan* (London: Methuen Drama, 1997)

LI   *The Lieutenant of Inishmore* (London: Methuen Drama, 2001)

PM   *The Pillowman* (London: Faber, 2003)

IB   *In Bruges* (London: Faber, 2007)

BS   A *Behanding in Spokane* (New York: Dramatists Play Service, 2011)

In addition, the abbreviation SS is used to refer to the film *Six Shooter* (Irish Film Board, 2005). The script of the film is not in print; quotations are taken directly from the film.

Abbreviations following other quotations in the text refer to titles listed in the Further Reading section at the end of this book.

INTRODUCTION

Martin McDonagh: facts and fictions

While I was completing the research for this book, I interviewed Garry Hynes, the great Irish director who introduced Martin McDonagh to the world when she premiered his first play, *The Beauty Queen of Leenane*, in 1996. We discussed a range of issues about McDonagh: his astonishing success both nationally and internationally, the hostile reaction he has received from many critics and academics, his ongoing popularity with audiences and performers everywhere, and so on. That discussion is reproduced later in this volume, but one point made by Hynes encapsulated perfectly the major argument that I wish to sustain throughout the book.

We'd been discussing the relationship between Mag and Maureen, the mother–daughter pairing at the centre of *The Beauty Queen of Leenane*. Those characters are now famous for their brutality towards each other: the mother Mag for vindictively destroying her daughter's chance of forming a loving relationship, and Maureen for beating Mag to death with a poker in reprisal. Yet one of the strangest features of *Beauty Queen* is that, despite their appalling treatment of each other, the two women clearly feel some sort of love for each other. 'There's no question that they love each other,' said Hynes. 'They are mother and daughter, after all.'

To illustrate that point, we began to talk about biscuits. One of the running jokes in the play is that Maureen keeps buying Kimberley biscuits for her mother, even though she considers them 'the most horrible biscuits in the world' (*BQ*, 24). 'I hate Kimberleys,' Maureen admits. 'I only get them to torment me mother' (24). Yet in the play's seventh scene, there's a brief moment when the two women appear to treat each other kindly: as I discuss in more detail later, Mag compliments Maureen's cooking, and she in turn appears to take some pleasure in her mother's being in a 'funny oul mood' (49). The pair continue to bicker with each other, but they do so without malice; there's a sense that they are almost enjoying the cut and thrust of the fighting. And then – 'smiling', as the stage directions state, Maureen offers Mag not a Kimberley but a shortbread finger.

It's easy to overlook this moment, but what Maureen is doing is offering her mother something *nice*: she is, in other words, not trying to 'torment' Mag as she normally does – she wants instead to break from that routine and to do something kind. Minutes later, of course, the interactions between the pair become more negative again, but Maureen's brief gesture allows the audience to understand that her instinct and desire is to treat her mother well: that she wants to behave better than she does, that she wants to change – that she may even be capable of changing.

This brief exchange also allows us to reconsider McDonagh's reputation. For many academic critics, McDonagh's inclusion of brand names such as Kimberley biscuits (not to mention his references to Australian soap operas, minor Irish celebrities, Hollywood movies and many other features of pop culture) shows that he is a typical postmodern writer, using a pastiche of styles to undermine the differences between high and low art. That style of pastiche – that throwing together of the kitsch with the literary – is often presented as evidence that McDonagh should be seen as doing for 1990s theatre what Quentin Tarantino did for 1990s film. Both artists, the argument goes, took apparently exhausted popular forms (Irish melodrama in McDonagh's case, the heist movie in Tarantino's) and revitalised them – often by knowingly and playfully putting clichés and other over-familiar motifs into strange new combinations. And because both McDonagh and Tarantino seemed playful, they were also open to the accusation that they were being insufficiently reverential – that by blending popular culture with high art they were trivialising the latter without elevating the former.

There is some value in thinking about McDonagh's work as exemplifying postmodern practices (as we'll see throughout this book, especially in José Lanters's essay in Part Five). Yet to see McDonagh as an indifferent *pasticheur* is to miss altogether his skill as a storyteller. The move from Kimberley biscuits to shortbread is a fine example of a technique McDonagh often uses more explicitly, whereby he establishes a pattern so that audiences will be inclined to predict what is going to happen – and he then achieves a strong emotional impact by suddenly deviating from that pattern. In performance, the reference to Kimberley biscuits is certainly funny *because* it seems so discordant with the sombre tone of most rural Irish dramas, *because* it seems so trivial and over-familiar. Yet when the play is directed and performed well, the sudden reference to shortbread can reveal Maureen's emotional depths, her hidden feelings, her potential to lead a better life – not to mention the possibility that there may be something in her mother that was once worth loving. For audiences around the world, such moments of poignancy and longing make *The Beauty Queen* and McDonagh's other plays much more than just simple black comedies.

As Hynes and I discussed this scene, she revealed that McDonagh had added the references to biscuits after the play had been drafted. We discussed the significance of the addition, and then Hynes suddenly paused and shook her head. 'How did someone who was only twenty-four years of age get to be such a skilled writer?' she asked.

And that question reveals the reason that I wanted to write this book: to show that, as Hynes put it, McDonagh is an extraordinarily skilled writer. For almost any other contemporary playwright or filmmaker of McDonagh's stature, such a task would be considered unnecessary – making an argument that is banal and obvious, while also adopting a very conservative approach to theatre criticism. Yet, one of the curious features of McDonagh's career to date is that he is admired far more by audiences and theatre-makers than he is by critics and academics. Of course, a great many writers enjoy popular success without being admired by critics – and, of course, there are many academics who love McDonagh's work, just as there are many theatre-goers who can't stand it. Nevertheless, there is a strange disconnection between McDonagh's reputation with audiences and his status among academics and critics. And this disconnection, I would propose, arises because we have yet to give sufficient attention to McDonagh's skills as a writer: to consider his work in terms of plotting, characterisation, patterning, language and so on. I don't have a definitive answer to the question of why he has not been given much credit for his accomplishments in those areas, but I will be making some tentative suggestions later in this book.

Yet it is worth reflecting on the amazing popular success of a writer whose first play appeared relatively recently, in 1996 – just a few weeks before McDonagh's twenty-sixth birthday. Since that time, his plays have been translated into more than forty languages; they have won dozens of awards, and they remain almost exceptionally popular with amateur and professional theatre-makers throughout the world. Indeed, it has been claimed that only Shakespeare is produced more often in America (though, as we'll see, it's best not to believe everything we read about McDonagh). His first short film, *Six Shooter*, appeared in 2005 and promptly won an Academy Award; his first full-length feature, *In Bruges*, was also nominated for an Oscar and won a Golden Globe. As I'll suggest throughout this book, the key reason for such success is McDonagh's talents as a storyteller. His plays and films are often inconclusive or ambiguous: but rather than frustrating his audiences, those features explain why his work is so popular. One of the conclusions I advance here is that this openness to interpretation is the major reason why McDonagh's work has so effortlessly crossed national and cultural boundaries, making him a truly global playwright. And I will also suggest that his success only makes sense when we think of McDonagh's work as functioning not on a page but in a theatre (or on a screen) – that is, before an audience.

This is not to suggest that I wish to dismiss or ignore the critical response to McDonagh; nor would I want to suggest that those who dislike McDonagh's plays and films are wrong to do so. Often, in fact, the features of his work that some people most love – his anarchism, his willingness to be provocative, his indifference to political correctness, his openness to interpretation – are the very reasons that others find his work so annoying. Indeed, as an academic who has written about and lectured on McDonagh often, I'm often amazed by the strength of the reactions his work generates. I first gave a paper on McDonagh in 2001, shortly after *The Lieutenant of Inishmore* premiered – and I put forward a version of the argument that appears later in this book: that the play is deliberately re-imagining some of the dominant tropes of Irish nationalism, that it demands of audiences that they think about their own tolerance of terrorism and the representation of violence through culture. In response, a delegate at the conference began to describe her experience of seeing the play in Stratford-upon-Avon earlier that year. As she tried to articulate her feelings of embarrassment and discomfort as an Irish person sitting in that English theatre, she became increasingly frustrated – until she finally declared that 'I just hate Martin McDonagh! Hate him!'

What struck me about that response is that there was no way for me to disagree with it: the person's sensation in the theatre was undoubtedly real, her views undoubtedly sincere. And in subsequent years, I have often been aware that the plays occasionally seem to produce such responses – not just among Irish people watching the work in Britain but in many other contexts. Notably (as I mention later), the distinguished American critic Hilton Als stated that he didn't know 'a single self-respecting black actor who wouldn't feel shame and fury' while watching *A Behanding in Spokane* (2010). If an Irish theatregoer or an African American actor feels 'shame and fury' while watching McDonagh's work, it is very difficult to claim that they are wrong.

But should they hold McDonagh responsible for such feelings? The key argument in this book is that the meanings of McDonagh's plays and films are only fully created when audiences engage imaginatively with what they see. But one consequence of that openness is that some members of the audience will construe the work's meaning in ways that can be offensive to *other* members of the audience, who may see the performance (and not the audience's reaction to it) as racist or bullying or anti-Irish or cruel or sexist. As I read the plays I fail to detect any evidence of anti-Irish sentiment, of racism, or indeed of cruelty – yet there is plenty of evidence that some productions of the plays have provoked precisely those reactions. Where does the responsibility for such reactions lie? This is a complex issue, and I will return to it in the Conclusion to this volume.

A further problem is that some of those responses have found their way into the academic scholarship. In particular, there has been an enormous amount of debate about whether McDonagh can be seen as an 'Irish' playwright – or, to put the idea more bluntly, whether he is laughing *with* the Irish (as great Irish dramatists like Synge, O'Casey,

Beckett and Friel have done), or *at* the Irish (as many English dramatists have done, from Shakespeare onwards). The major proponent of the latter view has been Mary Luckhurst, who wrote an article rather pointedly entitled 'Selling-(Out) to the English: Martin McDonagh's *Lieutenant of Inishmore*'. She argues that McDonagh is a 'thoroughly establishment figure who relies on monolithic, prejudicial constructs of rural Ireland to generate himself an income' (40). Quoting from a selection of McDonagh's interviews, Luckhurst presents the anti-Irish responses to *The Lieutenant* from the British press as evidence that the playwright is deliberately 'forging speech patterns and representations that build on prejudicial constructs [in Britain] of the Irish as little more than boneheaded buffoons' (38).

I don't agree with the points made in that article, but when I first read it I was struck by its similarity with the response to my conference paper, when the speaker did not say that she hated *The Lieutenant of Inishmore*: she said that she hated McDonagh. Similarly, Luckhurst attacks *The Lieutenant* not just on the basis of its form and content, but because of the actions of its author (as reported in the press). The major feature of her argument – and this is true of many of the people who attack McDonagh – is that she makes a link between audience response and authorial intention: she suggests that if McDonagh's plays promote anti-Irish prejudice in the theatre, he must himself be to blame. The question of whether an author is responsible for the many different responses his or her plays provoke is one of the key preoccupations of this book, as indeed it is a major feature of McDonagh's work from *The Pillowman* (2003) onwards. But what is also notable here is that the hostility is to McDonagh the man (and especially that he 'generates himself an income' from his work), and not to his plays. Indeed, it is notable that the most hostile responses to McDonagh tend to use audience response rather than textual analysis as evidence in support of their condemnation.

Such hostility probably owes something to McDonagh's media persona, and to the misrepresentation and misunderstanding of many of the comments he has made in press interviews. It's clear, both from his plays and from his public statements, that McDonagh can be flippant and perhaps somewhat sarcastic in conversation, especially when discussing his own work. So when he stated early in his career that he was interested in writing only because he wanted 'to avoid having a real job', it seemed likely (to me anyway) that he was joking. My assumption was that (as often happens with Irish people) his success was making him behave defensively, causing him to refute the accusation that he was taking himself too seriously before anyone had actually attacked him on those grounds. Yet such remarks are often presented as if they were intended to be understood literally, and so we find many critics rather sternly (and, to my mind, rather humour-lessly) complaining about what they perceive as McDonagh's arrogance. They react with fury to his suggestion that a lot of theatre is very bad (despite this being a fairly common complaint by other dramatists – Sam Shepard being a notable example). And when McDonagh said in 1997 that he'd only been to a handful of plays, the remark was construed as suggesting that he knew nothing about theatre (that is, that he had not *read* many plays). And again, that comment drew a great deal of negative criticism his way.

That said, many of the strongest claims against McDonagh arise from sloppy misreadings of his remarks. We are often told, for instance, that McDonagh has never read the plays of Synge, the Irish writer whose works seem to resemble his own so closely. That view comes from a misunderstanding of a statement made by McDonagh in 1997 – that he had not read Synge when he drafted his plays in 1994, but had certainly done so before the plays premiered (that is, while they were being re-drafted and rehearsed). I also constantly read newspaper articles and press releases that repeat the ridiculous claim that McDonagh is the first dramatist since Shakespeare to have four of his plays running simultaneously in London. That myth seems to have originated with a misreading of Mimi Kramer's remark that McDonagh was the only playwright, other than Shakespeare, to have four of his plays running simultaneously in London *during the summer of 1997*. One aim of this book will be quietly to refute such mis-conceptions, but I mention them now in order to point out that much of McDonagh's reputation arises from the preponderance of confus-ing, contradictory and often self-evidently absurd information in circulation about him.

The most controversial issues concerning McDonagh – Irishness, authorial intention and influence – are all presences in this book. I will suggest that his plays in particular engage with Irish society and culture in ways that are not often acknowledged – yet I also want to argue that the major significance of those works is their value for audiences internationally. For the most part, though, I have tried to sidestep the existing arguments about Irishness, hoping that by considering the basic issues of textual analysis and audience response I might highlight more important (and more interesting) features of the work.

Related to that strategy is my consideration of influence. I do occasionally note affinities and apparent allusions to other writers, Irish and non-Irish. There are, for instance, strong resemblances between McDonagh's plays and those of Synge – and there are also explicit references, as in McDonagh's choice of the name *The Lonesome West* for his fourth produced play: the line comes from Synge's *Playboy of the Western World* (1907). Yet the key presence that I want to trace is not that of an Irish author but of Harold Pinter. While there are obvious differences between these writers' works, I do want to assert the value of exploring areas of overlap between them, whether they seem coincidental (as in *The Beauty Queen of Leenane*), superficial (as in *The Pillowman*), or deliberate (as in *In Bruges*). What both writers share, I suggest, is a preoccupation with the relationship between authorial intention and audience interpretation: both, that is, set out to make us consider our own responsibilities as co-creators of the meanings before us.

Rather than organising the study thematically, I have instead opted simply to explore each work in turn. As is noted elsewhere, most of the plays were first drafted in 1994, so a strictly chronological ordering of the material does not seem necessary or useful. I have sought always to present the plays and scripts not just as words on a page but as lines to be delivered before an audience – but in order to make explicit the importance of the plays *as* plays, I have opted always to provide a section that specifically explores the works in production. My intention is that these sections should be seen as continuing the arguments advanced about the plays individually, and not as operating separately from them.

Given that a major purpose of this book is to stress the value of multiple interpretations of McDonagh, it seemed worthwhile to invite other scholars to contribute essays that would offer thematic perspectives on his work, especially when those perspectives differ from my own. Two of these essays present original approaches to subjects that are often considered in relation to McDonagh, as is the case with José Lanters's discussion of postmodernity and Eamonn Jordan's exploration of postcolonialism and Irish politics. I have also invited Joan Dean to consider issues of gender and Karen O'Brien to present an ecocritical reading of McDonagh – two approaches that have been presented occasionally in the past and which (it seemed to me) merited the kind of closer attention here provided.

A great many other approaches could have been included. There is a growing body of work on the representation of disability in McDonagh's plays – not just in the obvious case of *The Cripple of Inishmaan*, but also in the presentation of mental illness in *Beauty Queen* and *The Pillowman*. And there is also a fascinating body of work on the production of McDonagh around the world, which has traced the interpretation (and re-imagining) of his plays in Estonia, Belgium, Japan, Italy and elsewhere. I have included some references to this work in the list of Further Reading.

My hope, however, is that this study might stimulate new approaches to the performance, reception and analysis of McDonagh. I do argue that his plays and films are open to interpretation – but do not suggest that they are therefore meaningless or that all interpretations of the plays are equally valid. Nevertheless, I gladly concede that this book aims to present only one set of interpretations on the work, and that many other perspectives and counter-readings exist. As a theatregoer, the aspect McDonagh's work that I most love is that it sends people out into the street afterwards *thinking*, and often having to invent their own stories in response to what they've seen. While writing this book, I witnessed this phenomenon at a Galway production of *The Cripple of Inishmaan*, where I overheard long conversations in the bar afterwards – about what Billy *really* did in America, about how long he lived afterwards, about whether Jim Finnegan's daughter was really a slut, about what Helen did to the curate she ruptured. I'm also constantly struck by debates about *In Bruges* – about whether Colin Farrell's character survives after the action concludes, about whether his voiceovers are made from a hospital bed or London or the afterlife. Such acts of invention are to me the sign of a great story: that we, the audience, consider the characters to be just like real people, and are thus compelled to imagine the rest of the story for ourselves.

I
THE LEENANE TRILOGY

Leenane: murder capital of Europe

The village of Leenane can be found in northern Galway, just on the border with County Mayo. It's a very small place. There are a couple of narrow streets that are mostly used by tourist coaches on their way somewhere else. There's a hotel, a few shops (one of which doubles-up as a post office), a couple of pubs and a church with a small cemetery in front of it. There is no police station. Nor, strictly speaking, is there a lake: instead the village overlooks Killary Harbour, which is described by countless tourist guides as 'Ireland's only fjord'. Those books will also tell you that Leenane is one of Ireland's most beautiful places – and not inaccurately. The village is hemmed in by the Connemara mountains, its harbour creating an atmosphere of calmness and tranquillity that seems to reflect back outwards on to the landscape. There are a few small cottages dotted around the nearby fields, but the scene is otherwise unspoiled. It is a lovely place to visit, especially during summertime.

If you were to visit Leenane and stand on its main street, you'd probably find it very difficult to relate the real place to the dystopic hellhole conjured up by Martin McDonagh in the three plays that became known as *The Leenane Trilogy*: *The Beauty Queen of Leenane* (1996), *A Skull in Connemara* (1997) and *The Lonesome West* (1997). And if you got talking to any of the local people, you'd probably notice immediately that although their words are accented, they sound nothing like the characters in McDonagh's plays: you won't hear quite as many obscure slang words, the syntax isn't quite so disorderly – and you may wait a long time before anyone uses the word 'feck'. The people of Leenane don't seem to mind McDonagh's presentation of their village very much; as we'll see later, *The Beauty Queen* was actually performed there in 1996. That said, they don't exactly promote the association either.

One of the accusations most often levelled against McDonagh is that his plays misrepresent Ireland and the Irish. But standing in the real Leenane, it quickly becomes obvious how silly that accusation is: *of course* McDonagh's Leenane is not like the real place; *of course* his characters are not like the real people who live here. McDonagh's

Leenane – *of course!* – is an imagined location, bearing little resemblance to the real Galway village.

Why, then, does McDonagh set his plays in that recognisable locale? There are many possible explanations for his decision, but perhaps the most useful is offered by Shaun Richards, who suggests that the choice of Leenane allows McDonagh to engage in 'close intertextual referencing'. What Richards means by that is that the unified real-world setting allows 'characters and incidents seen in one play to become the topic of conversation in another' (Richards, 2003: 204). It is not necessary to have seen one play in the *Trilogy* in order to appreciate the others fully but, as Richards points out, there are some intriguing links between the three scripts. Hence, our understanding of one play can be conditioned by our knowledge of the other two. By locating the play in one real-world setting (the argument goes), McDonagh encourages us to make such connections.

And those connections can be very interesting. If we watch or read the three plays in order, we're likely to feel that they are becoming increasingly violent. In *The Beauty Queen*, a daughter kills her mother with a poker, but that event is shown offstage and occurs very late in the action. In *Skull*, most of the violence again occurs offstage, but there is a scene in which its main protagonist Mick Dowd joins with a young man called Mairtin Hanlon to smash several human skeletons to bits with mallets. By the time we get to *The Lonesome West*, we may feel that we've descended even further into anarchy. In that play much of the violence *is* performed on stage, yet it's often cartoonish and it rarely results in lasting damage to anyone.

Nevertheless, our expectations of what will happen in the final play are likely to have been conditioned by the violence presented in the previous two. In *Beauty Queen*, the violence comes as a shock: we see the forty-year-old Maureen torturing her aged mother, but we don't really expect the murder that concludes the play. And in *Skull*, we're never fully sure if Mick is guilty of having killed his wife. In both plays, then, murder is something that will surprise and confuse the audience. Yet in *The Lonesome West* we're faced with a reversal of that situation: the two mad brothers Valene and Coleman seem overwhelmingly *likely* to kill each other – but they don't actually do so. There are many ways of interpreting the development of the theme of violence across the three plays, but the important point is that such a development does actually take place.

Also important is that a character in one play will often be referred to in another. These allusions are usually brief – and they will probably go unnoticed by many audience members – but they can deepen our understanding of the characters. For instance, in *The Lonesome West* Valene reveals that Maureen Folan (from *Beauty Queen*) once wanted to ask Coleman to go on a date with her. That revelation changes the way we think about both Connor brothers, but it also changes our understanding of Maureen, showing that her desire to form a loving relationship in *Beauty Queen* had been thwarted at least once before. *Beauty Queen* and *Skull* also mention the lamentable Father Welsh, who is always referred to as 'Father Welsh Walsh Welsh'. That repeated joke in the first two plays shows that Welsh is not respected by any of his parishioners, adding weight to his claim that Leenane is a town in which 'God has no jurisdiction'. But it also means that audiences will be predisposed to find Welsh a little ridiculous even before he finally appears on stage in *The Lonesome West*: they've already been laughing at him during the previous two plays, after all.

This accumulation of such information allows us to compare characters, themes and situations across the three plays. For example, each of the three plays features conflict between brothers: Ray and Pato in *Beauty Queen*, Thomas and Mairtin in *Skull*, and Valene and Coleman in *Lonesome West*. Superficially, the three relationships seem similar. Yet Mairtin's reaction to the suicide of his brother in *Lonesome West* shows that even when two siblings appear to hold each other in contempt, they may still love each other. Audiences who have seen *A Skull in Connemara* are likely to be quite shocked by the tender way in which Thomas and Mairtin are discussed in *Lonesome West* – and that shock will in turn force them to reassess what they know about *Skull*, while also encouraging them to believe that Father Welsh might be right to think that Valene and Coleman can retrieve their love for each other.

The purpose of the Leenane setting, then, is to give unity, credibility and depth to the three plays by rooting them all in one location. It might be argued that McDonagh could have achieved this effect by setting the plays anywhere – and to an extent, that is true. But, in a way, that is exactly McDonagh's point. As we shall see, one of the key features of the development of the *Trilogy* is that McDonagh broadens his focus from one play to the next, moving from the individual in the first play to the community in the second, and then on to the whole of humanity in the final one. His point appears to be that the plays could indeed have been set anywhere: that, far from being anomalous, the people of Leenane are perhaps not all that different from the people of Galway city – or from the people of Dublin, London, New York, Sydney, Toronto or any the other places where the *Trilogy* has found an audience.

What follows, then, is a discussion of each of the plays in turn – an attempt to think about them *not* as realistic depictions of Irish life, but instead as collectively offering an analysis of the conditions that determine human relationships. In a final section on the *Trilogy* in production, I consider the plays both in their own right and together – and return again to the problem of the depiction of the 'real' Ireland. But the argument I wish to advance first is that the plays force a reconsideration of authorial intention. McDonagh, I want to suggest, is not attempting to convey a message about the real village of Leenane, but rather his plays use that setting to anchor an exploration of major themes: love, religion and the search for meaning. But what is essential is that those plays only become meaningful when audiences take upon themselves the responsibility of helping to create the plays' meanings.

Homecomings: *The Beauty Queen of Leenane*

Speaking in 1967, Harold Pinter described his great drama *The Homecoming* as being 'about love and lack of love'. His play explores the consequences that arise when a returned migrant arrives at his family home with a new wife – an incident that causes that family to engage in actions that will provoke both compassion and contempt in the audience. 'There's no question that the family behave[s] very calculatingly and pretty horribly to each other and to the returning son,' Pinter states. 'But they do it out of the texture of their lives and for other reasons which are not evil but slightly desperate' (quoted in Hewes, 1967).

There are many differences between *The Beauty Queen of Leenane* and *The Homecoming*, but Pinter's words offer us one useful way of thinking about Martin McDonagh's first produced work. At the heart of McDonagh's play is the appalling relationship between forty-year-old Maureen Folan (the eponymous beauty queen) and her mother Mag. Like Pinter's characters, Mag and Maureen are 'pretty horrible' to each other. And, as in *The Homecoming*, their already dysfunctional relationship is placed under irreparable strain due to the unexpected arrival of an outsider: the new wife Ruth in *The Homecoming* and, in *Beauty Queen*, the returned migrant Pato Dooley, who offers the possibility of love to Maureen but only if she abandons Ireland and her mother. Just as Pinter allows us to empathise with thoroughly unlikeable characters, McDonagh shows a remarkable ability to elicit sympathy for Mag and Maureen even as we condemn them for their brutality towards each other. Mag belittles and manipulates her daughter; she destroys Maureen's last (and possibly also her first) real opportunity to form a loving relationship with a man. In response, Maureen burns Mag's hand with boiling vegetable oil, and eventually beats her to death with a poker, showing no remorse afterwards. Yet the audience understands that these actions arise not out of 'evil' but from 'desperation' and from the 'texture' of these women's lives. This is because, to a great extent, the characters in *Beauty Queen* are as much motivated by 'love and lack of love' as are the characters in *The Homecoming*.

By focusing on those intense emotional states – the desire for love, the desperation that results from its absence – McDonagh intertwines the two major themes of *Beauty Queen*: emigration and the relationship between parent and child. In the play, the feelings of migrants for their home country and the feelings of children towards their parents are placed into a synecdochical relationship with each other. In other words, one theme illustrates the other: we learn something about the emigrant's attitude to Ireland by observing the relationship between Mag and Maureen – but their relationship in turn allows us to think of emigration from Ireland as operating in almost Oedipal terms, as involving a dysfunctional parent–child dynamic. Mag and Ireland have a similar impact on Maureen's life: both are damaged and repressive and ought to have been abandoned years before, but continue to exercise a disproportionate influence over the direction of her life.

McDonagh makes clear even before the action begins that Maureen's existence is dominated by things that should belong to the past, and which therefore prevent her from creating a decent future for herself. His description of the set features a television and radio (signifying the influence of the outside world), but also includes several old-fashioned icons of Irishness: a touristy tea-towel, a crucifix, photos of the Kennedy brothers. Those icons will quickly be exposed as empty signifiers – as signposts pointing the audience in wrong directions.

Hence, despite the presence of the crucifix, it soon becomes obvious that religion is not a significant presence in any of the characters' lives. Mag says bluntly that she doesn't like the local priest Father Welsh – who is defended by Pato's brother Ray, but only on the basis that Welsh is less violent than older priests are: 'It's usually only the older priests go punching you in the head,' Ray observes (*BQ*, 14). 'There was a priest the news Wednesday had a babby with a Yank!' announces Mag moments later (14). Mag's train of thought is interesting – she moves immediately from the idea of being punched in the head to having children – but her words are also an obvious reference to the Bishop of Galway Eamon Casey, who was forced to resign in 1992 when it was revealed that he had fathered a child. Casey's actions caused outrage in Ireland, but for Mag and Ray they are inconsequential, a boring subject even as gossip. 'It'd be hard to find a priest who hasn't had a babby with a Yank,' states the clearly unimpressed Ray (14).

Also on the wall are photographs of Jack and Bobby Kennedy. In Irish drama, the Kennedys are strongly associated with emigration, notably in the play *Conversations on a Homecoming* by Tom Murphy (premiered by Druid Theatre in 1985). And in Irish culture generally the Kennedy family are seen as representing an Irish success story: they left the country in relative poverty in the first half of the nineteenth century, and had made it to the White House within four generations. Yet that success story had a tragic ending: both J.F.K. and Robert Kennedy were assassinated, after all. So the presence of their photograph reminds us that the promise offered by emigration will not always be fulfilled. McDonagh reminds us of that fact throughout the play, especially in his characterisation of Pato – but he's also using the set requirements to signal to the audience that his characters are stuck in the past. The world of the play is the early 1990s, not the 1960s: just as the crucifix represents a barely remembered and increasingly irrelevant religion, so does the image of the Kennedys stand for a period of political optimism that is long past, and has no bearing on contemporary Ireland.

And just as the crucifix and photo seem like relics from a half-forgotten past, so will we find as the first scene develops that *all* forms of Irish culture operate similarly: they are not a vibrant part of the characters' lives, but are a barely remembered presence that really ought to have died off long ago. This attitude is made obvious in a debate between Mag and Maureen about the Irish language. Mag dismisses Irish as 'nonsense' (8), a suggestion that Maureen reacts angrily to, saying 'It's Irish you should be speaking in Ireland' (8). But, as we discover later in the play, Mag will always prioritise personal survival over sentimental attachments, so it is unsurprising that she values Irish only in practical terms: 'Where would Irish get you going for a job in England? Nowhere,' she says (9). For Mag, speaking Irish is an impediment to achieving financial security – something that can only be achieved through emigration to England or the United States. In contrast, Maureen's loyalty to Irish is based on a grievance that she is unwilling to forget: 'If it wasn't for the English stealing our language, and our land, and our God-knows-what, wouldn't it be we wouldn't need to go over there begging for jobs and for handouts?' she asks (9). The irony here, of course, is that the entire conversation is carried out in English: Maureen supports the Irish language in principle but appears incapable of supporting it in practice. It is also ironic that both women appear to agree on one point: that it is impossible to make a decent living in Ireland – a fact which both undermines and explains Maureen's apparently patriotic sentiments.

Another ghostly presence in the play is traditional Irish music, as is particularly notable with McDonagh's repeated use of 'The Spinning Wheel', a song recorded by Delia Murphy in 1939. Pato and Maureen agree that the song is 'creepy', and seem inclined to dismiss it as irrelevant: 'They don't write songs like that any more,' says Pato. 'Thank Christ' (28). He identifies much more with the music of the Pogues, the London-Irish group which blended punk and traditional Irish music in such songs as 'The Body of an American', which Pato sings in the play's third scene. Yet there is a curious affinity between Maureen's life and the story told in 'The Spinning Wheel'. Like *Beauty Queen* itself, Murphy's song is about two women living in rural Ireland: a blind old woman and her granddaughter Eileen. As the song develops, we learn that Eileen longs to escape from her grandmother's influence so that she can be with her lover. When it is first played in *Beauty Queen*, it seems to offer hope for Maureen and Pato (even if it does sound creepy). It tells of how Eileen successfully tricks her grandmother and is roving in the moonlight with her lover, seeming to suggest that Maureen herself might escape from Mag to be with Pato.

Yet when we hear the song for the second time, in the play's final moments, it takes on a different meaning. 'Maureen gently rocks in the chair until the middle of the fourth verse,' writes McDonagh in the play's last stage direction (65–6). By allowing the movement of Maureen's body to harmonise with the rhythm of the song, McDonagh suggests that Maureen is identifying with the past rather than seeking to create a new future – that is, he is signalling that, rather than escaping Mag, Maureen has effectively *become* her mother. This traditional Irish song seems to symbolise Maureen's entrapment – just as Pato's identification with the music of the Pogues foreshadows his own departure to America, and opens up the possibility of his having a better life (though as is mentioned later in the discussion of *Six Shooter*, it's not entirely clear whether things turned out well for Pato).

The need to escape the past is felt by all the play's characters, and is closely related to McDonagh's treatment of the theme of emigration. Both Pato and Maureen have spent time working in England, a place where neither felt at home, and in which neither found happiness. Their problems may have occurred because both characters were isolated by language. Maureen mentions sadly that she was often insulted due to her nationality. 'Half of the swearing I didn't even understand,' she admits. 'I had to have a black woman explain it to me. Trinidad she was from' (36). Similarly, when Pato struggles to spell the word 'gangerman' (a London colloquialism for a foreman on a building site), he reveals his isolation from his fellow workers. 'It is not a word we was taught in school,' he observes poignantly – and, by using the singular 'was' after the plural 'we', he reinforces our awareness of his difficulty with speaking English correctly (40). Such comments place Mag and Maureen's debate about Irish in an interesting context: even though Pato and Maureen have abandoned Irish, the language lingers on in their use of English – in their syntax, vocabulary and pronunciation. Like traditional Irish music, like Catholicism – like so many other forms of Irish culture in *The Beauty Queen* – the Irish language has a zombie-like presence in the lives of McDonagh's characters: it should be dead, but it continues to exert an influence. English may have allowed Pato and Maureen to emigrate, but the spectral influence of the Irish language prevents them from ever being fully at home there.

Yet Pato and Maureen do not feel at home in Leenane either. Pato often struggles to express himself, but he acquires a strange eloquence when speaking of his life in England:

> When I'm over there in London and working in rain and it's
> more or less cattle I am, and the young fellas cursing over
> cards and drunk and sick, and the oul digs over there, all pee-
> stained mattresses and nothing to do but watch the clock . . .
> When it's there I am, it's here I wish I was, of course. (26)

That simple repetition of the word 'and' brilliantly emphasises the monotony of Pato's life. Yet he knows that the Ireland he imagines in his London bedsit is nothing like the real place. 'When it's here I am,' he says, speaking of Leenane, 'it isn't *there* I want to be, of course not. But I know it isn't here I want to be either' (26).

Pato explains that his desire to leave Leenane is caused not by the place itself but by its inhabitants:

> Of course it's beautiful here, a fool can see. The mountains
> and the green, and people speak. But when everybody knows
> everybody else's business . . . I don't know. (*Pause.*) You

can't kick a cow in Leenane without some bastard holding a grudge twenty year. (27)

Several tensions are established in Pato's complaint. The attractiveness of the landscape is contrasted with the vindictiveness of the Leenane people; the way in which Pato feels like 'cattle' in London is reformulated in his suggestion that you can't 'kick a cow' in Leenane; the desire to be in Leenane when he is London is replaced by the desire to be anywhere *but* Leenane when he is actually in that place. For Pato, Ireland is a place that is bearable only when re-imagined from the safe vantage point of a foreign country.

That final rejection by Pato of his home town may remind the audience of something said earlier in the play by Maureen. 'Sometimes *I dream*,' she tells her mother, trailing off:

> **Mag**   Of being a . . . ?
> **Maureen**   Of anything! (*Pause. Quietly.*) Of anything. Other than this. (20)

Just as Pato rejects Leenane but cannot name an alternative destination for himself (until the end of the play, of course), so Maureen finds herself wishing she could *be* anything – except herself. These words imply that, to a great extent, Maureen considers herself to be totally without value. So there is a nihilism evident in Pato and Maureen's attitudes. Maureen's inability to imagine how to be someone else is what ultimately dooms her to become just like her mother. But Pato's ability to find a place to live – Boston (the home of the Kennedys) – gives him freedom.

Yet despite her negativity of outlook, Maureen is one of the most sympathetic characters in *The Leenane Trilogy*, at least until the penultimate scene of *Beauty Queen*, that is. She shows an interest in other people and places which marks her out as different from almost everyone around her, as evident (for example) when she claims to have preferred Bobby Kennedy to J.F.K. 'He seemed to be nicer to women,' she says, before qualifying her opinion with the statement that 'I haven't read up on it' (55). The audience will remember that Maureen has spoken already of her interest in reading. 'There has to be more to a man than just being good in bed,' she tells Mag. 'Things in common too you do have to have, y'know, like what books do you be reading, or what are your politics and the like' (50). It's true that Maureen's remarks are made in an attempt to deceive her mother about the failure of her relationship with Pato, but we also sense her capacity to engage with the outside world – and will note the way in which she appears to value the knowledge that can be gained from 'reading up' on things. And of course, we also glimpse briefly the loneliness she feels when she praises one of the Kennedys for being kind to women.

McDonagh gives many others signs of Maureen's intelligence. She uses fewer slang words than almost any other character in the *Trilogy* and (unlike Pato) is rarely lost for words. She appears to mock Mag's use of the diminutive 'biteen' in the play's first scene: again, unlike almost every other character in the *Trilogy*, she rarely uses the Hiberno-English convention of placing the suffix '-een' at the end of a word (described in more detail in the discussion of Hiberno-English later in this book). Later, she displays an intolerance of Mag's misuse of the word 'prerogative': 'Don't go using big words you don't understand,' she snaps (22). So it appears that McDonagh wants his audience to understand that Maureen is capable of transcending her circumstances – and that she is frustrated by being surrounded by people who are less intelligent than she is.

That capacity to change is revealed most movingly when Maureen dresses up to meet Pato, fleetingly allowing herself to believe him when he calls her a 'beauty queen' (25). By wearing a short black skirt, Maureen is asserting and calling attention to her own sexuality, but she is also rejecting her reputation within Leenane. As Ray later states, Maureen 'does wear horrible clothes. And everyone agrees' (44) – that is, she is seen as being anything *but* a beauty queen by the other inhabitants of Leenane. Our awareness of their contempt for her appearance is reinforced in *The Lonesome West* when Coleman describes her as a 'thin-lipped ghost, with the hair-style of a frightened red ape' (*LW*, 61) – harsh words from a man who believes that criticising someone's hairstyle is an insult that 'can never be excused' (*LW*, 34). So Maureen is not just trapped by her mother, but also by the small-mindedness of the people of Leenane. McDonagh suggests that the cruelty and violence in his plays is not caused by 'evil', but (to re-use Pinter's words) by the 'texture' of his characters' lives. Leenane, he shows, would drive any kind person to murder, suicide or insanity – as we discover again with Mick in *A Skull in Connemara* and Girleen and Father Welsh in *The Lonesome West*.

Even Ray Dooley – one of the most foolish people in the *Trilogy* – shows an awareness that Leenane has a corrupting influence on its inhabitants. 'There are plenty of other things just as dangerous' as drugs, he tells Maureen:

> **Maureen** (*wary*)   Things like what, now?
> **Ray** (*pause. Shrugging*)   This bastarding town for one.
> **Maureen** (*pause. Sadly*)   Is true enough.
> **Ray**   Just that it takes seventy years. Well, it won't take me seventy years. I'll tell you that. No way, boy. (*Pause.*) How old was your mother, now, when she passed?
> **Maureen**   Seventy, aye. Bang on. (59)

Maureen's 'bang on' seems to indicate some agreement with the point that Ray is making implicitly: Mag's death was primarily caused not by her daughter, but by the 'bastarding town' of Leenane.

So it's worth considering the extent to which Maureen can be held responsible for her mother's death: she killed Mag under the influence of a conversation with Pato which was entirely a hallucination, after all. In her fantasised discussion with Pato, he tells her that 'We do still have a problem, what to do with your oul mam, there . . . Would an oul folks' home be too harsh?' Maureen responds as follows:

> 'It wouldn't be too harsh but it would be too expensive.'
> 'What about your sisters so?' 'Me sisters wouldn't have the bitch. Not even a half-day at Christmas to be with her can them two stand. They clear forgot her birthday this year as well as that. 'How do you stick her without going off your rocker?' they do say to me. Behind her back, like. (*Pause.*)
> 'I'll leave it up to yourself,' Pato says. He was on the train be

this time, we was kissing out the window, like they do in films. 'I'll leave it up to yourself so, whatever you decide. If it takes a month, let it take a month. And if it's finally you decide you can't bear to be parted from her and have to stay behind, well, I can't say I would like it, but I'd understand. But if even a year it has to take for you to decide, it is a year I will be waiting, and won't be minding the wait.' 'It won't be a year it is you'll be waiting, Pato,' I called out then, the train was pulling away. 'It won't be a year nor yet nearly a year. It won't be a week! (56)

Audience members familiar with the real Leenane will suspect immediately that this entire scene is imagined: there is no train station in or anywhere near Leenane, so it appears that Maureen is inventing the incident based on (to use her own words) things that 'they do in films'. Yet the purpose of her fantasy is to justify the decision to murder her mother, who cannot be placed in a nursing home, and who won't be cared for by her other daughters. In her madness, Maureen is dramatising her conviction that the only way for her to live is to murder her mother. Her tragedy is that those actions are futile: killing Mag makes no difference – a point McDonagh grimly underlines by revealing in the play's last minutes that the other daughters did not forget Mag's birthday after all. So Maureen kills Mag not from hate, but because she feels she has no other choice: a form of entrapment which causes her to go mad.

This is an important point, since the success of any production of this play lies partially in audiences' belief that Maureen and Mag do appear to feel some sort of residual love for each other – even if those positive feelings have been perverted and overwhelmed by years of resentment, jealousy and bitterness. The trace of that affection is most evident in the play's seventh scene – which also happens to feature the play's most violent moment (emphasising McDonagh's ability to achieve dramatic effect by working with strong contrasts – something we encounter often in his plays). In this scene, Maureen has prepared dinner for Mag, who compliments her on the meal (possibly in response to Maureen's apparent threat to put her in a nursing home).

The pair begin to argue with each other – but the stage directions suggest that they are almost enjoying the sparring, rather like Beckett's Didi and Gogo taking pleasure in insulting each other because it passes the time in *Waiting for Godot* (Beckett, 2006: 70). Mag, we are told, 'smiles and nods' at Maureen, who says while 'laughing' that 'It's a crazy oul mood you're in for yourself tonight!' – and then, 'smiling', she offers her mother a shortbread finger (50–1). Maureen's smiling and laughing and her offer to her mother of a biscuit (a nice one, rather than one of those that she buys only to torment Mag) suggests that her attitude towards her mother is not entirely negative.

Of course, this scene soon takes a very nasty turn, as Maureen uncovers the fact that Mag had burned Pato's letter to her. Yet even in the ensuing argument there is a moment of empathy between the two when Mag explains how she knew that Maureen had been lying when she claimed to have lost her virginity to Pato. 'You still do have the look of a virgin about you you always have had,' says Mag, adding 'You always will' (52). Those last three words, importantly, are spoken 'without malice' according to the stage directions. This suggests that they must instead be spoken with something approaching pity or, at the very least, empathy.

Such moments have a powerful impact in performance because they contrast so strongly with the normal interactions between the pair. Perhaps again showing the influence of Pinter, McDonagh imposes an ambiguity of meaning upon all of the Mag and Maureen's early discussions, so that apparently innocent actions or words can take on an altogether more sinister tone when the audience watches or reads the play for a second time. For instance, when Maureen switches on a kettle in the play's second scene, her action seems innocuous enough – yet she is clearly trying to threaten that she will scald Mag again, as is obvious from the speed with which Mag stops lying and reveals that 'wee Ray Dooley' had called to the house once the kettle goes on (17). In the following moments, Maureen picks up on one of Mag's phrases – 'ah no' – and repeats it several times (17–19), each repetition making clearer that she does not believe a word her mother is saying, and building up towards the inevitable outburst of temper: 'Arsing me around, eh? Interfering with my life again? Isn't it enough I've had to be on beck and call for you every day for the past twenty year? Is it one evening out you begrudge me?' (19)

Mag, then, is obviously frightened of Maureen, but she in turn exploits Maureen's feelings of guilt for having scalded her. In the play's first scene, for example, Mag reacts to the suggestion that she should make her own Complan by telling Maureen that 'the hot water too I do be scared of. Scared I may scould meself' (6). We might form the impression here that Mag considers herself helpless. But the stage direction state that Maureen gives Mag a 'slight look' in response to this statement, implying that she knows that Mag's words are an allusion to the violence inflicted upon her previously (6). It seems apparent that Mag's revenge for that violence is to force her daughter to behave like her 'blessed fecking skivvy', as Maureen puts it (7). So both Maureen and Mag show an ability to use innuendo and ambiguity of language in an effort to manipulate and intimidate each other – and we also see how Mag transforms her position of apparent weakness (her physical frailty and the wound she suffered as a result of Maureen's rage) as a way of asserting her power over her daughter.

This ambiguity of meaning pervades the play. For instance, the audience might be charmed when Maureen turns up the radio to disguise the sound of her 'smooching' with Pato in the play's third scene (24) – yet McDonagh later reveals that this is a tactic she has used before, and will use again, to drown out the sound of her mother's screams (53, 55). And just as we must reconsider the characters' actions on a second viewing of the play, so must we re-evaluate the significance of certain objects. Ray's assertion that the poker is 'going to waste in this house' (45) – because, he says, it could be used to commit acts of violence – will seem sickeningly ironic by the end of the play. Indeed, McDonagh moves the action into the realms of Greek tragedy (as well as Irish melodrama) when Ray is asked to deliver a letter from Pato to Maureen, but gives it instead to Mag. 'May God strike me dead if I do open it,' Mag says. 'Only He'll have no need to strike me dead because I won't be opening it' (47). Like King Oedipus promising to punish the person who committed the crime for which he himself is responsible, Mag correctly but unwittingly predicts the consequences that will result from her interference in her daughter's life.

To watch *The Beauty Queen of Leenane* for a second time therefore involves a realisation that almost everything we believed to be true has proven false. The material objects in the set – the poker, the crucifix, the radio, the kettle, the stove – are all shown to function in ways that will surprise and unsettle the audience. Apparently offhand and innocent remarks turn out to have been thinly veiled threats; Mag's clichéd 'may God strike me dead' is shown to be an act of hubris; Ray's regret for the 'waste' of the poker appears cruelly ironic. And we are forced too to re-evaluate the characters. As mentioned above, Ray is clearly the play's least intelligent character, but he also has a more insightful understanding of Leenane than do any of the other people in the play. The apparent sincerity of Pato's feelings for Maureen is painfully undermined by the announcement that he has decided to marry someone else, only weeks after asking Maureen to join him in Boston (62). And our willingness to view Maureen as a victim of her mother's vindictiveness will inevitably be thrown into confusion by the play's last three scenes.

And we must, above all, re-evaluate the meaning of the word 'home'. Mag's treatment of her daughter is, of course, astonishingly bad. Yet it seems to be based to some extent on a fear of being institutionalized: she burns Pato's letter to Maureen not out of malice, but from fear of Pato's suggestion that she should be placed in care. 'I'd die before I'd let meself be put in a home,' Mag tells her daughter – prophetically, as it turns out (48). Her use of the word 'home' in this fashion again emphasises the links between Ireland and Mag: Mag refuses to be placed in a 'home'; Maureen's great shame was that 'I was in a home there a while, now, after a bit of a breakdown I had' (35). Throughout the play, the word 'home' has shifting meanings, from the literal sense to Ray's threatening use of the phrase 'close to home' (46), to the complex use of the word in relation to emigration. The word 'home' is used more often than almost any other in the play – but what is shocking is how negative its connotations are for Mag and Maureen. 'Home' for the Folan women is a place to be avoided at all costs, a place to be rescued from, a place quite like a prison.

The tragedy, then, is that Maureen ends the play still at home: she may have killed her mother, but because she has not also left Ireland, her problems remain unsolved. As stated earlier, the conclusion shows us Maureen sitting in her mother's rocking chair, listening to 'The Spinning Wheel'. She then stands up, picks up and caresses a dusty suitcase, and carries it into the hall of the house. McDonagh's audience will immediately see resonances from other plays. In Maureen's last message to Pato – 'The beauty queen of Leenane says *goodbye*' (65) – we find a woman lamenting the loss of an idealised male figure, with its slight echo if the finale of Synge's *Playboy of the Western World*, when Pegeen Mike laments the loss of Christy Mahon.

And of course another famous play that concludes with a woman walking offstage is Ibsen's *A Doll's House* (1879). But is Maureen, like Ibsen's Nora, departing, suitcase in hand, into an uncertain but more authentic future? Or does her removal of the suitcase from the playing area signify that the possibility of leaving Leenane is being discounted for ever? McDonagh tells us only that she walks into the 'hall', but we have no way of knowing whether she does so in order to leave the house or put away the suitcase for good. We listen to the song to its conclusion, watching the empty chair rocking as the lights slowly fade to black.

This ambiguity of meaning is one of the key features of McDonagh's work. As I argue throughout this book, his art aims constantly to confound his audience's expectations and assumptions; it repeatedly reveals to us our own capacity to be manipulated and deceived by lazy thinking, to be misled by our glib acceptance of the validity of over-familiar images and over-used literary conventions.

In its entirety, then, *The Beauty Queen of Leenane* works to re-educate the audience, to force us to think again about what we know, about how we interpret reality. By giving his play an inconclusive ending, McDonagh is passing over to the audience the responsibility for creating meaning for ourselves: it is up to us to determine what happens next for Maureen. For as we see in his next play, *A Skull in Connemara*, ambiguity and uncertainty impose responsibilities not just on McDonagh's characters – but on his audiences too.

All the dead voices: *A Skull in Connemara*

The Beauty Queen of Leenane portrayed Ireland as a place where things that ought to be dead are still clinging desperately to life – from the Irish language to Catholicism to Mag Folan herself. *A Skull in Connemara* pushes that vision of place one step further, showing that in Leenane even the dead cannot rest in peace: their graves will be violated, their memory defamed and their remains stripped of all dignity. The murder that concludes *Beauty Queen* appeared an act of madness and desperation: Maureen seemed like an exceptional and therefore almost tragic figure. But in *Skull* we begin to face a much grimmer possibility: that Maureen is far from anomalous, that her murder of a family member is actually one in a series of vicious acts that have been committed by the people of Leenane. As we try to make sense of our suspicion that Mick Dowd murdered his wife, McDonagh is slowly leading us towards the realisation that Leenane is a place in which 'God has no jurisdiction', as Father Welsh will put it in *The Lonesome West* (8). Where *Beauty Queen* seemed tragic because it dealt with one individual, *The Lonesome West* will seem tragic because of what it seems to say about all of humanity. *A Skull in Connemara* thus has a crucial role in the *Trilogy*, leading us from the individual to the wider community and thus showing how the people of Leenane are products of their environment and their community. In doing so, it bridges the gap between the *Trilogy*'s first and third parts.

Because of its importance for those two plays, there has been a tendency to ignore the inherent value of *Skull*. It is less frequently produced than McDonagh's other plays, and the academic literature tends to deal with it only in the context of the *Trilogy* generally. We certainly need to be appreciative of its function in relation to *Beauty Queen* and *Lonesome West* – and also of its relationship with other of McDonagh's works, especially *The Pillowman*. But *A Skull in Connemara* raises important issues in its own right: about morality, about audience interpretation and about the impact of reputation on the construction of a person's sense of self.

Ostensibly, *A Skull in Connemara* is a mystery of sorts; it has even been described occasionally as a blackly comic detective story. But the question of whether Mick Dowd did or didn't murder his wife will prove irrelevant for McDonagh's larger purposes: the play aims to puzzle the audience but, to borrow a phrase from *The Pillowman*, it is a 'puzzle without a solution' (*PM*, 17). Its function is not to expose a truth, but to invite us to question why we were so preoccupied with solving the puzzle in the first place.

Just as individual directors adopt different approaches to Maureen's actions at the end of *Beauty Queen*, so there are a variety of opinions about whether Mick really did kill his wife Oona. Mick sticks rigidly to the same story about her death:

> The only aspersions that could be cast are the ones I've already
> admitted to, and the ones I've already served me time over.
> That I had a drink taken, and a good drink, and that she had
> no seat-belt on her, and that was the end of it. (*SC*, 18–19)

Mick certainly caused his wife's death and, unusually for Leenane, he has actually spent time in prison as a result. But he rejects the rumour that Oona was already dead when he crashed into the wall: that he had staged the accident in order to cover up her murder. 'All that came out at the time . . . and didn't the inquest shoot every word of it down,' he tells the hapless policeman Thomas Hanlon in the play's second scene (36).

Mick's explanation might seem reassuring, until we remember that Mag Folan's death was also the subject of a 'hundred bastarding inquests [which] proved nothing' (*BQ*, 58). And those audience members who haven't seen *Beauty Queen* will soon have reason to doubt the reliability of the Leenane authorities anyway: if Thomas is an example of Irish law enforcement, then it seems reasonable to assume that the inquest into Oona's death might well have been flawed.

One reason why Mick has failed to shake off the suspicions of the people of Leenane might be his rather grisly occupation. His job is to exhume the bodies in the local graveyard every year, in order to make room for new corpses. This role gives him an unusual status within the community, so it is understandable that he is resented and somewhat feared. As his drinking companion Maryjohnny Rafferty points out, suspicions about Mick's relationship with his wife are far less urgent than the question of how Mick treats the remains of the villagers' loved ones:

> Questions about where did he put our Padraig when he dug him up is the kind of question, and where did he put our Bridget when he dug her up is the kind of question, and where did he put my poor ma and da when he dug them up is the biggest question! (12)

Again, Mick has a story that he repeats whenever he is faced with such antagonism. Once he has exhumed the bodies, he says, he seals the remains in a bag and 'let[s] them sink to the bottom of the lake and a string of prayers I say over them as I'm doing so' (14). Yet when he is goaded, Mick has a different explanation: 'I hit [the remains] with a hammer until they were dust and I pegged them be the bucketload into the slurry,' he says (13). The audience, understandably, will be unsure of which story to believe. It makes sense that Mick, in his frustration, would say something sarcastic but untrue to shock and offend Maryjohnny and Thomas's brother Mairtin. Yet Mick gives few indications of being the kind of man who would have the piety to say 'a string of prayers' over anyone's remains.

As the plot develops, the audience will begin to assume the worst about Mick – especially in the play's third scene when he and Mairtin use mallets to smash several skeletons into 'skitter', as Mick calls it (43). (Skitter, by the way, is a Hiberno-English slang for 'shit'.) And once Mick realises that Mairtin was responsible for stealing his wife's body, he decides to murder him in exactly the way he had been accused of killing Oona:

> **Martin**   I'll be sure and remember to be putting me seat-belt on too, Mick, knowing your track record . . .
> **Mick** (*quietly*)   Be doing what you like, ya feck. (*He picks up his mallet and rolls it around in his hand a little.*) It'll make no difference in the end. (51)

In both cases, then, we see Mick doing exactly the things he has been accused of doing earlier in the play.

Yet Mick claims that that he commits those acts not because he is *repeating* his past crimes, but from a desire for revenge against the people of Leenane. 'If it's whispering about me they're going to be through the years, what more should they expect when they wind up in my hands than batter?' he says (43). He later claims that his decision to kill Mairtin was also provoked by the negative opinions of the Leenane people: 'Do you want to hear something funny?' he asks Maryjohnny. 'I *didn't* butcher my wife . . . I never butchered anybody 'til tonight . . . A pure, drink-driving was all my Oona was, as all along I've said, but if it's a murderer ye've always wanted living in yere midst, ye can fecking have one' (58).

Some audience members might hear a faint echo of Synge's *Playboy of the Western World* in such remarks. In Synge's play Christy Mahon has been made a 'mighty man' by the 'power of a lie': because the villagers in *Playboy* believe Christy killed his father (which is a lie, albeit not a deliberate one), he gains the confidence to murder his father a 'second time' (Synge, 1982: 165). Mick is claiming that he too has been shaped by the views of the people of Leenane, his point appearing to be that since everyone believes he is a murderer, he has nothing to lose by acting like one. And just as Christy's father will make a surprise reappearance, his head bandaged from a still-bleeding wound, so will Mairtin reappear unexpectedly with his own bloody injury. The irony in both cases is that although Christy and Mick try to transform the lies told about them into realities, both fail in their attempts to do so: their intended victims refuse to stay dead.

Mick also makes clear that his bad reputation predates Oona's death. One of the things Mick loved about his wife, he says, was that 'she'd always stand up for me against people. Y'know, in a fight or something, or if people were saying things agin me' (54). It seems, then, that regardless of whether Mick is guilty, the people of Leenane were predisposed to assume the worst about him: they said things 'agin' him even when Oona was alive.

In any case, the people accusing Mick of murder hardly seem reliable. This is particularly true of Thomas, who views the death of Oona as one of a number of unsolved crimes that merit further attention – crimes which, he hopes, might finally earn him the professional status that he craves. Yet those other cases are self-evidently ridiculous, the first involving a fat man who was found dead with only 'a pot of jam and lettuce' in his fridge (30), and the second a drunk man who drowned in a 'potty of wee' (46). These events seem suspicious to Thomas not because he has great insight into the workings of the criminal mind, but because he has watched too much television: 'It isn't knowing the difference between hearsay and circumstantial evidence that makes you a great copper,' he shouts. 'No. Detective work it is, and going hunting down clues, and never letting a case drop no matter what the odds stacked against you are, no matter how many years old' (57). As Maryjohnny suggests, that attitude to policing makes Thomas seem just like the hero of *Petrocelli*, a 1970s TV show about a lawyer who solves crimes in small-town America. 'Like *Petrocelli* is right,' agrees Thomas immediately. His frame of reference is not the real world: it is American crime drama like *Starsky and Hutch*, *Quincy* and *Hill Street Blues*.

Given that he bases his sense of self on fiction rather than reality, it makes sense that Thomas always seems to be trying to be someone that he's not. When he first appears, he is presented 'in full uniform, sucking, at intervals, on a cigarette and an asthma inhaler,' writes McDonagh (28). That contrast between smoking and needing assistance to breathe is very funny in performance, but it also indicates one of the central features of Thomas's personality: he is always trying to do things that he lacks the ability to do properly.

The most interesting feature of Thomas's characterisation is his total conviction that Mick is guilty of killing Oona – a belief that he continues to hold even after he digs up her body and finds that her skull displays no evidence of violence. Rather than seeing that absence as evidence as suggesting that Mick might be innocent, Thomas chisels a gash into Oona's skull in the hope of forcing a confession. Thomas clearly is not interested in the truth about Mick; he simply wants to gather (or create) enough credible evidence to make it seem that he has solved a crime. And he's doing this not from any desire to remedy injustice, but because he hopes he's going to be promoted (17).

There is a clear link here to *The Pillowman*, which gives us not one but two detectives – who actually don't detect anything, but argue over who should be the 'number one' in the next case and extort a confession from someone who is (more or less) innocent. But aside from that similarity in terms of characterisation, there is also a shared preoccupation in both plays with the theme of how evidence is never interpreted dispassionately, and how objectivity will always be undermined by self-interest.

Just as the word 'home' dominates *Beauty Queen*, so does the word 'fact' recur in interesting ways throughout *Skull*. 'You don't know the full facts,' says Martin, trying to explain his reasons for having smashed bottles in the faces of two girls because, it turns out, they laughed at his trainers (11). Later Martin will tell Mick that he ought to get his 'facts right' when speaking about the identity of the person who microwaved a hamster in his school (23). Mairtin blamed that incident on the (obviously innocent) Blind Billy Pender, providing us with another example of how the people of Leenane will often scapegoat villagers who (like Mick) are vulnerable because of their obvious deviations from the norm. Thomas also speaks often about how 'a fact is a fact' (31), though as we have seen earlier he is perfectly willing to invent 'facts' to suit his own purposes. He also uses the facts of 'statistics' about children's deaths to deceive his brother (38–9). In short, every time we hear the word 'fact', we are being confronted with an obvious untruth.

One impact of McDonagh's focus on the difference between facts and lies – or appearance and reality – is to emphasise something that should be obvious from the characterisation of both Mick and Thomas: the lives of both men are strongly determined not by *who* they are (the facts or 'reality' about them) but by *how they appear* (their reputations). Mick claims that he is not a killer, but that he has been provoked into the attempted murder of Mairtin by 'the power of a lie'. Similarly, Thomas is not concerned with truth or justice but with *seeming* to be a great detective. Thomas is trying to live a lie – but Mick claims that he is trying to refute a lie about himself. This characterisation returns us to the point that Ray made at the end of *Beauty Queen*: that it is not the decisions of individuals but the 'bastarding town of Leenane' that leads people to commit acts of horrible violence. If we believe Mick – and it not clear whether we should – then it seems that he has been corrupted by his environment, by the malice and suspicion of his community.

We certainly do learn more about the immediate environment of Leenane from this play, which ventures out from the Folans' cottage in *Beauty Queen* to the outdoor space of the village graveyard. Even the play's title seems to gesture towards a wider environment – and indeed it is notable that as the *Trilogy* progresses, the titles move from specific locations to general ones, starting with Leenane, moving then to the bigger space of Connemara, before finishing with the generalised lonesome 'west'. The title of *Skull* is taken from a line in Samuel Beckett's *Waiting for Godot* (1955), appearing at the end of a long speech by Lucky, who speaks of:

> . . . the flames the tears the stones so blue so calm alas alas on on the skull the skull the skull in Connemara in spite of the tennis the labours abandoned left unfinished graver still abode of stones in a word I resume alas alas abandoned unfinished the skull the skull in Connemara . . . (43)

There has been considerable debate among Beckett scholars about the meaning(s) of Lucky's speech, and a variety of possibilities have been put forward about the phrase that gives McDonagh's play its title. One of those possibilities has been suggested by Andrew Gibson, who points out that:

> In the nineteenth century, Connemara was a land of skulls. This is clear from the travel narratives of English 'improvers' visiting the west in the wake of the Famine. Thus the anonymous author of *The Saxon in Ireland* (1851) evokes the Abbey at Cong as having been a 'mere charnel-house, blocked up with rubbish, and strewed with human skulls and bones'. True the images of Connemara as boneyard frequently seem to feature almost by accident . . . But the Famine supplied only the most recent images of historical devastation. (Gibson, 2010: 191–2)

I don't wish to suggest that Beckett was certainly thinking of the Famine when he wrote Lucky's speech. Nor is there any evidence that McDonagh chose the title because he was thinking of the Famine. However, Gibson's point is helpful because it reminds us that, while Connemara and the west of Ireland are *generally* associated with natural beauty, there is *also* a tradition of presenting the place as a 'boneyard' or 'charnel house'. That tradition is based partly on the impact of the Great Irish Famine of the late 1840s, in which over a million people (many of them living in the west of Ireland) starved to death. It is therefore notable that, while in the graveyard, Mick finds himself thinking of the Famine, if only as a way of playing a practical joke on Mairtin (27). Girleen in *The Lonesome West* will also find herself thinking about the Famine when confronted with death in the present (*LW*, 41). The point in both cases – and one possible explanation for McDonagh's choice of title – is that Connemara is a place where the memory of mass death remains a strong presence in the lives of his characters.

Whatever the reason for the title, we are certainly being given a rather morbid image of the west of Ireland – one that contrasts with the romanticised West of John Ford's *The Quiet Man* (1952), a film which draws countless 'eejit yanks' (7) to Connemara each summer. McDonagh's treatment of the play's environment is, then, another example of his creation of a tension between appearance and reality: the west of Ireland may on the surface appears to be a place of great natural beauty – but the memory of a million Famine dead lurks just below that surface.

There is also a warning to audiences here. One of the things that leads Thomas astray is that he is so determined to confirm a pre-existing suspicion that he completely ignores the facts in front of him. In a similar way, we as audience members can become so caught up with the question of *reality* – with the issue of Mick's innocence or guilt – that we may lose sight of what is actually true about the play. We know for a fact that the person responsible for enforcing the law in Leenane is not competent to do so (something which will contextualise Father Welsh's guilt for the moral standing of his parishioners in *The Lonesome West*). We know too that the only genuinely happy person in the entire *Trilogy* is Mairtin – who is by far the most idiotic character in those plays: ignorance, it seems, is the only way to experience bliss in Leenane. Mairtin's name also provides one of the best jokes in *Skull*: the *Trilogy*'s stupidest character has the Irish version of McDonagh's own given name, suggesting that if we seek out the presence of the author in the work, we might not find it in the obvious places. And we learn something finally about Maryjohnny Rafftery: she appears to believe that Mick really did murder his wife, yet is perfectly happy to keep visiting him, because he gives her free booze. In other words, we know that whatever Mick did, he is probably more admirable than any of the play's other three characters.

Perhaps, then, the key symbol in this drama is the empty grave at the end of the second scene. It is fascinating that McDonagh gives us that image of people digging in search of 'facts' at the halfway point of the *Trilogy*'s middle play. His characters strip away layers and delve deeper – only to find an empty space where they expected to uncover a hidden truth. It is tempting to see that act of digging as analogous to the audience's search for truth. As we will see in many of McDonagh's works, *Skull* suggests that audiences need to be aware of – and perhaps even to resist – their desire to find meaning. A play should not be seen as a hiding-place for an author's message, but instead as a space in which audiences can create their own meanings.

The empty space at the centre of *Skull* is the question of Mick's guilt or innocence. There is no way of knowing whether he really did kill his wife, but McDonagh makes clear that the people of Leenane have made up their minds anyway. The challenge for us as audience members is to consider where we stand, how we fill the empty space ourselves. Do we sink to the level of the people of Leenane, assuming the worst without sufficient evidence? Should we think well of Mick, despite all the hints that he doesn't deserve our admiration? Or should we instead seek to remain in a state of uncertainty, knowing that even if McDonagh's puzzle has no solution, we can still identify some important truths? It doesn't really matter which of those options we choose; what is essential is that we leave the theatre asking those questions – not accepting passively what we have been told, but instead trying to piece together the evidence for ourselves.

A sainted glory: *The Lonesome West*

As *The Leenane Trilogy* moves towards its conclusion, McDonagh's moral and thematic focus broadens. As mentioned in the last section, the titles of the three plays hint at this movement, bringing us from a very particular local setting to a more general one: from Leenane in the first play's title, to Connemara in the second, and then to the west in the last. I've also suggested that the ethical focus shifts in a similar way, from the specific to the general. The audience begin by considering the individual culpability of Maureen in *Beauty Queen*, before judging the community of Leenane in *Skull*, until we are faced with human nature generally in *The Lonesome West.*

But perhaps the most significant broadening of focus in the plays relates to the theme of authority. The first play in the *Trilogy* questions authority within the home, asking what responsibilities a parent has for a child, and a child for its parents. The second analyses authority in the community, exploring the legal authority that the police have over the people of Leenane, while also reminding us of the moral authority that individuals wield when we tolerate (or condemn) our neighbours' wrongdoing. *The Lonesome West* operates in a similar way, showing again that authority works in both directions: it is something that we both submit to *and* a responsibility that we wield. In this play, however, the authority figure being challenged is God himself: we are being invited, then, to consider what we owe to God, and what God owes to us. The thematic ambition of *The Lonesome West* explains why it is one of McDonagh's most admired plays: it is satisfying in its own right, it allows us to judge the first two plays in *The Leenane Trilogy* in a new light, and it anticipates the detailed treatment of Catholicism and morality in McDonagh's later work.

Another significant feature of the play is that its title appears to gesture towards America. It has often been suggested that McDonagh modelled *The Lonesome West* on Sam Shepard's 1980 masterpiece *True West*. There is of course the obvious resemblance between the two titles, but the theme and structure of both plays are similar too. In McDonagh's play, two middle-aged brothers, Valene and Coleman Connor, live in isolated part of western Ireland; they fight endlessly with each other, but seem inseparable. In Shepard's play, two middle-aged brothers called Lee and Austin are forced to live together in their mother's house in the American West. As both stories unfold, the brothers move from ill-humoured competitiveness with each other to outright hostility – a mood that is worsened by their consumption of large quantities of alcohol. In both plays, the conflict is intensified by the intervention of a well-meaning outsider (Father Welsh in McDonagh's play, a Hollywood agent in Shepard's); and, in both plays, some of the events are witnessed by a likeable but powerless woman – Girleen in *The Lonesome West*, Mom in *True West*. Kitchen appliances play an important role in both dramas, with toasters appearing in Shepard's and a stove in McDonagh's. And each writer explores – and perhaps seeks to undermine – a national myth: the idea of the American frontier West in *True West* and the centrality of Catholicism to Irish life (and indeed the idea of the West also) in *The Lonesome West*.

But if the play appears indebted to an American writer, it is also deeply engaged with an Irish one. Where McDonagh had borrowed the title of *A Skull in Connemara* from Beckett, he turned to J.M. Synge for the title of *The Lonesome West*. In Synge's *Playboy of the Western World*, Christy Mahon famously arrives at a pub in the west of Ireland claiming to have killed his father. That story so impresses the pub's owner – the drunken and self-centred Michael James Flaherty – that he instantly offers Christy a job. Christy will be employed as the pub's pot-boy, and will therefore be able to protect Flaherty's daughter Pegeen while the old man spends the night getting drunk at a wake. Pegeen's fiancé, the effeminate and priest-fearing Shawn Keogh, has already been asked to occupy that role, but fled from the pub when asked to do so. A respectable young man would never allow himself to be left alone with an unmarried woman, thinks Shawn; besides, he might get into trouble with the local priest. Shawn's cowardice has provoked a disgusted response from Flaherty: 'Oh, there's sainted glory this day in the lonesome west,' he says to Pegeen, 'and by the will of God I've got you a decent man!' (Synge, 1982: 65). Flaherty is being sarcastic about his future son-in-law here: Shawn's 'saintliness' is regarded as a negative rather than an admirable trait by Flaherty and his fellow villagers. Having a 'decent' man for a husband is thus seen as a misfortune for Pegeen.

What is evident in that line from *The Playboy* is a dangerously skewed sense of morality. The arrival in Flaherty's pub of a man who has murdered his father should provoke a negative reaction: fear, outrage, a desire to see justice done. Yet as Flaherty's sarcasm indicates, it is Christy's willingness to be violent rather than Shawn's sense of morality that is seen as a blessing – as a 'sainted glory' enacted through the 'will of God'. To Synge's original audiences in Ireland, such lines seemed blasphemous. But what makes these words provocative even now is that they reveal a clash between the appearance and the reality of religious faith within Irish culture. The language of Synge's villagers is rich in religious allusion, yet it is also obvious that all have failed completely to understand and internalise the central tenets of Christianity: forgiveness, compassion, charity, selflessness and, above all, love for others. The absence of those traits has a corrosive effect: it is manifested in their tolerance for violence and their fear of (rather than respect for) religious authority – and it also explains why Pegeen Mike seems doomed to a life of unfulfilled desires.

McDonagh offers a similar critique of the west of Ireland in his own play. Like Synge, he is showing that the West should not be idealised as a place of stunning natural beauty (as it is generally seen to be); it is also a place that has been marginalised and impoverished in many ways – not just economically, but culturally and (perhaps) intellectually. In both writers' plays, characters who are ambitious or talented have just two options: to leave their communities for ever or, as happens more frequently, to surrender to frustration and bitterness.

It is to be expected, then, that both Synge and McDonagh's most admirable characters feel so isolated, despite being surrounded by countless other people. It is for this reason that the word 'lonesome' and its variants appear thirty-three times in *The Playboy of the Western World* and nineteen times in *The Lonesome West*. And that 'lonesomeness' – the isolation, the marginalisation of McDonagh's central characters – is shown as having significant moral consequences.

That treatment of morality in *The Lonesome West* is developed mainly through the characterisation of Father Welsh – another McDonagh character who has been portrayed in a surprising variety of ways from one production to another. For some actors and directors, he is sympathetic: flawed, not especially intelligent, but certainly well-meaning. For others, he is a drunken buffoon, a character designed largely to mock the self-importance of the Catholic Church in Ireland. While the first interpretation is more likely to be correct – and it certainly results in a more satisfying play in production – it is easy to understand how both opinions are formed.

From the beginning of the play, audiences will struggle to decide what to think of Welsh. They are likely to form a negative impression of the priest due to his obvious dependence on alcohol even while they sympathise with him for having to endure Coleman's insults in the first scene. Welsh claims that Leenane has driven him to drink: 'I never touched the stuff before I came to this parish,' he claims (4). Leenane, as he points out, does seem rather like 'the murder capital of fecking Europe' (36), and Welsh is certainly not very highly respected by his parishioners. As mentioned already, the first two plays in the *Trilogy* feature a running joke about the people from the village not calling Welsh by his correct name, referring to him as 'Father Welsh Walsh Welsh' – a joke repeated fourteen times in *The Lonesome West* alone.

So Welsh's life is quite difficult. Yet it seems likely that his fondness for alcohol arises from a desire to avoid facing a deep-rooted sense of his own inadequacy. Another possibility, of course, is that Welsh is just making excuses (as many alcoholics do), blaming Leenane for his own failings. As Coleman suggests, Welsh may have been driven to drink, but 'some people don't need as much of a drive as others. Some need only a short walk' (4).

Indeed, it is unclear whether Welsh drinks because he is a bad priest or if he is a bad priest because he drinks. It is even unclear whether Welsh should be seen as a good or bad priest. Early in the play he violates one of the fundamental rules of his own church when he breaks the seal of confession (that is, he reveals the sins that some of his parishioners have confessed). 'About betting on the horses and impure thoughts is all them bastards ever confess,' he says, referring to Maureen Folan and Mick Dowd. The embarrassed Coleman has to point out Welsh's error to him: 'Em, only I don't think you should be telling me what people be confessing, Father. You can be excommunicated for that I think' (9). Welsh also reveals that he is not very familiar with holy scripture. 'Thou shouldst share and share alike the Bible says,' he suggests in the play's third scene (28). Although such words are consistent with Christian teaching, they appear nowhere in the Bible.

Familiarity with rules and regulations and the ability to quote scripture are not necessarily requirements for being a good priest, of course. Girleen clearly sees something worth admiring in Welsh – not just as a man, but also in his clerical capacity. She praises his sermon at the funeral of Thomas Hanlon, for instance: 'Almost made me go crying, them words did,' she admits (34). And Welsh also seems keen to see the best in his parishioners – though it's not clear how we're supposed to react to this feature of his personality. When he learns of Thomas's suicide, he describes him as someone who 'never had a bad word to say about anybody and did his best to be serving the community every day of his life' (24). Yet the audience – and McDonagh's characters – know that this description is inaccurate. As we have seen, Hanlon is vindictive and malicious, in search of self-advancement at all costs. Welsh, then, is either hopelessly naive or is instead being deliberately dishonest in describing Thomas as he does.

It must also be pointed out, of course, that at the moment when Thomas committed suicide, Welsh was 'sitting pissed on me own in a pub' (28). '[Thomas'] father had to haul me drunk out of Rory's to say a prayer o'er him, and me staggering,' says Welsh (20). So his desire to speak well of Thomas could be seen as an attempt to compensate for his inability to do something meaningful: to prevent the suicide or adequately to console Thomas's family. Throughout *The Lonesome West*, then, Welsh proves himself able to talk about what he *should* have done, but is rarely able to act for anyone's benefit, including his own.

The difference between Welsh's words and actions is probably most apparent in his decision to take his own life. As a Catholic, Welsh believes that a person who commits suicide will be condemned to hell. He hopes to escape that fate by restoring Coleman and Valene's love for each other: his suicide is intended as a sacrifice that will shock the brothers into behaving well towards each other – a 'miracle' that will in turn save Welsh's soul.

This seems very noble. Welsh appears to imagine himself as being like one of the Christian martyrs whose statues Valene collects so enthusiastically. Yet it's probably worth asking whether he's being entirely sincere. After all, he regards himself as a 'shite priest' (4), and seems to have nothing to live for. He is by his own admission 'maudlin' (38); he's also obviously very lonely, and all the characters mock him for his regular crises of faith (10, 12). In his suicide note (recited in Scene Five), Welsh suggest that the Connor brothers' anger with each other arises because they are 'lonesome' and because of the absence of women from their lives. Mightn't we suggest instead that Welsh is describing his own problems in this letter? Welsh believes that Thomas Hanlon's suicide was inspired by courage, Guinness and stupidity – but isn't it possible that his own suicide results from exactly the same causes? Despite his attempts to make his actions seem self-sacrificing, is Welsh just surrendering to his own sense of despair, using alcohol to fortify himself and religion to justify himself?

Characteristically, McDonagh leaves those questions unanswered.

Perhaps the most tragic aspect of Welsh's suicide is its impact on Girleen. Before his death, Welsh had said that Thomas Hanlon took his own life because he had no one to tell him that his life was worth living. 'Where were his friends when he needed them in this decent world?' he asks. 'When he needed them most, to say, "Come away from there, ya daft, we'd miss ya, you're worthwhile, as dumb as you are." Where were his friends then?' (44) Welsh appears to identify with Thomas's isolation; indeed, it seems partially to inspire his own thoughts of suicide.

What he doesn't realise – through self-absorption or stupidity – is that he, unlike Thomas, has someone who believes that his life *is* worth something. Girleen tells him that he certainly will be missed when he leaves Leenane, and asks him to keep in contact with her. Welsh thanks her for her company – 'It's meant something to me' he says (41) – but it doesn't stop him from going through with his plan. Welsh's suicide, then, is not just a rejection of his life; it's a rejection of the faith that Girleen places in him.

Girleen of course is horrified by the news of Welsh's death – not just by the revelation that he committed suicide, but that he died in an attempt to redeem Valene and Coleman while never even mentioning her in his letter. 'You notice he never asked me to go saving his soul,' she says. 'I'd've liked to've saved his soul. I'd've been honoured, but no . . . Only mad drunken pig-shite feckbrained thicks he goes asking' (50). The real tragedy for Welsh, then, is that he lacks the self-awareness to realise that redemption is available, not through his act of self-sacrifice, but through the love of Girleen.

It's difficult to determine precisely how we're supposed to react to Welsh. Is he a bad priest but a good Christian? Does he commit suicide from noble motives, or is he simply trying to justify an act of gross selfishness? Does he ignore Girleen's love for him because he is too self-absorbed – or because he is so full of a sense of his own failures that he has become blind to the possibility that someone else might care for him? Or is he aware of her feelings but indifferent to them? And is he right to blame Leenane for making him what he is? These are all difficult questions to answer – but as we have seen in the discussion of *A Skull in Connemara*, the impact of Leenane on its inhabitants is worth exploring in a little more detail, especially in relation to the portrayal of Girleen.

As we've come to expect, McDonagh's presentation of Girleen reminds us that we need to be mindful of the difference between appearance and reality: Girleen's actions are a key example of how McDonagh's characters often reveal much more about themselves through their actions than their words. She seems at first to be an assertive and strong-willed individual. Despite being a schoolgirl, she shows in the first scene that she is perfectly willing to speak frankly about sexual matters to the three male characters. The local postman fancies her, she claims: 'I think he'd like to be getting into me knickers, in fact I'm sure of it' (11). Later in that scene, she proves herself well able to stand up to Valene when he tries to under-pay her for her poteen: 'You're the king of stink-scum fecking filth-bastards you, ya bitch-feck, Valene,' she tells him (11).

However, Girleen is not as tough as she might at first seem. She sells poteen to the people in her community – which was against the law in Ireland when the play premiered. But she does so not because she is deliberately setting out to break the law, but rather because she wants to save enough money to buy Father Welsh a gift. And it seems likely that her sexual frankness arises not from experience but from a desire to get the attention of Father Welsh, with whom she is clearly infatuated. This is made clear in the play's fourth scene, when a depressed Welsh states to Girleen that 'You have no morals at all, it seems', referring to her attitudes to sex and sexuality. Her response asserts her own value while implicitly rebuking Welsh: 'I have plenty of morals,' she says, 'only I don't keep whining on about them like some fellas' (35).

The three male characters in *The Lonesome West* show an indifference to the value of life: Father Welsh commits suicide for reasons that are (to say the least) questionable, and Valene and Coleman appear to think nothing of the death of their father – or to worry much about the prospect of killing each other. But Girleen sees the value of life: 'Even if you're sad or something, or lonely or something, you're still better off than them lost in the ground or in the lake, because . . . at least you've got the *chance* of being happy, and even if it's a real little chance, it's more than them dead ones have.' And 'At least when you're still here [alive] there's the *possibility* of happiness, and it's like them dead ones know that, and they're happy for you to have it. They say "Good luck to ya"' (39–40). Although expressed in simple language, this is another unusually eloquent passage (reminding us of Pato's speech in *Beauty Queen*). It reveals Girleen's ability to do two things that the other characters are largely incapable of: she can empathise with others, and is able to define her life in relation to something positive – the possibility of happiness.

In many ways, then, Girleen is the most admirable character in the play, perhaps even in the entire *Trilogy*. She talks like someone who is immoral and tough – yet she is much more vulnerable in reality. She can call Valene insulting names, and can tease a priest about condoms, but claims to be too shy to give a gift to Father Welsh: 'I'd've never've got up the courage to be giving it him to his face. I'd've blushed the heart out of me,' she admits bitterly (49). In *The Lonesome West* it is only Girleen who seems capable of acting entirely on behalf of others, of loving others more than she loves herself. And it is notable that she feels obliged to hide these aspects of her personality, pretending instead to be as immoral and rough as everyone else.

For that reason, audiences are likely to be upset by what happens to Girleen in the play's final scenes. Upon learning of Welsh's death, Girleen flings the heart and pendant she had bought for him to the floor of the Connors's living room. 'Feck me heart. Feck it to hell. Toss it into fecking skitter's the best place for that fecking heart,' she cries (51). These words are probably intended to function both literally and metaphorically. Girleen's optimism – her belief in other people, and her love for Welsh – have been betrayed: she has, to use the cliché, had her heart broken. She now claims to regret having wasted her money on Welsh. 'I should've skittered it away the boys in Carraroe, and not go pinning me hopes on a feck I knew full well I'd never have,' she says (50). These words may sound like a dismissal of the priest, but alert audience members will know that Girleen is quoting almost exactly Welsh's earlier words to her (37). By repeating these words about herself, Girleen reminds us that Welsh's opinion of her was much lower than it should have been. What is upsetting here is that she seems inclined to think that he might have been right.

As Welsh had suggested at the start of the play, Leenane seems like a place in which 'God has no jurisdiction' (7). The barbaric behaviour of its under-twelves football team suggests that the next generation of Leenane people will be every bit as vicious as their elders. So the presence of Girleen might initially be seen as offering some hope that perhaps the future for Leenane is not quite as bleak as it might seem. Yet we learn at the end of the play that Father Welsh's suicide has had an appalling impact upon her. 'Her mam two times has had to drag her screaming from the lake at night . . . there where Father Walsh jumped, and her just standing there, staring,' Valene reports. 'It's the mental they'll be putting Girleen in before long if she carries on' (55).

This is a very grim ending for this character: the suggestion is that she too has finally been defeated by her environment – like Maureen in *Beauty Queen*, somewhat like Mick in *Skull*, but different from both in that her actions only harm herself. Watching these events unfold, audiences may form the conclusion that if Girleen has behaved better than the other characters during the play, this could be because she has not yet lived long enough to be worn down by Leenane.

The characterisation of Girleen brings into focus a theme that has been mentioned several times already: the difference between appearance and reality, which in this play is presented in relation to religion. We've seen already that Father Welsh might be using the rhetoric of religion to justify actions that aren't especially virtuous, notably his suicide. Valene and Coleman also seem to use religion to justify their actions. 'I'm sure to be getting into heaven,' says Valene, referring not to the way that he lives his life, but instead to his extensive collection of religious figurines (45). Coleman too is blithely confident of his salvation: 'Me, probably straight to heaven I'll go, even though I blew the head off poor dad. So long as I go to confessing it anyways. That's the good thing about being Catholic. You can shoot your dad in the head and it doesn't even matter at all' (55–6). The fault of both brothers here is to confuse a symbol with the reality – to believe that the possession of religious figurines is more important than genuine holiness, to believe that an act of confession can result in absolution, even if it is made without any genuine penitence.

Central to this exploration of religion is a re-imagining of two of the central features of the Catholic church: confession and a belief in the redemptive power of suffering. The theme of confession and absolution runs through *The Lonesome West* (indeed, it features in different ways in many of McDonagh's works, especially *In Bruges*). We've seen already that Coleman seems to understand the rules of confession better than Father Welsh does, and there are some very good jokes about that sacrament at the start of the play. Yet in order to save his soul, Welsh encourages the brothers to confess their sins not to him, or directly to God – but to each other. As Welsh asks,

> Couldn't the both of ye, now, go stepping back and be
> making a listeen of all the things about the other that do get
> on yere nerves, and the wrongs the other has done all down
> through the years that you still hold against him, and be
> reading them lists out, and be discussing them openly, and
> be taking a deep breath then and be forgiving each other

them wrongs, no matter what they may be? . . . Would that
be so awful hard, now? (43)

As we learn in the play's final scene, such an act of confession and
forgiveness is indeed 'awful hard' for the two brothers. Their com-
petitive nature quickly overcomes their desire to abide by Father
Welsh's request, and they attempt to outdo each other, each trying to
make a revelation more outrageous and hurtful than the other's. Just
as the sacrament of confession is meaningless unless there is genuine
repentance, so is Valene and Coleman's attempt to 'step back' and for-
give each other revealed to be pointless, because neither brother really
regrets his actions. McDonagh is not questioning the validity of the
sacrament of confession here; rather, he is showing how that sacrament may be used by immoral people to convince themselves that
their actions are without consequence.

A similar scrutiny is given to another of the central features of the
Christian faith: the belief that Jesus suffered and died to redeem the
sins of mankind. That belief has in turn given rise to the notion that
certain forms of suffering can have a redemptive power – an idea that
is explored in some detail in *The Lonesome West* (and later developed
in *The Pillowman* and *In Bruges*). That idea is introduced in the third
scene, when Welsh burns his hands in the molten plastic of Valene's
saints. It seems at first that his act is provoked by despair at the news
that Coleman deliberately murdered his father – and that Valene
deliberately profited from that terrible event. 'Welsh stares at the two
of them dumbstruck, horrified,' writes McDonagh. 'He catches sight
of the bowl of steaming plastic beside him and, almost blankly . . .
clenches his fists and slowly lowers them into the burning liquid, holding them under' (33). These actions seem irrational, even involuntary:
Welsh carries them out 'almost blankly', we're told.

Yet Welsh soon re-imagines that pain, giving it a symbolic importance. 'I have been thinking about ye non-stop since the night I did
scald me hands,' he tells the brothers in his suicide note. 'Every time
the pain does go through them hands I do think about ye, and let me
tell you this. I would take that pain and pain a thousand times worse,
and bear it with a smile, if only I could restore to ye the love for each

other as brothers ye do so woefully lack' (43). The pain that Welsh experiences encourages him to commit suicide: he believes that his pain – his death, in fact – can redeem Valene and Coleman. This, Welsh believes, would be 'the greatest achievement of his whole time' in Leenane (43). So in addition to redeeming the brothers, Welsh is seeking to redeem himself.

But what does Welsh's suffering actually accomplish? By the end of the play, Valene and Coleman have few secrets from each other, but they seem totally unchanged from the way they were in the first scene. Girleen on the other hand has changed utterly, transformed from someone with a sense of hope to becoming almost ghost-like, haunting the place where Father Welsh committed suicide, and likely to be sent to a hospital for the mentally ill. If Welsh is a saintly martyr, like one of Valene's plastic saints, McDonagh seems to be questioning seriously whether his sacrifice was worthwhile.

It may be useful to see McDonagh's critique of Catholicism in the context of the time and place where this play was premiered: Ireland in 1997. This was a time when Irish society was just learning of the institutionalised abuse over many decades of thousands of the country's most vulnerable by members of the Catholic Church. Priests and nuns had systematically abused children and young adults, both sexually and physically – and, to make matters worse, church authorities had actively facilitated that abuse by moving guilty clergy from one parish to another and refusing to report their actions to the police. So for many members of McDonagh's first Irish audiences, his jokes about Catholicism must have been extraordinarily provocative. Seeking to reassure Father Welsh, for instance, Coleman says, 'You're a fine priest. Number one you don't go abusing five-year-olds, so, sure, doesn't that give you a head-start over half the priests in Ireland?' (9) Later, Valene will describe Welsh as the 'laughing stock of the Catholic Church in Ireland,' vindictively adding that this 'takes some fecking doing, boy' (29).

Those first Irish audiences were forced to think about the fact that clerical abuse in their country lasted for several decades, and that its impact is evident everywhere: not just in the brothers' twisted sense of morality, but also in their father's strange habit of screaming at nuns.

This is not to suggest that the focus on suffering within Catholicism caused the physical and sexual abuse of children by priests. Rather, there is an attempt here to reveal the extent to which the public appearance of Catholicism in Ireland – the use of religious statues, the public acts of faith – were disguising acts of horrendous violence.

For its original Irish audience, then, the play's most powerful moment – perhaps its most transformative moment too – occurs when Valene's religious figurines are placed in the stove. McDonagh is literally showing us these emblems of religion in meltdown, suggesting that these public presentations of saintliness can be destroyed. It's at this moment that the clash between appearance and reality works most effectively: McDonagh shows that the appearance of religious power and authority (the statues) can melt away. The play is literally iconoclastic.

Does that iconoclasm mean, however, that the play is amoral? McDonagh presents us with an environment in which people who are good or admirable (like Girleen and Father Welsh) are doomed, whereas those who behave badly seem to be rewarded (as are the Connor brothers). It would be wrong, however, to believe that simply because McDonagh presents a particular vision of the world he is saying that this is how things ought to be. Indeed, the power of *The Lonesome West* lies in the fact that it challenges its audiences to account for, react against and resolve the problems that it dramatises.

Perhaps the most significant moment in the play, then, is a discussion between Father Welsh and Girleen in the fourth scene. Welsh has realised that Maureen Folan killed her mother, and suspects strongly that Mick Dowd killed his wife (though as I have argued in *A Skull in Connemara*, it is possible that Welsh ought to give Mick the benefit of the doubt). So the news that Coleman is also responsible for a murder has deeply affected him. But even more shocking to him is that Girleen was aware of these events long before he was – and that she did nothing. 'I think I did hear a rumour somewhere' about the murder, she concedes. 'A fecking rumour?' he replies. 'And you didn't bat an eye or go reporting it?' (36).

This is a key moment in the play. Violence, abuse and brutality can arise from many causes, but Welsh shows his awareness that good people who do nothing to stop wrongdoing are themselves morally culpable.

This suggestion resonated with the play's original Irish audience, reminding us that clerical child abuse was not simply a result of the Church's covering up of its members' crimes – it was also enabled by a culture of silence that pervaded an entire society. Like Girleen, people in Ireland had for decades heard 'a rumour somewhere' about what was happening and (with some notable exceptions) had done nothing to prevent it. If McDonagh shows us that Irish Catholicism is in meltdown, he also challenges us to consider how the Church's power to enact atrocity was enabled by the silence of its own members. McDonagh is not representing the 'real' Ireland in his plays, but what he has to say certainly has real consequences for that country.

This is not to suggest, however, that the play is relevant only for Ireland and only for the year 1997. Welsh's demand that good people react when they witness wrongdoing helps us to understand the play's final moments. As the lights fade, a spotlight rests for a moment on three objects hanging on the wall centre-stage: a crucifix, the letter by Father Welsh and the chain bought for him by Girleen. These three symbols mean nothing to Valene and Coleman. The crucifix signifies a kind of self-sacrifice that neither man can achieve, the letter is a call for a peace that neither man desires and the chain is a symbol of the love that neither will ever experience. And all three are emblems of the suffering of innocent people. Why then does the light linger on this part of the set? Should the audience leave the theatre feeling hopeless, convinced that Valene and Coleman will never change? Perhaps.

But perhaps the purpose of those images is instead to force the audience to think about their own lives and their own responsibilities. *The Lonesome West* is of course primarily a comedy – and it presents us with characters and situations that exaggerate reality for comic effect. Nevertheless, the dilemmas at the heart of *The Lonesome West* are real enough. Like Synge before him, McDonagh is reminding us that *seeming* to be good and *being* good are rarely the same thing. We must, then, leave the theatre facing the question asked so poignantly by Father Welsh and Girleen. When we are confronted with intolerable brutality, what must we do in response? Will we sit quietly when confronted with disturbing infomation – or will we do something to change matters?

We are back again to the issue of ambiguity here, to the need for audiences to bring their own creativity to bear on what they have watched. But what makes *The Lonesome West* different from the other plays in the *Trilogy* – and indeed what makes it a satisfying conclusion to it – is that McDonagh has shifted the focus from drama to morality. The empty grave at the middle of *Skull* and the question of what Maureen does at the end of *Beauty Queen* are both challenges to the audience: they show us that McDonagh's plays are not seeking to convey one message to us, but that they instead create empty imaginative spaces that we must fill for ourselves. In *The Lonesome West*, the empty space is not physical or imaginative but ethical: it is the space that is left vacant when people who 'hear a rumour' about wrongdoing say nothing. Just as an audience must not watch a play passively, waiting to be told what to think, so must we as individuals not adopt a passive attitude to morality, following rules without really understanding them.

Taken together, what the three plays in *The Leenane Trilogy* show us is that our obligation is to be creative: not just in terms of art, but in our lives generally. We should leave each of the three plays asking questions – and the plotting alone will ensure that this will happen. But the spirit of questioning needs to extend into other areas as well. As we shall see, this is a theme that dominates McDonagh's other work. But before exploring the later plays, it is important to consider a question that arises from this discussion: if McDonagh's plays are deliberately ambiguous, how do audiences actually respond to them in production?

Staging *The Leenane Trilogy*

The first production of a Martin McDonagh play took place on the first day of February in 1996 in the small city of Galway on Ireland's west coast. The day was one of celebration – not because of the premiere of the play itself, but because it was being staged in a new venue: a civic theatre called the Town Hall, which was opening its doors for the first time. Druid Theatre, a highly respected local company founded in 1975 (and thus celebrating its twenty-first birthday), had been selected to produce the first play in the new venue. Much to everyone's surprise, its artistic director Garry Hynes had decided to present a new work from a then entirely unknown playwright. The playwright was McDonagh, and the play was *The Beauty Queen of Leenane*.

It might have seemed to that first audience that they were about to see a play with a surprisingly old-fashioned title. Galway, like the rest of Ireland, had only recently begun to experience a series of transformations that seemed to signal an abrupt rupture from the past. The old authorities of Irish life – church, state and family (each of which would of course be undermined in one of the plays in the *Trilogy*) – were being challenged by ongoing revelations of corruption, cover-up and the systematic abuse of the vulnerable. And there were signs of positive change too. Only three months before the play opened, in November 1995, the Irish people had signalled their society's growing liberalisation when they narrowly voted in favour of the introduction of divorce. Homosexuality had been decriminalised in 1994. And at the beginning of the 1990s, Mary Robinson had become the first woman to be elected president of the Republic of Ireland. Unemployment was falling rapidly, as was the rate of emigration. And although the IRA had broken the ceasefire it had declared in 1994, there were encouraging signs that peace in Northern Ireland might yet be attainable. Ireland, it seemed, was beginning the slow process of replacing an obsession with the past with a sense of hope for the future.

The title of Druid's new play seemed rather at odds with the feeling in the air – that Ireland was looking forwards rather than backwards – becoming cosmopolitan, prosperous and, in every sense, at peace with itself. Leenane, the audience knew, is a small and relatively isolated village in the north of county Galway; to be crowned the 'beauty queen' of such a tiny community would be an achievement so trivial as to be almost meaningless. The title of McDonagh's play thus seemed to call to mind an Ireland that was parochial, old-fashioned and full of an exaggerated sense of its own importance. In other words, the title seemed to recall the Ireland that the audience thought they had left behind for ever.

As they filed into their seats in the Town Hall, some of those theatregoers might have taken a moment to look at the set, which was designed by Francis O'Connor. What they saw was an image of Ireland that seemed outmoded. Like hundreds of Irish plays before it, *The Beauty Queen* takes place in a kitchen in a rural cottage. The usual paraphernalia was exactly where one would expect to find it. As has already been mentioned, on the wall was a crucifix, beside it a framed photograph of the Kennedys. Of course, the furniture was shabby: there was a small TV in the corner, a bare table centre stage and at stage left a long black range with a stack of turf – and beside it a seemingly innocuous black poker. And of course, there was water running down the windows at the back of the set, signifying rainfall. So before the action had even begun, the audience felt securely located in the world of the play, which seemed indistinguishable from so many Irish plays that had come before.

What most members of that audience didn't realise was that Hynes had deliberately chosen to open the new theatre with *The Beauty Queen* not because it was old-fashioned but, on the contrary, because she knew that its apparent familiarity would lull viewers into a false sense of security. She knew her audience would arrive at the theatre 'expecting a particular kind of play' – that is, a work similar to Druid's signature productions of plays by Synge and Tom Murphy. 'For the first few moments,' stated Hynes, 'the audience will feel *oh lovely, this is a Druid play, we know where we are*. And then . . . ' Hynes left unspoken her ideas about what would happen next, but it was clear that she too wished to signal a radical break from Ireland's past – and that she intended to use *The Beauty Queen of Leenane* to mark that rupture (quoted in Woodworth, 1996: 10).

Hynes's strategy proved remarkably effective. As the play opened, the audience was presented with a scene that seemed instantly to recall Tom Murphy's *Bailegangaire*, the classic Irish play first produced by Druid in 1985. Both plays are set in a rural Irish cottage, and both focus on a hostile but interdependent relationship between two women of different generations: a woman called Mary and her grandmother in *Bailegangaire*, and Mag and Maureen in *Beauty Queen*. Hynes emphasised the resemblance between the two plays by casting Marie Mullen, who had played Mary in *Bailegangaire*, in the role of Maureen.

But as the action progressed the audience slowly began to realise that this was definitely not a typical Irish play. Many of its themes and techniques had been seen before, but there was a bleakness in the author's outlook, a cruelty in his humour, and a jarring blend of traditional Irish culture on the one hand and global pop culture on the other that would have unnerved many that evening. By the time the play had moved into its shockingly violent and hopeless final scenes, the audience would largely have abandoned their expectations, becoming entirely immersed in the action. And, as *The Beauty Queen* concluded, they must have been aware that they had seen something that was simultaneously over-familiar and alienating: a play that was full of codes and signals that seemed to promise conventional meanings, but which instead had led them down several interpretative blind alleys. It was clear already that some of the people present were excited by this experience, while others were deeply irritated.

McDonagh has not produced a new play with Druid since 1997, so it might be tempting to underestimate the extent to which that company – and Hynes in particular – had an impact on his career. Yet as the description above sets out to show, there are a number of ways in which Druid set the terms against which all of that subsequent work would be judged.

There is, first, the fact that the reception of the play was determined both by Hynes *and* McDonagh. Both at Druid (which she co-founded in 1975) and at the Abbey Theatre (which she ran from 1991 to 1993 before returning to Druid), Garry Hynes has had a major impact on the development of contemporary Irish playwriting. As I suggest above, many members of McDonagh's first Irish audiences picked up on the echoes in his work with earlier plays directed by Hynes – notably her signature productions of Synge's *Playboy of the Western World* and such plays by Tom Murphy as *Bailegangaire* and *Conversations on a Homecoming* (1985). Questions about McDonagh's influences should thus include a consideration of Hynes's own interests as an artist.

The style of performance employed by Hynes is also important. As Fintan O'Toole observes, McDonagh's plays are an ideal vehicle for Druid's acting style, which is famous for exploding 'naturalism from within, starting with the apparently familiar and making it very strange' (Chambers and Jordan, 2004: 384). Hynes's style of direction during the *Trilogy* therefore presented the absurd naturalistically. When she directed *The Lonesome West*, she stated that actors and director 'have to absolutely believe that Valene will not allow his brother to eat a packet of his Tayto. If you think of that as a joke, and take that attitude to it in rehearsal, then the play doesn't exist,' she states (quoted in Ross, 1998).

Another essential feature of Hynes's influence on the plays is her company's dedication to working as an ensemble. As a result, many of the actors in the *Trilogy* played more than one role. Brian F. O'Byrne, for example, took the role of Pato in *Beauty Queen*, Thomas Hanlon in *A Skull in Connemara* and Valene in *The Lonesome West*. Hence the intertextual echoes that Shaun Richards identified (as alluded to earlier) were also represented in the staging. As has been noted, the plays appear to become both more bleak and more violent – and this was represented in the gradual transformation of O'Byrne's roles: from good-natured lover to feckless copper to downright psychopath. Similarly, the fact that Anna Manahan played both Mag in *Beauty Queen* and Maryjohnny in *Skull* tended to predispose audiences against the latter character from early on. And, as we have seen already, the casting of Marie Mullen in the role of Maureen would have encouraged audiences to think of other roles played by that great actress, including that of Mary in *Bailegangaire* – but also the Widow Quin in Synge's *Playboy*.

But perhaps the most important impact of Druid on McDonagh is the company's touring policy. I have argued earlier that one of the main features of *The Leenane Trilogy* is that McDonagh's deliberate ambiguity was employed in order to create a number of different reactions in the audience. There is no central 'meaning' to, say, *A Skull in Connemara* – no way of decoding the text to determine the innocence or guilt of Mick Dowd. Instead, the meaning of the play will be determined by the context in which it is performed, by the willingness of each audience member to decide how he or she will react to Mick. By taking McDonagh's plays on tour to a variety of different locations, Druid fully activated that feature of his work – showing definitively that many different meanings can be found in his drama.

Druid's tours of *The Leenane Trilogy* took place from 1996 to 2001. Aa a co-production with London's Royal Court Theatre, the *Trilogy* played in thirty-one venues in Ireland, north and south. It was also produced (either collectively or in individual productions) in England, Australia, the United States and Canada. Having premiered in Galway on 1 February 1996, *The Beauty Queen of Leenane* then toured to Longford, Kilkenny and Limerick, before transferring to the Royal Court Theatre Upstairs in May 1996. Following its London premiere, *The Beauty Queen* went on one of Druid's famous 'Unusual Rural Tours' (known as URTs by the company), playing in Skibbereen, Portmagee, Lisdoonvarna, each of the three Aran Islands, Arrain Mor, Rathlin Island and Erris Island. Druid also visited larger venues in Tralee, Enniskillen and Derry, before concluding in Leenane itself. A week later, *Beauty Queen* transferred to the West End.

In June 1997, again in Galway, *A Skull in Connemara* and *The Lonesome West* premiered, joining *Beauty Queen* to become *The Leenane Trilogy*. After transferring to the West End, the *Trilogy* ran for a week in Cork, and then played for ten days at the 1997 Dublin Theatre Festival, where it was named 'Reuters Play of the Year' (by a three-person jury that included Marina Carr) in a festival that also featured new work from Robert Lepage and Thomas Kilroy.

McDonagh's international profile grew throughout 1998 as Druid brought his work to other audiences. The *Trilogy* was staged at the Sydney Festival in January of that year, and then *Beauty Queen* opened in New York, where it later won four Tony Awards. *The Lonesome West* opened with its original cast on Broadway in 1999 and, although it was less popular than *Beauty Queen*, it too was nominated for four Tony Awards. In the same year, Garry Hynes directed local casts in Australian and Canadian productions of *The Beauty Queen*. The plays finally received a sustained run in Dublin in 2000, when *The Beauty Queen* played at the Gaiety, a large commercial theatre, where in 2001 *The Lonesome West* was also staged. The final Druid production of McDonagh's Leenane plays was a two-week run of *The Lonesome West* in Galway in October 2001.

This five-year tour involved a variety of venues and audiences, and achieved many objectives. The premiere of *Beauty Queen* in Galway was an act of localised, civic celebration. The *Trilogy*'s tours in Ireland – including visits to some of the most isolated parts of the island – are an excellent example of the capacity of subsidised theatre to operate as a force for cultural inclusion. As a co-production with the Royal Court, the *Trilogy* formalized a partnership between Irish and English theatre that has since been a feature of the career of other Irish dramatists, such as Conor McPherson and Sebastian Barry. The *Trilogy* can also be seen as an example of event-driven theatre, which made it ideal for the Sydney Festival and the Dublin Theatre Festival – and which (as I discuss later) may have influenced the decision to use celebrity casting in McDonagh's later plays *The Pillowman* and *A Behanding in Spokane*. The 1999 productions of *Beauty Queen* in Sydney and Toronto – with local casts directed by Garry Hynes – offer an interesting way of thinking about Irish theatre on tour: the Druid aesthetic remained in place, but audiences received the plays as local productions. And on Broadway and in Dublin, the plays appeared in commercial rather than subsidised venues.

This meant that the plays were received in a variety of ways by audiences throughout the world, and indeed throughout Ireland itself. As I have written elsewhere (in *Theatre and Globalization*, 2009: 115), one excellent example of this variety is the contrasting responses of audiences in Leenane and the Aran Islands to Druid's tour of *Beauty Queen*. As we have seen, during the first scene of that play, Mag and Maureen debate the merits of the Irish language. Uinsionn Mac Dubhghaill explains that Mag's criticisms of Irish expose a 'deeply felt conviction, held in many Gaeltacht communities, that Irish is of no value'. This feeling, he suggests, is 'not often articulated openly in public, for fear of jeopardising the community's chances of getting any grants that might be going'. The performance of this line on the Aran Islands meant that someone 'on stage [is] saying what many privately feel, and the audience is loving it'. However, when the play was performed in Leenane, the audience was silent during the same scene, because, Mac Dubhghaill proposes, Mag's opinion came as 'an unwelcome reminder in an area where the decision to abandon Irish as a community language is still uncomfortably close' (1996: 12).

There are numerous other examples of this kind of diversity. In her review of the Belfast production of *A Skull in Connemara*, Joyce MacMillan points out that 'some of the audience . . . clearly found the tone objectionable, and one or two walked out' (1997). Presumably the objectionable tone was not helped by the play's reference to an IRA bombing. When Thomas says that 'I would like there to be bodies flying about everywhere, but there never is,' Mick suggests that he should 'Go up ahead North so. You'll be well away. Hang about a bookies or somewhere' (SC, 29). Understandably, this line generated different responses in Belfast, Armagh, Sligo, Tralee and Dublin.

When Druid took the *Trilogy* abroad, the company already had a well-developed reputation which again had an impact on the reception of the plays. Druid first toured internationally in 1980, bringing four plays to the Edinburgh Festival. Visits to London, the United States and Australia soon followed, with works such as *The Playboy of the Western World, Bailegangaire* and *Conversations on a Homecoming*. This meant that the arrival of Druid at the Royal Court in 1996 marked the *return* of a company whose style was familiar to many London critics and theatregoers. To an extent, this was also the case in Sydney, where the company had a following after tours of *The Playboy of the Western World* and Vincent Woods's *At the Black Pig's Dyke* (1992). *The Leenane Trilogy* would probably not have reached London, New York and Australia if Druid had not already developed relationships with producers and audiences in those places. So Druid toured McDonagh with a reputation behind them, and put a great deal of energy into maintaining the integrity of that reputation. The company ensured that the premiere of the play in several major Anglophone theatrical centres was directed by Garry Hynes, illustrating its commitment to determining the reception of McDonagh's work internationally. The evidence suggests that these efforts were for the most part successful, and that (once again) the plays were received in terms of local issues – social, cultural or political – in each location on the tour.

British responses to his plays, for example, seem to have been influenced by anxieties about the place of Ireland in British society during the late 1990s. Particularly in *The Beauty Queen*, the *Trilogy* highlights the existence of anti-Irish prejudice in England. McDonagh has said that many aspects of Maureen's description of her time in London 'came from stories my mum told me – she worked in similar jobs when she first came over from Ireland. And, like the play, she had to have a black woman explain what those abusive words mean' (quoted in Hoggard, 2001: 11). It appears that McDonagh's consideration of the role of the Irish in Britain confused many, especially when they realised that the playwright did not conform to prevailing images of Irishness.

Similarly, in New York both *The Beauty Queen* and *The Lonesome West* were received in the context of American preoccupations. Whereas in Britain and Ireland, McDonagh was presented as the 'bad boy' of contemporary theatre, American journalists celebrated him as an example of the American 'rags to riches' narrative, just as in the 1960s Brian Friel's origins as a rural schoolteacher who had conquered Broadway were repeatedly emphasised (see Harrington, 1997: 145–65). *The Beauty Queen* was also seen as one of a number of foreign imports needed to shake Broadway out of a perceived lethargy. 'Sometimes you don't even know what you've been craving until the real thing comes along,' wrote Ben Brantley in the *New York Times*, adding that watching *The Beauty Queen* was 'like sitting down to a square meal after a long diet of salads and hors d'oeuvres' (1998: E.1.1). Brantley thus suggests that the function of the play is not to represent Ireland, but to transform American drama.

The Lonesome West was also received in terms of American society. Because it opened shortly after the tragic 1999 high-school shootings in Columbine, it became part of the debate about the relationships between violence and art in America, with Garry Hynes being called on for her opinion on American gun-control laws in pre-publicity for the show by Philip Hopkin (1999: 17). And there is little evidence that audiences took either of the Druid productions on Broadway at 'face value'. Maeliosa Stafford, who played Coleman in *The Lonesome West* on Broadway, states that 'New York audiences "get" everything, they are with us, they understand Martin's dark humor' (quoted in Barth, 1999: 26). Dawn Bradfield, who played Girleen in the same production, agrees, but was surprised by the conservatism of American audiences: 'There was a huge reaction to the bad language and to taking the piss out of the priest' (quoted in Ross, 2003: 16).

Druid's productions of his plays reached Australia at a time when that country was undergoing a growth in cultural self-confidence: like

Ireland, it was becoming more aware of itself as occupying a role on the global stage, and culture was an element of its attempt to come to terms with this development. Hence, media coverage both of the original 1998 visiting Druid production of the *Trilogy* and the 1999 touring Sydney Theatre Company production of *The Beauty Queen* directed by Garry Hynes focused more on what the plays might be saying to Australia, than on what they might be saying about Ireland. The Irish origin and setting of the plays was certainly considered, but when the question of authenticity arose, it was treated as if the reader would understand that the plays are self-evidently inauthentic.

One report of the visit of the touring production to Canberra encapsulates this well, telling readers that 'of course it's not an Ireland that exists any longer', and that 'one might argue that *The Beauty Queen of Leenane* is actually a postmodern play written about the stage Irish more than the real people' (Eccles, 1998: A12). Considerably more attention was paid to McDonagh's use of Australian soap opera. In the 1999 tour of *The Beauty Queen*, the lead role was given to Maggie Kirkpatrick, one of the stars of the soap opera *Prisoner: Cell Block H*, implying that McDonagh's interest in Australian culture was an aspect of the play that the producers wanted to highlight. While Irish critics worried about Australians taking McDonagh literally, in Australia his plays appear to have become part of that country's debate about how its own cultural exports play out for overseas audiences.

This is not to suggest that every interpretation of McDonagh is a positive or indeed a valid one. In 1999, the rights were released to *The Leenane Trilogy*, after which some versions of the plays were produced independently of Druid, and in ways that might be troubling for an Irish audience. For example, when Bernard Bloch directed and translated *The Lonesome West* as *L'Ouest Solitaire* for the 2002 Avignon Festival, he stated that 'the directorial approach will be to look at the fratricidal combat of the Connor brothers as a conflict reminiscent of the Northern conflict between Protestants and Catholics' (quoted in Kilroy, 2001). Similarly, when one of the earliest regional US productions of *The Beauty Queen* took place in Virginia in 1999, the director described the play as 'a true representation of Ireland, particularly in the north'. This suggestion that the senseless violence portrayed onstage might serve as a direct analogy for political violence in Northern Ireland would probably be regarded as offensive by many Irish audiences.

What emerges from this production history is an overlap between the construction of the plays and their reception. The inherent ambiguity of the work – and in particular the inconclusive nature of each of the three plays' endings – resulted in a situation where audiences were able to interpret the plays in different ways. In Ireland, that interpretation was occasioned by a familiarity with previous productions by Druid, and it is thus understandable that many of McDonagh's first Irish audiences found plenty of Synge and Murphy in the *Trilogy*. And internationally, the plays acquired a number of different meanings, few of which had anything at all to do with their Irish origins. But one consequence of that ambiguity was misinterpretation: there may be no single 'right' description of any of these plays' meanings, but there are plenty of wrong ones.

As we shall see, the question of whether McDonagh himself was responsible for such misinterpretations would have a bearing on his later work, notably *The Pillowman*. But first it's necessary to turn our attention from McDonagh's three Irish productions, to consider his work in the UK. As we'll see, his two Aran Islands plays are on the surface very similar to *The Leenane Trilogy* – yet they achieve something very different in production.

2
THE ARAN ISLANDS PLAYS

'A life that has never found expression': Imagining the Aran Islands

One of the key moments in the history of Irish drama occurred in Paris in the late 1890s, when W.B. Yeats met John Millington Synge for the first time. 'Give up Paris,' Yeats told Synge. 'Go to the Aran Islands. Live there as if you were one of the people themselves; express a life that has never found expression' (Synge, *Plays 1,* 1982: 20).

Many scholars now suggest that Synge probably would have made his way to those three small islands off the west coast of Ireland even without Yeats's advice. Either way, his visits there from 1898 to 1902 were momentous. He developed his knowledge of spoken Irish on the islands, met many kind and interesting people, and gathered the stories that would later be transformed into his great plays *The Shadow of the Glen* (1903), *The Playboy of the Western World* (1907) and *Riders to the Sea* (1904). Synge also published a fascinating prose account of his visits, which appeared in 1907. Only one of Synge's plays (*Riders to the Sea*) is actually set on the Aran Islands, but as Yeats's words imply, Synge could not have become so great an artist without having been inspired by that place.

Yeats's words also tell us a lot about the status of Aran within the Irish creative imagination. There is firstly an obvious tension in Yeats's remarks between Paris and Aran. Paris in the 1890s was (as it would be through much of the twentieth century) the world's artistic capital, yet it seemed to Yeats that Synge's presence there was having an inhibiting impact on his imaginative development; he needed instead to move away from the metropolis, away from the cosmopolitan, to the most marginalised community in one of the most marginalised countries in Europe.

And there's also a tension between the real and the performed in Yeats's advice: Synge should live not *as* one of the people (becoming one of the community), but *as if* he were one of the people. Yeats thus casts Synge not as an artist but as an agent: as someone who will give voice to what is already there. Synge's task, then, is to act *as if* he were something that he's not – but through that performance he will retrieve an underlying truth which Yeats believes to exist, even though it has 'never found expression'.

The Aran Islands were thus constructed as the site where an authentic Irish identity might be retrieved and then re-transmitted, first to Ireland and then to the world. Part of that construction involved seeing the place as not just regional but as the very opposite of the metropolis – as offering an alternative to the city's materialism, to its emphasis on speed, to the forced individualism of its inhabitants. And part of that construction betrayed an awareness that the role of the artist was to *perform* and, in a way, to falsify – but by doing so to reveal a deeper truth.

Synge showed a far more complex attitude to the Aran Islands than is evident in Yeats's description. But that association of the islands with an authentic Irish identity – and the desire to represent the place as embodying everything that was absent from the city – has persisted. It is there prominently in Robert Flaherty's 1934 documentary *Man of Aran*, and has been both reproduced and contested by dozens of Irish artists since that time, from Máirtín Ó Díreáin to Tim Robinson to Paul Keogan to (of course) Martin McDonagh.

In a 2001 interview, McDonagh claimed that the decision to locate three of his plays on the Aran Islands had happened rather arbitrarily. He had been drafting the play that would later become *The Lieutenant of Inishmore*, and, for plot purposes, needed to set the action somewhere in Ireland that would take 'a long time to get to from Belfast'. As Penelope Denning explains, 'Inishmore fitted the bill. Three Aran islands prompted the idea of a trilogy' (Denning, 2001). This in turn led to *The Cripple of Inishmaan* and the as-yet unproduced *Banshees of Inisheer*.

The plays' relationship with the Aran Islands may appear a fluke, but it would an enormous mistake to disregard the setting. One of the major features of the Aran plays is that McDonagh sets out to challenge Ireland's presentation of itself to the world – and one of the essential aspects of that presentation is to represent the Aran Islands as primitive in order to root an authentic Irish identity there. So *The Cripple of Inishmaan* is engaged directly in dialogue with Flaherty's *Man of Aran*, though Synge is in all sorts of ways also an important presence. McDonagh is scathing about the Hollywood misrepresentation of Ireland in that play, yet he is equally critical of Ireland's presentation of itself – as friendly, generous, creative, beautiful and unspoiled.

That critique of Ireland's capacity for myth-making (or for national self-delusion?) is given further bite in *The Lieutenant of Inishmore*, which not only attacks the rhetoric and iconography of Irish republicanism (that is, Irish militant nationalism), but also aims to rewrite one of the key tropes of Irish drama: the idealisation of woman as an icon of the nation.

We don't yet know what *The Banshees of Inisheer* is about. McDonagh has stated that he doesn't consider the play to be very good, but that he hopes to rewrite it for production at some stage. Yet the various rumours that circulate about the play suggest that it too is focused on Irish myths (some rumours suggest that it is set in the 1950s, that it is about a writer and that it investigates the Easter Rising of 1916). Nevertheless, because this play remains unpublished and unproduced, it seems best to refer to the 'Aran Islands plays' rather than seeing *Lieutenant* and *Cripple* as part of an unfinished second trilogy.

The Leenane Trilogy has a universal quality, but as I've mentioned it was also seen in Ireland as an attack on what were then the major authority figures of that country: the family (as considered in *Beauty Queen*), the state (as in *Skull*) and the Catholic Church (as in *Lonesome West*). The two produced Aran Islands plays were both premiered in England: *Cripple* at the National Theatre, London, in 1997 and *Lieutenant* in Stratford-upon-Avon in 2001. Those plays therefore don't have quite the same immediate relevance to Irish life, but instead consider the representation of Ireland within international or global culture – by Hollywood cinema, by music and indeed by the theatre also. This is entirely appropriate: given that the plays were written to consider Ireland from a non-Irish vantage point, it seems appropriate that both would be preoccupied with Ireland's presentation of itself to the world. And as we'll see, one of the major features of these plays is that they take up the tension implicit in Yeats's description – between the city and the country, between the performed and the authentic and, most importantly, between the real and the false.

'Ireland mustn't be such a bad place':
The Cripple of Inishmaan

The plot of *The Cripple of Inishmaan* is, on the surface, a very familiar one. A Hollywood film crew descends upon a sleepy village in a remote rural location. They are initially greeted with excitement and enthusiasm: they offer the locals relief from the monotony of their daily lives and for some they hold out the promise of escape. But gradually attitudes shift. The villagers begin to suspect that they are not being celebrated but exploited, and soon turn against the outsiders – before finally deciding to take control of their representation by telling their own stories.

It's a tale we've have heard before, both before and after the premiere of McDonagh's play in early 1997. It's appeared in many Irish plays, from Dennis Johnston's *Storm Song* in 1934 to Marie Jones's *Stones in His Pockets* in 1996 and 1999; it's featured in at least two different episodes of *The Simpsons*; and it's a major element of David Mamet's 2001 film *State and Main*, while McDonagh's own first film, *In Bruges*, takes up where *Cripple* leaves off, giving us a film that happens on the fringes of a film set. And of course, there are dozens (perhaps hundreds?) of Hollywood films about aspiring actors who achieve success against the odds, while stories about country-dwellers who outwit visitors from the city have been a recurring feature of Irish theatre at least since the time of Goldsmith and Sheridan, if not earlier.

McDonagh's play seems to fall easily into the pattern of such works. It is set against the backdrop of the filming of Robert Flaherty's *Man of Aran*, a documentary that was shot on Inishmore in the early 1930s, and which achieved international success when it was released in 1934. The play's eponymous protagonist is 'Cripple' Billy Claven, whose dreams of making it in Hollywood are thwarted when it is discovered that he can't act particularly well. Instead, he returns home from America to Inishmaan, hoping to gain the love of Slippy Helen, the girl he'd left behind – and, perhaps, to uncover the truth about his upbringing from the local gossip, Johnnypateenmike. Typically, McDonagh refuses to give his hero an entirely happy ending, concluding with the suggestion that Billy is suffering from tuberculosis – an example of the 'fashionably downbeat ending' that he would later celebrate in *The Pillowman*. Nevertheless, the plot seems to follow a mostly predictable course, albeit with a few twists along the way.

Yet *The Cripple of Inishmaan* is in some ways McDonagh's most surprising play. It is a damning critique of Flaherty's documentary, which is attacked for misrepresenting life on the Aran Islands. Yet rather than presenting an alternative vision of that life – rather than revealing 'the truth' – McDonagh instead criticises *all* forms of representation that lay claim to authenticity, emphasising instead the importance of storytelling. He thus highlights the subtle differences between terms that are often considered synonymous: the true, the real, the factual and the authentic. And he suggests that his self-evidently fictional play might be closer to the truth than other forms of cultural expression, such as journalism, history, national mythology, folk customs and even religious scripture. *The Cripple of Inishmaan*, then, offers a defence of the theatrical and of storytelling generally. As such, it anticipates *The Pillowman*, while also combining with *The Lieutenant of Inishmore* to offer a detailed analysis of the problems that arise due to Irish myth-making.

In order to appreciate the achievement of the play, it's important to understand its relationship with the documentary that it so thoroughly deconstructs – and indeed, the two are compared in further detail in Karen O'Brien's essay later in this book. *Man of Aran* is one of the key films of early Irish cinema, establishing many of the motifs that came to dominate the visual representation of Ireland during the latter half of the twentieth century. It presents a few days in the life of an apparently typical Aran family. We are shown their traditional stone cottage (where they sleep side by side with their livestock). We watch the film's 'hero' repairing his curragh (a small boat used for fishing). We see his wife gathering seaweed, which is used to fertilise the family's tiny crop of potatoes. The son of the family is shown perched on a cliff ledge, catching fish with an improvised line; later, he tries to join his father on a fishing expedition but is sent home because of his youth. In that relationship between father and son we have a strong sense that this way of life will persist, that the customs and traditions of Aran will be carried on through the generations for ever. This has the effect of giving the film a timeless quality: it was shot in the early 1930s, but might just as easily be set in the 1890s (when Synge first visited), or even the 1790s. Yet while the film celebrates the resilience of these people, it also shows how precarious their lives are – how much their safety is at the mercy of the weather, the landscape and, in particular, the sea.

The documentary presents itself as authentic, as revealing the truth about the islanders' lives and customs. But it is now widely understood that Flaherty contrived and invented many of the film's most important moments. The cottage was built specially for the film, for example – and the 'family' were unrelated to each other. The 'Man of Aran' was Colman 'Tiger' King, who is described in *Cripple* as being 'ugly as a brick of baked shite and everybody agrees' (*CI*, 7) – a remark that shows how Johnnypateenmike is wrong about almost everything, since King was handsome enough. King's 'wife' was Maggie Dirrane and their 'son' was a boy called Michael Dillane (Michaeleen). Michaeleen's real mother had initially refused to allow her son to participate in the film, but because Flaherty believed that Michaeleen was the only person who could play the role, he dedicated considerable energy to wearing down the mother's resistance. Finally, Flaherty convinced the local priest to intervene on his behalf (giving him a big present in return); it was only then that the mother gave way.

Flaherty adopted an exploitative approach towards the islanders in numerous other ways. As the film progresses, the action becomes more dramatic and less illustrative: this is because Flaherty deliberately created scenes that would excite his audience rather than merely inform them. Perhaps the best example of his artifice is the movie's final scene, which shows King and two other men rowing back to Inishmore in a terrifying storm that threatens to smash their boat to pieces. Not only did Flaherty send the men out into that storm so that he could shoot the scene; he also made them return to sea several times so that he could film them from different angles. As we watch the film, it seems nearly miraculous that the men survived the attempt to return to Inishmore even once; Flaherty's insistence that they repeat the attempt several times thus seems utterly unethical.

Flaherty also deliberately falsified information about the islanders. Most famously, he showed the men hunting and killing a shark – even though he knew that the islanders had not hunted the creatures for more than fifty years. Yet he knew that his scene would be considered dramatic, especially by his audience in America. After all, with its focus on a heroic male figure hunting an enormous fish, *Man of Aran* looks back to Melville's *Moby-Dick* (1851) just as it anticipates Hemingway's *The Old Man and the Sea* (1952) and even Spielberg's *Jaws* (1975). The film may have had an Irish setting, but it was clearly attempting to channel an American myth.

Despite (or perhaps because of) these deliberate acts of invention, Flaherty seems to call attention to the artificiality of his film in subtle ways. Its opening credits emphasise that the score is based on authentic Irish folk music, for instance – yet those credits also name King, Dirrane and Dillane as 'the characters'. More interesting still is the presentation of Maggie, who is not just a subject of the film, but also a kind of surrogate for the audience. Flaherty's camera seems constantly to linger on Maggie as she *watches*: we often see her staring through the frame of a window, or standing on a cliffside awaiting her husband's return. Pointing here, gesturing there, Maggie seems to direct the audience's gaze towards the scenes that Flaherty's camera records. By inviting the audience to watch her as she watches King, Flaherty seems to ask us to think about the process of *seeing*. And he also seems to suggest that the camera's gaze is not his, but Maggie's – deliberately distancing himself from what he represents, as if to create the illusion that the images on screen are an unmediated presentation of life as Maggie sees it. As we shall see, McDonagh makes interesting use of such techniques himself.

Perhaps one of the most distressing consequences of *Man of Aran* was that the experiences of King and Michaeleen are matched by Billy's – but only to a point. Both men toured internationally with the film after it was released, earning the escape from Aran that Billy dreams of. But unlike McDonagh's character, the two men found it impossible to return to Inishmore afterwards: they were too big for Aran, but unable to make a decent living anywhere else. They finally drifted to England, and Michaeleen disappeared altogether. So while these two real people achieved the success that eludes Billy, it is McDonagh's hero who ultimately seems better off.

One of the central aims of *Cripple* is, then, to challenge the validity of Flaherty's presentation of the Aran Islands. The play enacts that challenge most explicitly in the eighth scene, when we see the islanders sitting in a church hall where *Man of Aran* is being shown. Immediately notable (and immediately funny) is the film's failure to capture its audience's imagination: the characters talk throughout the screening and seem only half interested in what they're watching. They're also sceptical about the authenticity of the shark-hunting scene. 'It's mostly off America you do get sharks,' says Helen's brother Bartley, again showing how the film's imagery is American rather than Irish – and, to underline the point, he adds that 'this is the first shark I've ever seen off Ireland' (55). The islanders also seem to disapprove of the decision to kill the fish: as Johnny's Mammy says, 'They should give the shark a belt, then leave the poor gosawer alone' (58). In Flaherty's film, the hunt for the shark is presented as a necessity – as a metaphor for the islanders' constant battle for survival against the natural world. But McDonagh's people can afford to be compassionate – to animals, if not to each other.

This scene does something very important, not just for the play, but for McDonagh's whole *oeuvre*: it shows us what an engaged and genuinely critical audience looks like. Flaherty invited us to look at Maggie Dirrane as she watched Tiger King – and he did so as a way of subtly asserting the authenticity of his vision. But McDonagh instead uses the islanders' critical distance from the film as a way of warning us not to accept everything we see uncritically. The 'audience' in *Man of Aran* (that is, Maggie) is passive, accepting and mute; the 'audience' onstage in *Cripple* is active, unruly, outspoken and unwilling to allow an outsider to represent them falsely. McDonagh's audience is, in other words, exemplary, at least insofar as the reception of his own work is concerned.

McDonagh also challenges the apparent timelessness of *Man of Aran* by making visible what is invisible in the documentary: the presence of the film-making technology. He places a film screen and projector onstage, showing how the image is created. The moment towards the end of the scene when Billy steps out from behind the cinema screen can thus be seen (albeit momentarily) as a 'real' Aran Islander breaking through the mediated image of his people to assert the truth. But the truth that Billy asserts is not about the real Ireland, but the real Hollywood.

Billy's return is likely to come as a surprise to many people in the audience, since we will (most likely) believe that he had died in the previous scene. We had watched him sitting in what appears to be a run-down American motel, and had listened to his long and seemingly heartfelt monologue about the death of his parents, and his decision to abandon Inishmaan.

> Can't I hear the wail of the banshees for me, as far as I am
> from me barren island home? A home barren, aye, but proud
> and generous with it, yet turned me back on ye I did, to end
> up alone and dying in a one-dollar rooming-house, without
> a mother to wipe the cold sweat off me, nor a father to curse
> death o'er the death of me, nor a colleen fair to weep tears
> o'er the still body of me. (52–3)

As this scene comes to a conclusion, Billy appears to die – an event intended to have a major impact on the audience's emotional state. His reappearance from behind the screen shows that what we had taken for a tragic moment – his achievement of self-awareness and then his death – was actually a performance. And it was not a *real* performance, in a studio before cameras, or in a theatre before an audience, but a rehearsal for a screen test. To make matters worse, Billy was not just acting, but acting so badly that he didn't get the part for which he was auditioning. As he admits later, the producer's attitude was that it would be 'better to get a normal fella that can act crippled than a crippled fella who can't fecking act at all' (66). So what we had taken for 'the real' was in fact (at least) four times removed from the real: a rehearsal for an audition for a performance of a script that would be made into a film that will mediate the real world through art.

Billy seems relieved that he was unsuccessful. 'It wasn't an awful big thing at all to turn down Hollywood,' he tells Bartley, laughing at the

'the arse-faced lines they had me reading for them,' which he describes as a 'rake of shite . . . "An Irishman I am, begora! With a heart and a spirit on me not crushed be a hundred years of oppression" ' (63). Bartley – who, even for a McDonagh character, is not exactly gifted with discernment and insight – recognises that this dialogue is obviously daft. 'Them was funny lines, Cripple Billy,' he says. 'Do them again' (63). McDonagh's audience should feel a little foolish at this point: if the play's stupidest character can identify stage Irish nonsense when he hears it, why can't we?

Yet Billy is not in a position to criticise Hollywood for misrepresenting reality. Billy had falsified the truth himself, pretending that he had TB in order to persuade an islander called Babbybobby to row him to Inishmore – a particularly manipulative story, since Bobby's wife had died of TB herself. 'In the long run, I thought, or hoped, that if you had a choice between you being codded a while and me doing away with meself, once your anger had died down anyways, you'd choose you being codded every time,' says Billy by way of explanation. 'Was I wrong, Babbybobby? Was I?' (66). The answer, as Billy probably knows, is that he *was* wrong: Bobby beats him brutally with a length of lead piping in retribution for the deception. In many productions of the play, that act of violence is framed by the film screen, usually being performed either in front of it or immediately behind it (often in silhouette). In a 2008 Druid Theatre production, that screen was streaked with Billy's blood. Such directorial decisions clearly link Billy's manipulations of reality with Flaherty's.

The irony, of course, is that Billy's lies turn out to be true: in the play's final scene, the doctor tells him that he probably *does* have tuberculosis – though, in common with almost every other piece of information in the play, the doctor's diagnosis is uncertain. Billy's reaction is rather muted: 'That's a coincidence,' he says 'quietly' (69). Here again we find faint echoes of Synge, whose Christy Mahon became a 'mighty man' from the 'power of a lie': in both *Cripple* and *The Playboy of the Western World*, a well-told story has more power than a mundane truth. Johnny (and by extension McDonagh) shows an awareness of that power early in the play, when he suggests that the film crew will surely want to recruit him, due to his 'fine oratory skills

[that] could outdo any beggar [on] the Dublin stage' (8). Those words again resound with *Playboy*, and may remind some of a moment in that play when Synge's villagers award Christy several prizes: 'A fiddle was played by a poet in the years gone by! A flat and three-thorned blackthorn would lick the scholars out of Dublin town!' (1982: 154). In both *Playboy of the Western World* and *The Cripple of Inishmaan*, we learn something true about the characters based on the lies they choose to tell – and the lies that they choose to believe about themselves.

Yet as McDonagh makes clear, even when we are presented with 'the truth', we must still interpret it. For example, the audience is reminded early in the play not to believe everything they read in the newspapers – which are usually (though of course not always) seen as providing an objective account of the events of the day. 'There's a fella here, riz to power in Germany, has an awful funny moustache on him,' states Johnnypateenmike, reading the paper to his mother. 'Ah he seems a nice enough fella, despite his moustache. Good luck to him' (36). Clearly, anyone who can form the impression that Hitler was a 'nice enough fella' has rather missed the point of what he is reading.

We see a similar inability to interpret facts correctly in the islanders' superstitions. 'A Cripple fella's bad luck in a boat, and everybody knows' says Bobby (again, that phrase *everybody knows* should warn us that we're about to hear something inaccurate). He explains that this belief arose because one of the other islanders took a 'Cripple fella in his boat and it sank' (24). But given that the person who owned the boat was called 'Poteen Larry', it seems safe to assume that his death was caused by his own drunkenness rather than his passenger's disability. McDonagh reminds us again of how people who are seen as different will often become scapegoats within their communities. But he also shows how the apparent facts of any situation are always subject to interpretation – and so to misinterpretation.

That kind of skewed interpretation recurs throughout the play, especially in relation to religion. 'I always preferred Pontius Pilate to Jesus,' says Helen at one point. 'Jesus always seemed full of himself' (58). Bartley too seems unimpressed by Christ, criticising him because he drove a 'thousand pigs into the sea one time [and] drowned the lot of the poor devils' (58). Bartley uses the word 'devil' in its Hiberno-English sense, to describe a person who has experienced a misfortune (though as we see below, it is also sometimes used as a mark of grudging admiration). Yet Bartley's choice of the word is inadvertently accurate, of course. In Matthew's Gospel, Christ had encountered people possessed by devils; he banished the spirits from their human hosts into the bodies of pigs – and through destroying the pigs, he saved the people. Not for the first time, one of McDonagh's characters shows more sympathy for animals than humans; not for the first time, one of his characters says something accurate without meaning to do so.

McDonagh repeats that trick of contrasting a positive use of the word 'devil' with a negative reference to God in the play's ninth scene, when Johnny asserts that 'from God I'm sure that TB was sent Cripple Billy, for claiming he had TB when he had no TB' (70). Johnny agrees not to spread the story of Billy's illness around the island, calling himself a 'kind-hearted, Christian man' before admitting to giving his mother poteen earlier that day. 'I don't know where she got hold of that poteen,' says Johnny. 'She's a devil, d'you know?' he adds, half admiringly. For Johnny, being 'Christian' is not incompatible with attempting to kill his mother. Helen has a similar view of religion: she tells her brother that tormenting Billy's aunties 'wouldn't be a very Christian thing to do . . . but it'd be awful funny' – a contrast that says much about the use of humour in the play, and about Helen herself (48).

A similar reversal of our expectations can be found in the treatment of Irish history and politics. Michael Collins is referred to as 'one of the fat ones' in the annals of Irish history (50), a very unexpected (and unlikely) description for the man who had led the War of Independence against Britain from 1919 to 1921, before being assassinated in 1922 – only twelve years before the time in which the play is set. That story of national liberation is further re-imagined, not as the heroic struggle of a small nation against an empire, but as a rather cruel game involving eggs.

Helen   Do you want to play 'England versus Ireland'? . . . Stand here and close your eyes. You'll be Ireland.
Bartley *faces her and closes his eyes.*
Bartley   And what do you do?

Helen I'll be England.

Helen *picks up three eggs from the counter and breaks the first against* **Bartley***'s forehead.* **Bartley** *opens his eyes as the yolk runs down him, and stares at her sadly.* **Helen** *breaks the second egg on his forehead.*

Bartley That wasn't a nice thing at all to . . .

Helen Haven't finished.

Helen *breaks the third egg on* **Bartley**.

Bartley That wasn't a nice thing at all to do, Helen.

Helen I was giving you a lesson about Irish history. (50–1)

The 'lesson' being taught to Bartley is that the narrative of Ireland being oppressed by England is often deployed to excuse bad behaviour. This links *Cripple* with *The Lieutenant of Inishmore*, of course; but it also shows us that something we had taken as 'the truth' – the history of Ireland's independence – is (again) subject to interpretation and mediation, and so to manipulation.

McDonagh's harshest satire is for the Irish propensity towards national myth-making, especially in the commonly held notion that the country is a friendly place that the rest of the world is keen to visit. There is a recurring joke in the play about how Ireland 'mustn't be such a bad place' if German or French tourists – or sharks – want to visit it. This belief in Ireland's international reputation, McDonagh suggests, serves as a form of self-delusion, and thus as a distraction from the realities of the islanders' life and the responsibilities they face. This is probably best illustrated in a scene in which Johnny speculates about whether Billy is ill, but is distracted momentarily by an article in the newspaper. 'They all want to come to Ireland, sure. Germans, dentists, everybody,' he tells his mother, before offering the following explanation for the country's international popularity: 'In Ireland the people are more friendly. Everyone knows that. Sure isn't it what we're famed for?' He pauses for a moment before resuming his deliberations on Billy's health. 'I'd bet money on cancer,' he muses (37). McDonagh thus juxtaposes the illusion that Ireland is a friendly place against the reality that Johnny sees Billy's possible terminal illness as a story that he can spread around the island for financial gain.

Only one character in the play shows himself committed to the truth: the island's doctor. In one of the few moments of compassion during the play, Billy calls for an end to malicious gossiping in his community, citing the example of Jim Finnegan's daughter, who has a reputation for being promiscuous. 'It's only pure gossip that Jim Finnegan's daughter is a slut,' he protests. 'No,' says the doctor. 'Jim Finnegan's daughter is a slut . . . Just take me word' (67). Soon afterwards, the doctor refuses to allow Billy to exaggerate the positive qualities of his parents.

> **Billy**   Would you tell me something, Doctor? What do you remember of me mammy and daddy, the people they were? . . .
> **Doctor**   As far as I can remember, they weren't the nicest of people. Your daddy was an oul drunken tough, would rarely take a break from his fighting.
> **Billy**   I've heard me mammy was a beautiful woman.
> **Doctor**   No, no, she was awful ugly.
> **Billy**   Was she?
> **Doctor**   Oh, she'd scare a pig. But, ah, she seemed a pleasant enough woman, despite her looks, although the breath on her, well, it would knock you.
> **Billy**   They say it was that Dad punched Mammy while she was heavy with me was why I turned out the way I did.
> **Doctor**   Disease caused you to turn out the way you did, Billy. Not punching at all. Don't go romanticising it. (68–9)

We've seen throughout the play a scepticism about storytellers who claim to be telling the truth, from Flaherty's making of hi documentary to Johnypateenmike's dodgy news reports. Yet the doctor's assertion of the truth seems one of the cruellest acts in the play: he denies Billy the chance to believe something positive about his parents, and also the opportunity to 'romanticise' his disability.

That cruelty contrasts with the final story told by Johnny, which is about the death of Billy's parents. 'They'd . . . been told you'd be dying if they couldn't get you to the Regional Hospital and medicines down you. But a hundred pounds or near this treatment'd cost,' he claims (74). Johnny's story is that Billy's parents took out a life insurance policy and then killed themselves so that Billy would inherit the money, thus being able to afford his treatment. This news gives comfort to Billy immediately after the revelation that he probably has TB. 'So they *did* love me, in spite of everything,' he says, implying that his new awareness of his origins can compensate him for the grim (and all too short) future ahead of him (74).

As we find out moments later, Johnny's story is false. Or, more accurately, Johnny's story is contradicted by a new version of the tale, told by Billy's aunts Eileen and Kate, who say that his parents had tried to kill Billy but that he was rescued by Johnny. Again, we have no way of knowing whether *that* story is true: it must have been told to the aunts by Johnny himself, and there are no particular grounds to believe that he would have put his own life at risk to save Billy's. Yet most audiences assume this final version of the tale is the true one – perhaps because it is more in keeping with the tone of the play, or perhaps because it is simply the last iteration of the story. What McDonagh is showing us, however, is that our search for the truth is always bound to end in frustration: the best we can hope for is a more satisfying revision of an earlier fiction – whether that revision is a more credible version of the story of Billy's parents or McDonagh's response to Flaherty's depiction of the Aran Islands.

But if these layers of fiction frustrate our attempts to determine what is true, we should be aware of one feature of *Cripple* that is indisputable – which is that Johnny's claim that Billy's parents loved him is one of the play's only moments of kindness. We are being shown that a compassionate lie is far better than a cruel truth. Perhaps, then, the phrase that best sums up *Cripple* is one used by Eileen in the play's last minutes: she suggests that some day they must tell Billy the 'true story' about his origins. Those words seem contradictory: a story by definition is usually seen as *untrue*. But the play shows that a work of fiction can *reveal* a truth – even if that truth is only that the story-teller means to be kind.

So McDonagh draws intriguing parallels between Flaherty's mediation of reality in his documentary and the stories that are told by his characters – and especially by Johnypateenmike. That character, like

Flaherty, tells stories for economic gain and, although he is despised by his fellow islanders for his manipulations of reality, those stories are revealed as necessary – precisely because the truth of the islanders' lives is so unbearable. Likewise, although Billy is probably the most likeable character in the play, he lies constantly: about his illness, about his reasons for leaving Ireland and about his reasons for returning home.

The play thus has a double function: it attacks Hollywood for misrepresenting reality, but then celebrates the role of the artist-storyteller in providing solace from that reality. Perhaps, then, *Cripple* can be seen as an illustration of George Bernard Shaw's maxim that 'The honest artist does not pretend that his fictions are facts; but he may claim . . . that it is only through fiction that facts can be made instructive or even intelligible . . . The writer rescues [facts] from the unintelligible chaos of their actual occurrence and arranges them into works of art' (quoted in Holroyd: 443). Or, as Robert Flaherty puts it, rather more bluntly, 'Sometimes you have to lie. One has to distort a thing to catch its true spirit' (quoted in O'Brien, 2004: 47).

But if we accept that the artist will never tell the truth, but may ultimately *reveal* a truth, there is still the issue of responsibility for others. We can form ethical as well as aesthetic judgements about Flaherty's film, just as we can admire Billy while condemning his lies. To transform reality does not justify or excuse the manipulation and exploitation of others.

McDonagh will again take up the theme of artists' responsibility, both to their audiences and their subjects, in *The Pillowman*. But the impact of *Cripple* is (once again) to shift the focus away from the intentions of the storyteller and to point to the responsibilities of the audience itself. Like the islanders who laugh at the 'rake of shite' presented by film-makers, we must be critical, sceptical and active in our engagement with culture. And when we are misrepresented – or when we witness a misrepresentation – we must *act*. As we see with *The Lieutenant of Inishmore*, this focus on the responsibilities of an audience is particularly urgent when culture becomes politicised.

'A political what-do-ya-call-it': *The Lieutenant of Inishmore*

The Cripple of Inishmaan is set 'circa' 1934, at a time when modernity was beginning to make its presence felt in the Aran Islands. The encroachment of the new is made evident many times during that play, most obviously by the arrival of Robert Flaherty and his film-crew to Inishmore. But the change is apparent in more subtle ways too, such as the gradual replacement in Kate and Eileen's shop of home-grown foods like eggs and bacon with imported products such as canned peas – not to mention the yalla-mallows and other American 'sweeties' that Bartley craves so much. That change is evident too in the attitudes of the islanders to national identity: they seem to reject the importance of Irish history and its legacies, and turn instead towards America. So if Flaherty's *Man of Aran* suggested that the life of the Aran Islanders would endure for ever, *The Cripple of Inishmaan* instead seeks to present that location at a moment of transition from tradition to modernity.

The Lieutenant of Inishmore is set some sixty years later, probably in the months immediately prior to the declaration in 1994 of the first IRA ceasefire – a key moment in the development of the Northern Irish peace process. In one sense, the shift from tradition to modernity appears to have been completed. For instance, the characters seem to have fully accommodated themselves to global culture: they sing along to the music of Motorhead; they watch such British TV shows as *Top of the Pops*; they are comfortable with technological innovations such as mobile phones; and they go to the cinema to watch Academy Award-winning Irish films such as *In the Name of the Father* (a movie that shows the Irish finally telling their own stories rather than having them told by outsiders).

In fact, one of the key differences between *Cripple* and *Lieutenant* is the impact of cinematic culture on each play's characters. In *Cripple*, the Hollywood film crew seemed glamorous because they were inherently different from the islanders, but *The Lieutenant* gives us people whose lives are so saturated in pop culture that they behave like characters in Hollywood blockbusters. This difference is most evident in the presentation of the play's protagonist, 'Mad' Padraic. He shoots his victims at point-blank range, using two guns in the style of Keanu Reeves in *The Matrix* (1999), or of Nicolas Cage and John Travolta in John Wu's *Face/Off* (1997). Like a sheriff in an old-fashioned Western, Padraic confronts his enemies at high noon; those enemies camp out on the roadside by night, eating beans from a can like old-fashioned cowboys. And, like the crazed Mister Blonde in Tarantino's *Reservoir Dogs* (1992), Padraic traps one of his victims in a warehouse and tortures him with a cut-throat razor. So one of the most unexpected features of *Lieutenant* is that the characters share a popular culture with the rest of the Anglophone world: the play could easily be set anywhere in Ireland, and might very easily be transferred to a great many other locations internationally with only a few minor alterations of the language.

Yet despite the encroachment of global culture on the lives of the Aran Islanders, one feature of Irish tradition has not just survived but become stronger since the period of *Cripple*: Irish nationalism. In 1934, Anglo-Irish relations could be represented as a game involving eggs; the heroes of Irish nationalism (such as Michael Collins and Kevin Barry) could be dismissed as irrelevant to ordinary life. In *Lieutenant*, however, the conflict between Ireland and Britain is used to justify acts of violence that have horrendous consequences for every character in the play. So whereas in *Cripple* the impulse to turn Irish nationalists into heroes was gently mocked and ultimately dismissed, here that impulse will be subjected to a fiercely satirical assault.

It is perhaps because of the harshness of its satire that *The Lieutenant* has never been popular in Ireland. In *The Cripple*, the force that threatens to change the lives of the islanders is external and therefore can easily be mocked and (perhaps) resisted, if only symbolically. But in *The Lieutenant* the destabilising force is entirely home-grown. Mad Padraic may fight in Northern Ireland but he was shaped by Inishmore, and we often see how his actions are made possible by the indifference, cowardice or passivity of the other islanders. McDonagh's target is not just Irish terrorism but also the compliant and complacent culture that makes Irish terrorism possible.

Perhaps, then, the difference between the two plays could be characterised (if a little glibly) as a tale of two Clavens. In *Cripple*, Billy

Claven yearns to escape to Hollywood but, having experienced American culture at first hand, decides to return home because he realises that America is 'just the same as Ireland really' (*CI*, 64). In *Lieutenant*, Mairead Claven, the play's only female character, has also idealised a culture that exists outside her own immediate experience: the culture of Irish republicanism as it exists in Northern Ireland. Yet, her confrontation with reality, unlike Billy's, does not lead to dis-illusionment but, on the contrary, to her decision to appoint herself leader of her own terrorist army (opening up the question of whether the 'Lieutenant' of the play's title is Mairead or Padraic). Both of McDonagh's Aran Islands plays attack the use of popular culture to glamorise Irish life. But what is challenging about *Lieutenant* is that here the myth-making is by the Irish themselves – and it has consequences that are far worse than anything Robert Flaherty ever did.

So the Ireland that emerges from *The Lieutenant* is not a small country that suffers from being misrepresented by a large one (which, it could be argued, is what happens in *Cripple*). Rather, it is a place that has entered a state of profound moral crisis, largely as a result of its own people's actions. *Cripple* forced us to differentiate between the real, the true, the authentic and the factual; here McDonagh will show a similar need to redress a confusion between morality, ethics, prin-ciples, military tradition, political doctrine and Irish custom.

That confusion is apparent from the play's second scene, when Padraic sadistically tortures a drug-dealer, but then justifies his vio-lence on ideological grounds. James (his victim) has been 'keeping our youngsters in a drugged-up and idle haze, when it's out on the streets pegging bottles at coppers they should be' (*LI*,12). Padraic nevertheless considers himself a 'nice fella' because he takes two 'small' toenails from James's foot – and he took them both from the same foot, meaning that James will only have to hobble on one leg (rather than being confined to a wheelchair) on his way to the hospital. Padraic then allows James to pick his 'favourite' nipple, agreeing then to cut off the other one, before offering him the bus fare to pay for a visit to hospital, because 'the last thing you want now is septic toes' (16).

Padraic's sense of morality is shown to be thoroughly out of joint: selling marijuana to students is intolerable, he believes, but his acts of brutal retribution are entirely appropriate. Those acts might seem mindless and barbaric (and of course they are), but McDonagh is also using this scene to attack the 'punishment beatings' that were carried out by paramilitary groups on both sides of the Northern Irish conflict throughout (and after) the Troubles. Generally such beatings were inflicted upon 'anti-social' elements (such as joyriders and drug-dealers) within the paramilitary groups' own communities. McDonagh is expo-ing the obvious hypocrisy involved in such beatings, whereby acts of violence are used to 'punish' comparatively minor offences. He also shows how these acts of 'punishment' were used by paramilitary groups to terrorise their own communities. To take on the responsibility of 'punishing' anyone is to confer upon oneself a capacity for moral judgement – but a 'beating' is simply the use of superior physical strength by one person over another. So even the term 'punishment beating' reveals the confusion that existed at the heart of Irish paramilitarism, on both sides.

Christy, the storytelling INLA man who comes to Inishmore in order to murder Padraic, is similarly confused about his principles. He quotes on one occasion from Marx and on another from the Jesuits, a combination of Christianity with Communism that suggests that he doesn't think very deeply about the source of his ideas. His colleague Joey is equally perplexed, complaining that the terrorist organisation he has joined is forcing him to commit acts of violence against cats, while also suggesting that Airey Neave didn't deserve to die, because of his 'funny name' (29). Christy's response to such complaints is to draw on a ridiculous version of Irish history. 'Do you know how many cats Oliver Cromwell killed in his time?' he asks, justifying his own actions on the basis of something that may have been done by an Englishman more than three hundred years earlier (30).

Mairead shows a similar confusion in her discussion of 'valid targets', another oxymoronic phrase from the Irish republican lexicon. The notion of 'validity' suggests that there are circumstances under which violence can be justified. McDonagh exposes this view as self-contradictory, telling us that Mairead used to shoot cows' eyes out as a form of 'political protest' against the meat trade, but that her 'thinking has gone full tilt since then and they are valid targets no longer' (19). The notion of blinding animals to protest against the meat trade is a very good joke, but it is also a harsh criticism of the way in which terrorist organisations justify their destruction of human life in terms of such abstractions as the resistance of oppression, the search for freedom, and so on. The fact that Mairead describes her illogical activities as resulting from 'thinking' only adds to the irony. And of course the fact that Mairead's thoughts 'tilt' wildly between extremes tells us something about her inability to intellectualise anything.

The problem, however, is that this moral confusion is evident in all the characters in the play, even those who are not politically engaged. We see it in the play's comic double act of Donny and Davey (Padraic's father and Mairead's brother). They object that Padraic shoots his victims with two guns from point-blank range – not from a sense of compassion for those victims, but because Padraic's use of these weapons does not involve enough skill. They contrast Padraic with Mairead, who, because she shoots her victims from long range, 'sees more of the sport' involved in maiming and killing people (56). The pair go on to express respect for the IRA as 'more established' than the INLA; they 'travel further afield . . . They go to Belgium sometimes [and] you never see the INLA shooting Australians' (55). Even Padraic grudgingly respects the IRA for their 'skill': 'One thing about the IRA anyways, as much as I hate the bastards, they know how to make a decent bomb,' he concedes (14).

The cause of this confusion has been mentioned briefly above: the characters form their moral responses to terrorism under the influence of images of violence from film, song, literature and other forms of culture. At many times during the play, McDonagh contrasts the brutality of the action onstage with his characters' references to popular representations of violence. The play therefore reminds us of how violence is presented – and often sanitised and made pretty – by culture. McDonagh attacks that beautification of violence by providing a series of jarring contrasts between culture and reality. Jaunty Irish rebel songs are played to the rhythm of hacksaws dismembering real bodies. The film *In the Name of the Father* is proposed as suitable entertainment for a romantic night out. Mairead and Padraic propose that their list of valid targets should be organised like *Top of the Pops*. Even theatre is contrasted with terrorism, as McDonagh emphasises by having Padraic object to the Irish authors Dominic and Brendan Behan. 'If they'd done a little more bombing and a little less writing I'd've had more respect for them,' he says, alluding to the fact that Brendan Behan gave up membership of the IRA and turned to writing in the 1940s (48). One consequence of that presentation of violence through culture is to desensitise the characters. As we've seen already, most of the people in the play seem to be more sympathetic to animals than towards each other (another link with *Cripple*, of course).

Indeed, McDonagh's characters repeatedly use human traits to refer to animal characters. Davey complains that all the cats in Inishmore are 'full of themselves' (5), but notes that Wee Thomas 'would always say hello to you were you to see him on a wall' (6). Padraic's loving description of Wee Thomas is even more sympathetic. He remembers how his cat would

> pooh in a corner when you were drunk and you'd forget to
> let him out, and he'd look embarrassed the next day then, as
> if it was his fault, the poor lamb. How in through the hole
> in the wall there he'd come, after a two-day bender chasing
> skirt the length of the island, and pulling your hair out for
> fear something had happened to him you'd be, and him
> prancing in then like 'What was all the fuss about? I was off
> getting me end away.' (47–8)

The audience has been trained by cinema and advertising to relate to this sentimental treatment of animals, as McDonagh indicates by having his character use the word 'lamb' as a term of endearment. The emotional range of the cat, which is capable of both embarrassment and exuberant promiscuity, is considerably wider than that of most of the human characters in the play. This humanisation of animals is intended to contrast with the presentation of the humans, who shoot, torture and dismember each other – apparently without any reservations or moral qualms. Padraic, for example, is willing to murder his own father because of the death of his cat, while Mairead kills Padraic in revenge for his shooting of her cat Sir Roger. And while Donny and

Davey show no great sympathy for the three people whose bodies they are forced to dismember, they cannot bring themselves to shoot Wee Thomas.

If McDonagh's characters are confused about the difference between animal and human, they also appear deeply anxious about issues of gender and sexuality. As Lionel Pilkington points out, in the Irish theatre 'political commitment, most especially the kind of anti-state political activity demanded by the IRA is [frequently] exposed as a subterfuge of domestic and/or sexual failure' (2001: 146). That is, Irish dramatists often suggest that militant nationalism arises not from political ideology, but from sexual dysfunction. This symbolism can be traced back to Sean O'Casey's *The Plough and the Stars* (1926), in which the political convictions of the play's protagonist Jack Clitheroe are shown to be directly related to the deterioration of his sexual relationship with his wife Nora. This symbolism is brought to a conclusion in the play's second half, when Nora has a miscarriage due to Clitheroe's decision to keep fighting in the 1916 Easter Rising. For O'Casey, military activity and sexual success (as represented through reproduction) appear incompatible.

The representation of terrorism in Ireland as arising from sexual dysfunction may be seen as serving ideological aims, and indeed can be read in the context of postcolonial ideas about Ireland (as Eamonn Jordan show later in this book). Such representations attempt not only to emasculate terrorists and nationalists, but also take the societal problem of militant violence and translate it into a private failure by an individual. This de-legitimises the terrorist while reinforcing the position of the state. The trope is to be found in many Irish plays, from O'Casey's *Plough* in 1926 to Rosemary Jenkinson's *The Bonefire* in 2006.

McDonagh explores this mode of representation through his characterization of Davey and Mairead. Davey's femininity is emphasised throughout the play: he rides his mother's pink bicycle and his hair is called a 'girl's mop' (4). He does not express his concern for the murdered cats in the play from fear that his friends would 'call me an outright gayboy, and they do enough of that with me hairstyle' (18). His femininity is also shown in his declaration that 'I love my

Mam . . . Love her more than anything' (26). Mairead, in contrast, is often mistaken for a boy (33, 51), and gains acceptance from Padraic only when she has proven her masculinity. Padraic initially rejects her request to be admitted into his terrorist cell: 'We don't be letting girls in the INLA No. Unless pretty girls' (35). Mairead's development during the action can thus be seen as a pseudo-feminist narrative, in which she proves her right to be admitted to the INLA. From that perspective, it is significant that Padraic acknowledges that she has 'some balls, anyways' (35) before finally allowing her to join his splinter group.

This obsession with gender is revealed as an anxiety about the instability of sexual identity (a point explored in more detail by Joan Dean later on). Padraic responds strongly to Mairead's suggestion that he might he gay: 'I do not prefer boys! There's no boy-preferers involved in Irish terrorism, I'll tell you that!' (33). Similarly, when Mairead kills Brendan and Joey, they are more concerned about the gender of their assailant than their own imminent death. Brendan thinks that Mairead appears to be 'a boy with lipstick' and Joey that she is 'a girl with no boobs'. In response, Brendan prays not to be 'killed by a girl, Sweet Jesus! I'll never live it down' (51).

In O'Casey, sexual dysfunction and confusion about sexual identity are symbolic of the inherent futility of republican violence, but McDonagh brings his two most violent characters – Mairead and Padraic – into a romance. Mairead entertains romantic ideals about Padraic, and McDonagh attempts to gain the audience's sympathy for her by having Padraic initially reject her advances. Their relationship becomes sexual only after Mairead saves Padraic's life, by assassinating Joey, Christy and Brendan. Terrorist violence is shown not to impede sexual expression, but actually to make it possible. So McDonagh has taken a common presentation of the Irish terrorist – and uses it in ways that are unexpected and disorientating.

One possible explanation for this strategy is that McDonagh is attempting to reject the idealising of women within Irish literature – particularly in Irish literature with a nationalist or republican bias. In such writings, the nation is personified as a passive female figure who requires the protection – and usually the blood sacrifice – of young men. This personification has been given several names: Roisin Dubh, Dark Rosaleen, the Shan Van Vocht (the poor old woman), and so on. One of the most famous presentations of such idealised female figures features in the play *Kathleen ni Houlihan*, which was produced by W.B. Yeats and Lady Augusta Gregory in 1902, in which an old woman visits an Irish farmhouse to complain that her 'four green fields' (a metaphor for the four provinces of Ireland) have been stolen from her. She appeals to the young men in the family for help and, after some debate, one of them chooses to follow her, knowing he will meet with certain death by doing so. Due to his willingness to sacrifice his life for her, the old woman is transformed at the end of the play into a beautiful maiden with the 'walk of a queen'. The symbolism suggests that through the blood sacrifice of young male patriots Ireland will be regenerated.

Many Irish dramatists have sought to undermine that personification of Ireland as a woman. Again, O'Casey's *The Plough and the Stars* rejected the motif, infamously comparing the idealised female version of Ireland with a real prostitute – an affront so offensive that Irish nationalists rioted in the theatre upon the play's premiere. In 1958, Brendan Behan would go a step further, setting *The Hostage* (his play about the IRA) in a brothel. The suggestion being made by both men was that, if Ireland was to be seen as a woman, the country appeared more like a whore than a queen.

McDonagh's presentation of Mairead can be seen as operating in the tradition of O'Casey and Behan (two writers with whom he shares much more). Yet, characteristically, McDonagh adds something new to the old image, presenting a female character who does not want to *inspire* acts of Irish patriotism (as in Yeats and Gregory) or to be a passive conduit for male desire (as in O'Casey and Behan). Instead, he emphasises the political and sexual agency of his heroine.

Mairead's attraction for Padraic appears to arise because he can help her to become a member of a Republican paramilitary group – to become, in effect, what she has wanted to be since she was the eleven-year-old girl who begged Padraic to bring her with him to 'free' the north of Ireland. As the play continues, we witness Mairead's attempts to be taken seriously by a group of men who think of women only as symbols. Her eventual acceptance by Padraic – not to mention the fact that she is the only Republican character left standing at the play's conclusion – refutes the notion that women cannot be active participants in the nationalist cause. Ultimately, Mairead comes to realise that much of that cause is founded on empty values. 'I think I'll be staying around here for a biteen,' she declares at the play's conclusion. 'I thought shooting fellas would be fun. But it's not. It's dull' (66). But before leaving the stage, she promises to launch an investigation into the death of her own cat. Her implication is clear: she will be back the next day to extract revenge against Donny and Davey, setting her own rules and dispensing her own version of justice. The presentation of Mairead therefore challenges the idealising of women within Irish drama.

This brings us back to the link between Billy and Mairead. As stated at the beginning of this chapter, the two characters are very different from each other, but they have in common a desire for self-definition – and a refusal to be defined by others. McDonagh's sympathy (as ever) seems to be with characters who choose to take creative responsibility for the direction of their own stories. This is not to suggest that Mairead is intended to be seen as admirable in any way, but to point out that, just as McDonagh attacks the mythologising of Aran in *Cripple*, so in *The Lieutenant* he undermines the mythologising of women in Irish drama and Irish republican rhetoric.

If *The Cripple of Inishmaan* sets out to reveal the fictions that underlie Flaherty's *Man of Aran* documentary, *The Lieutenant* thus reveals the facts that are obscured by Republican rhetoric. The play features an almost sickening number of references to specific events from the Troubles – and many victims of the IRA and INLA are alluded to, sometimes for humorous purposes. For instance, Padraic's reference to attacking 'chip shops' can be seen as a reference to the 1993 bombing by the IRA of a chip shop on the Shankill Road, which led to the death of nine civilians. He also mentions shooting builders, a reference to a real IRA atrocity in which eight Protestant builders were murdered by the IRA in 1992 because they were working on a military base. There are also references to Airey Neave, murdered by the INLA in 1979; to the Guildford Four, who were wrongfully accused of membership of the IRA and spent fourteen years in prison as a result; to Richard Heakin, an off-duty British soldier who was murdered by the IRA in Belgium in 1988; to Nicholas Spanos and Stephen Melrose, two Australian tourists killed by the IRA in the Netherlands in 1990; and to Jonathan Ball (aged three) and Timothy Parry (aged twelve), killed when the IRA bombed Warrington in 1993. In total, twenty-three innocent victims of Irish terrorists are alluded to during *The Lieutenant*; there is also a joke about the thirteen people killed in Derry by the British army during Bloody Sunday.

It is difficult to know how to react to McDonagh's inclusion of those thirty-six real people – just as it can be difficult for some Irish people to understand why McDonagh decided to set his obviously imagined Irish plays in the real location of Leenane. Is he laughing at the expense of victims of Irish terrorism, thereby intensifying the pain of those still mourning them? Some critics believe so. But perhaps, just as the Leenane setting of the *Trilogy* forces the audience to consider the real consequences of those plays, the function of the references to victims of Irish terrorism in *Lieutenant* is to remind the audience that the events on stage have a real political context. The Troubles may seem farcical, the ideology of terrorists may seem ridiculous – but the tragedy is that real people were actually killed. Furthermore, *The Lieutenant* is not simply an attempt to criticise the IRA and the INLA; it is instead addressing the problem of terrorism and political violence generally by exploring how it is represented culturally, and inviting us to think again about our own responses to it.

The Lieutenant of Inishmore thus reimagines many common representations of Irish terrorism. McDonagh shows his audience that they will condemn terrorists as animals, while also caring about the fate of a cat that wanders around a stage covered in human body parts. He shows us that we may confuse terrorism and sexual dysfunction, even as we sympathise with a heroine's attempts to gain the love of a man who does not seem to notice her. He will invite us to laugh at jokes about Irish terrorism before reminding us that we are laughing about the deaths of real people.

This means that the confused morality of McDonagh's characters will almost certainly be mirrored by the confused responses of audiences at his play. This confusion often provokes consternation and irritation, but it *should* also provoke thought. McDonagh's work is often described as 'empty', but *The Lieutenant* illustrates that a better word might be 'vacuous': the play leaves spaces that demand to be filled. Faced with the amorality onstage, the only response for an audience is to react *morally*; faced with representations that attempt to manipulate, the response it to mistrust *all* representation. McDonagh is again demanding that his audiences start to think more critically about the images of violence and terrorism that they are presented with on a daily basis.

This tactic makes the play very funny, but *The Lieutenant* should not be seen only as comedy. McDonagh is offering a response to his audiences' willingness to let sentimentality and lazy thinking determine their actions. It should be shocking for any audience to realise that terrorists have been humanised, just as it should shock them that they can care more about animals than people. As happens with every McDonagh play, the audience will inevitably find itself experiencing the guilty pleasure of laughing at something that we just should not find funny. No member of McDonagh's audience should go away feeling comfortable with his or her responses.

Perhaps, then, this play is genuinely dangerous, not because of Irish terrorism, but because its theatricality challenges audiences in a way that some will find uncomfortable, and perhaps even intolerable. It forces us to think about what we have seen, and reminds us of our willingness to be influenced by culture ourselves – like McDonagh's characters, we too may have been desensitised to violence by cinema, song and theatre.

What, then, has changed between 1934 in *Cripple* and 1993 in *Lieutenant*? We might initially have formed the impression that modernity and nationalism are incompatible: that while the Aran Islands become more awash with global culture, Irish atavism will weaken. What is fascinating and perhaps even challenging about *Lieutenant* is that it shows how global culture and nationalism are not incompatible but complementary. McDonagh's point is that our tolerance of violence in society must in some way be linked to the beautification of violence in global culture: by song, film and theatre; by Irish rebel songs, by Motorhead, by spaghetti westerns, by *The Matrix*. The contrast between the highly aestheticised representations of violence alluded to by his characters, and the brutality and ugliness of McDonagh's final scene in the play arises from a desire to make a very serious point. By covering his stage in blood, gore and human body parts, McDonagh is showing us what happens to human bodies when people are killed – and reminding us that murder is not glamorous or beautiful but sordid, revolting and fundamentally unacceptable. By pointing out to his audience that his characters are manipulated and influenced by the representation of violence through culture, McDonagh draws attention to the artificiality of his own play in a way that asks his audiences to consider whether they themselves have been influenced by mass-mediated representations of terrorism and violence.

We return briefly to the question of whether McDonagh is a political playwright when discussing *The Pillowman* (a play from which the present chapter takes its name). But as we have seen already, the strategy of forcing the audience to think is a central feature of all McDonagh's plays. Deployed in a satire about terrorism, however, it shows us that his work also has important social consequences – not just for how we see terrorism, but how we see the interlinking of violence with politics.

The Aran Islands plays in production

I've suggested earlier that McDonagh's reception in Ireland was (at least initially) influenced not so much by his own skills as a writer as by the reputation of Druid. That is, his work was seen as a continuation of that company's productions of Synge and Tom Murphy, and his plays were judged in the context of earlier Irish drama. Something similar happened in England, where McDonagh's reputation was founded on the context in which his work was initially produced rather than being seen in terms of what he was doing in his own right.

The Beauty Queen premiered in Galway in February 1996, as we've seen, but soon transferred to London's Royal Court Theatre, which co-produced *The Leenane Trilogy* in the following year. McDonagh's plays appeared at the Royal Court at a time when it was experiencing a significant renaissance, thanks to new work which included Sarah Kane's *Blasted* (1995) and Mark Ravenhill's *Shopping and Fucking* (1996). Because McDonagh's work appeared at around the same time, as those other new plays, he was seen not just as the heir to an Irish dramatic tradition but also as one of a group of exciting young writers who were forcing British theatre into a new era.

Much of that work is now known as 'in-yer-face' theatre – a term coined by Aleks Sierz, who defines such plays as including 'any drama that takes its audience by the scruff of the neck and shakes it until it gets the message', often by using 'shock tactics' (2001: 4). The term 'implies that you are being forced to see something close up, that your personal space has been invaded' (4), so that audiences 'either feel like fleeing or are suddenly convinced [the play is] the best thing they have ever seen, and they want all their friends to see it too' (5). The value of this kind of theatre, according to Sierz, is that shock disturbs the 'spectator's habitual gaze' (5), and that it can renegotiate the relationship between the audience, performers and performance space. Many of those characteristics have existed throughout the history of drama, of course, but Sierz argues that 'never before had so many plays been so blatant, aggressive or emotionally dark' and that 'although drama has always represented human cruelty, never before had it seemed so common' (30).

A notable feature of Sierz's terminology is that the experiences he describes all involve spontaneous emotional reactions. A play such as *The Lieutenant of Inishmore* certainly *can* provoke such responses: it *is* shocking, it *does* disturb one's 'habitual gaze' – and it has undoubtedly made many people feel like fleeing the theatre. But what happens afterwards? My suggestion about all of McDonagh's plays is that, whatever we experience in the theatre, we have an opportunity to think about and analyse those experience *afterwards* – and it may be that we have an obligation to do so. In other words, we should not take 'in-yer-face' theatre only at face value, but should consider what our immediate reactions tell us about the plays – and about ourselves.

Yet because audiences and critics found the plays of Kane, Ravenhill, McDonagh and others *so* shocking, they tended to focus only on those immediate affective responses. Kane's work only began to receive detailed consideration after her death in 1999, and to a great extent much of McDonagh's work remains underrated and under-explored, as I've argued in the introduction to this book. McDonagh may have gained a lot of positive short-term notice in England for his use of 'shock tactics' – but, once the shock had worn off, many people assumed there was nothing left that might be worth thinking about.

A further impact of the 'in-yer-face' movement was that some dramatists became celebrity figures, albeit reluctantly. This problem was especially evident in the media presentation of Sarah Kane, who was forced only three years after her debut to produce her play *Cleansed* (1998) under the pseudonym 'Marie Kelvedon', which, according to David Greig, was 'partly a private joke and partly a serious attempt to allow her work to escape, briefly, from the shadow of being [written by] 'Sarah Kane, the controversial author of *Blasted*' (Greig, 2001: xii).

If Kane was often spoken of as a new Sylvia Plath, then McDonagh quickly became a new Johnny Rotten for British drama. He first came to the attention of the general British public when, presented with the George Devine Award for most promising newcomer in December 1996, he had a disagreement at the award ceremony in London with the actor Sean Connery. That incident was quickly picked up by the tabloid press, with the result that, in the words of Fintan O'Toole, McDonagh became famous overnight, not for his plays but for 'telling Sean Connery to fuck off'.

That incident had a disproportionate impact on the construction of McDonagh's reputation in England (which in turn affected his reputation in Ireland), so that he soon became known as the 'bad boy of British theatre'. As Karen Vandevelde points out:

> Extensive reviews and interviews in popular magazines . . .
> which generally devote little column space to drama or
> dramatists, presented Martin McDonagh as an upcoming
> enigmatic pop star and the most innovative playwright
> Ireland or England had ever witnessed. 'A theatrical star'
> (*Hot Press*), 'a sensation' (*Sunday Telegraph*), 'a white-knuckle
> roller coaster' (*Daily Telegraph*) and 'the shocking dark-comic
> phenomenon (*Newsday*). Descriptions such as these are

generally attributed to radical contemporary art, pop stars or
notorious film directors, and it is quite surprising to meet
them in the rhetoric of theatre criticism. (2000: 292)

The premiere of *The Cripple of Inishmaan* at London's National Theatre
was somewhat overshadowed by such controversy. This was regrettable, because the production was directed with wit and dynamism by
Nicholas Hytner, and it gathered together one of the finest Irish casts
seen on a London stage in many years, featuring such distinguished
performers as Ray McBride, Anita Reeves and Dearbhla Molloy, while
also introducing promising young actors Rúaidhrí Conroy and
Aisiling O'Sullivan (both of whom would later appear in *Six Shooter*).
It also featured a marvellous set and costume design by Bob Crowley
(brother of John, who would direct *The Pillowman* and *A Behanding
in Spokane*). The setting of each scene was established by the use of
free-standing structures that rolled on- and offstage, sometimes merely
being turned around to present new environments. In a review for
Variety, Matt Wolf praised the 'gently absurdist . . . sloping lines of
Bob Crowley's gliding sets' (1997), and in doing so captures well their
impact. By showing audiences how each scene was created – by requir-
ing the performers literally to set each scene by moving the set around
– Crowley reproduced McDonagh's strategy of rendering the filmmaking technology visible. That is, he showed the audience how the
play's theatrical effects were constructed. As a result, audiences were
always being reminded that they were watching a play – not a
reproduction of reality, but a work of fiction.

Yet as *Cripple* became more popular, McDonagh found his reputation rapidly deteriorating in London. This seems to have been due
(in part) to his audiences' inability to reconcile their enjoyment of the
cartoonish Ireland seen in *Cripple* with the media presentation of
McDonagh himself. Richard Eyre and Nicholas Wright relate
McDonagh's decline in popularity to the British public's concern that
he was not as 'Irish' as they first thought. 'When McDonagh, in his
many media appearances, turned out to be a chic young guy, wearing
the nicest Armani suit you've ever seen and sporting a marked South
London accent, bemusement turned to fury,' they write. ' "If this is an

Irish playwright, I'm a banana," cried the chorus' (2001: 277). Aleks Sierz offers a slightly different suggestion – that McDonagh's apparently arrogant style in his 'many media appearances' might be to blame for the backlash: 'After he compared himself to the young Orson Welles, claiming to be "the greatest" and attacking older playwrights for being "so ugly" and "really badly dressed", his sudden decline seemed like a comeuppance' (225). Whether we agree with Eyre and Wright or with Sierz, all three writers illustrate one point clearly: McDonagh was clearly 'getting up the nose of the theatrical establishment' as Penelope Denning accurately put it (2001).

The 'sudden decline' that Sierz refers to is that McDonagh found himself in a strange situation whereby, despite his having four plays in production in the West End simultaneously, no one wanted to produce a new work, *The Lieutenant of Inishmore*. Much to McDonagh's disgust, the play had been rejected by the two English theatres that had championed his work, the National Theatre and the Royal Court – and it was also rejected by Druid. McDonagh was in no doubt about the causes of that rejection: censorship. He told Sean O'Hagan that 'the National's Trevor Nunn thought the play so inflammatory that its production might threaten the Northern Irish peace process' (2001). And, as Penelope Denning relates in a 2001 interview:

'The National refused to do it for political reasons.' McDonagh's easy smile flicks off. 'I can't quite accept the whole political question that the play's too dangerous to be done. The point of writing it was to be dangerous, so not to do it for those reasons smacked of crass stupidity and gutlessness.' He had the same response from the Royal Court. 'Just as gutless. I would have thought it would have been up their alley, the hip young theatre that they're supposed to be. We tried continually for the last four years. We could have done it at a smaller place; the Tricycle in Kilburn said yes to it a while ago. But it is quite an expensive show: guns, bodies and so on. It's a good play anyway, a good story. It pushes the boundaries of violence and animal exploitation quite far.' (2001)

The Lieutenant of Inishmore was eventually premiered by the Royal Shakespeare Company at its Other Place studio theatre in Straford-upn-Avon in 2001, seven years after McDonagh had written it and four years after his previous UK premiere. By that time, the 'peace process' in Northern Ireland was well established, following the signing of the Good Friday Agreement of 1998. The so-called 'Real' IRA has perpetrated one of the worst atrocities of the Troubles in August 1998, when their bomb in the town of Omagh killed twenty-nine people – but that tragedy aside, terrorist acts in Northern Ireland had generally reduced in severity and frequency since *The Leenane Trilogy* had premiered. In a review of the play for BBC Radio, Germaine Greer warned that it might yet provoke reprisals: 'A play-house is a very soft target, and terrorists are very good at attacking soft targets,' she said, gloomily. But most commentators agreed that *The Lieutenant* was unlikely even to be noticed by Irish Republicans, or to have any serious impact on Northern Irish politics.

Nevertheless, the RSC avoided focusing on the Troubles in its pre-publicity for their production – and there was also some evidence of nervousness that the show might provoke protests from animal rights groups, and that its violence be seen as objectionable. The company took the unusual step of warning audiences about its content prior to its opening. As David Ward reports:

> In a letter to all ticket holders, Kate Horton, the RSC's director of marketing, makes it clear 'no cats or people are hurt in reality', but says the show is unsuitable for children under fifteen because of its violence. She also warns of a large number of gunshots. 'The sound generated is within the legal limit for noise exposure. However, if you or anyone in your party is very young, elderly, pregnant or visually or hearing impaired, you should be aware of the significant noise.'

These warnings continued to be issued well into the play's run. As Joan FitzPatrick Dean reports in her review of the production for *Theatre Journal*, 'When I booked by phone, I was advised not to sit in the front row because of the risk of being spattered with stage blood' (2002).

This cautious attitude is somewhat difficult to explain. The RSC's repertoire has included a number of violent Jacobean tragedies – not to mention Shakespeare's *Titus Andronicus*, a play that concludes with a mother being fed her own sons, who have been murdered and then baked in a pie. The suggestion that the play is not suitable for children certainly makes sense, but the assertion that it might be dangerous for pregnant women seems sensationalistic. Also notable is the attempt to reassure audiences that 'no cats or people' (not, one notes, 'no people or cats') are hurt during the production.

In fact, the status of the animals in the original Stratford production, together with the play's excessive violence, were the most controversial aspects of its initial run. Reviews and features tended to avoid serious consideration of both the politics and the quality of the play, instead focusing on its sensationalistic and affective elements, under generally facetious headlines such as 'Sick Buckets Needed in the Stalls' or 'Animal Harm'.

It's possible that the theatre's marketing may have encouraged such responses. One of the most common publicity images for the premiere shows a faceless woman with a rifle, kneeling bare-legged in front of an exploding armoured vehicle, as a cat walks by. What is being highlighted here are sex (as implied by the stance and dress of the woman), violence (the explosion) and farce (the incongruous appearance of the cat). Perhaps it would be unfair to describe that image as misleading, but let's remember that the play involves no explosions; that the only vehicle shown on stage is a pink bicycle; and that its only woman character is described in the stage directions as 'plain' and by the other characters as like 'a boy wearing lipstick' (*LI*, 51).

The Lieutenant was well received by its first reviewers, though it didn't generate quite the same level of enthusiasm as McDonagh's earlier work. Its director was Wilson Milam, an American whose style appeared heavily influenced by the work of Steppenwolf Theater, as evidenced in his skill at directing fast-paced action, involving overlapping dialogue and speedy scene changes. He also had an impressive ability to generate tension through the use – or, more frequently, the threat – of violence. He had been responsible for the first production of Tracy Letts's *Killer Joe*, a 1993 play which is thought to have been an important influence on McDonagh (and which, with its focus on small-time crooks who find themselves out of their depth when they try to con a much more dangerous character, can be seen as a possible influence on *A Behanding in Spokane*).

The performances were generally well received, with the actors playing Padraic and Mairead receiving particular praise. The part of Padraic was played by David Wilmot, who would later appear in *Six Shooter* in the role of Pato. Mairead was played by Kerry Condon, who attracted positive reviews for her performance as Octavia in the HBO–BBC TV series *Rome*, and who also starred in Australian movie *Ned Kelly*, which was scripted by McDonagh's brother John. Owen Sharpe, who had appeared in the premiere of *The Cripple of Inishmaan* as Bartley, took the part of Davey, for which he also reviewed positive notices – though he was later replaced by Domhnall Gleeson (whose father Brendan appeared in *Six Shooter* and *In Bruges*).

If *The Cripple* marked the beginning of a backlash against McDonagh, *The Lieutenant* showed that his career was not over yet – so there is an obvious contrast between the two plays in terms of their British reception. As they toured internationally, however, both met with a wide variety of reactions – in terms of the issue of authenticity in the case of *Cripple* and (unsurprisingly) of terrorism in *The Lieutenant*. In November 1998, for instance, an *LA Times* critic, reviewing an American production of *The Cripple of Inishmaan* at the Geffen playhouse, stated that, as a Londoner, McDonagh had no right to portray the Irish as he did. This statement led to a well-informed debate in the letter pages of that newspaper about the Irish elements of the play.

In the same year, the Court Theatre of Christchurch, New Zealand, also produced *The Cripple*. That theatre's show programme featured background information about McDonagh, the Aran Islands, Robert Flaherty and many other features of the play; and it pointed out the play's resemblances to the works of Synge and Pinter. The theatre also produced an education resource kit, which included an innovative 'before and after' exercise: student readers were asked before the show to write down three stereotypes commonly associated with the Irish; then they were asked to consult their list at the end of the show, and consider how McDonagh had undermined their preconceptions. Drawing attention to the difference between the world that 'we live in' and the 'world [that] is imagined by others', the booklet asked student audiences to consider how the play might apply to New Zealand.

On the other hand, there were (again) some serious misinterpretations of the play's satire. For example, in a programme note for the Theatre of Western Springs' 2003 production of *The Cripple of Inishmaan*, director Dorothy Parlaw introduces the play as follows:

> Beautiful Ireland . . . the modulations of the light, the surprising moments of the rain. Tonight we are telling a great little story; one-half laughter, one-half tears. [. . .] When two or three Irishmen get together, whether in the kitchen or a pub, a song-fest is inevitable. As in a junket of storytelling, these song-fests reveal two sides of the Irish: the laughter and the tears. They create a beautiful whole, like the weaving together of the glorious colors in an Irish shawl, the purples, the roses, the greens, and the blues. So sit back and relax, and enjoy the Cripple's adventures. No great lesson, no great theme – just a story. The laughter will come of itself. The tears are inevitable.

Anyone who lives in (or has even briefly visited) Ireland will smile ruefully at the use of the words 'rain' and 'surprising' in the same sentence above, and it thus seems apparent that the writer's understanding of the country might be lacking in some important respects. Nevertheless, she considers herself qualified to direct her audience's reception of the play. There is 'no great lesson' in this 'little story', Parlow writes, promising to use the 'Cripple's adventures' to show audiences the two halves of the Irish character – laugher *and* tears – that together make up our beautiful, shawl-like, whole. This is not the kind of language likely to encourage an audience to seek out a sophisticated interplay of images, clichés and stereotypes.

The reception of *The Lieutenant* was overwhelmingly influenced by the 'War Against Terror' that began soon after its April 2001 premiere; the play's treatment of terrorism seemed to resonate with people who were struggling to come to terms with the world after 9/11. When the play appeared in London's West End, for instance, Wilson Milam recalls seeing 'American tourists milling around after performances: 'They would talk about how it was a marvellous thing for them to see. That it did help them to go through their own experience and come out with a viewpoint of what was valuable in life.'

Not every production of the play has had a political context, however. Hiroko Mikami reports that the August 2003 Japanese premiere, which was renamed *Wee Thomas*, was 'totally apolitical'. Its director Keishi Nagatsuka had 'little interest in contextualising the play in a particularly Irish setting,' she writes, so he focused on the moral question at the heart of the play: why a cat's life can seem more valuable than a person's. Mikami suggests that by diminishing the play's historical and political elements, the production allowed its moral core to emerge more clearly.

Another notable 2003 production was *Il tenente di Inishmore* by Teatro della Corte di Genova in Italy. According to Debora Biancheri, that version of the play again ignored the Irish elements of the script, aside from briefly playing U2's classic song about the Troubles *Sunday, Bloody Sunday*. Instead, its director Marco Sciaccaluga drew on circus, puppetry and cinema, presenting the play as a straightforward farce. By using explicitly theatrical gestures in the direction of his actors, Sciaccaluga was able to explore the way in which the play undermines the distinction between reality and fiction.

Perhaps the play's finest moment arrived in 2006, when it opened first in New York's Atlantic Theater, and then transferred to Broadway. The production was again directed by Milam, and again starred Wilmot, Condon and Gleeson. An undoubted context for the production was the terrorist destruction of the World Trade Center. For many commentators, the appearance of McDonagh's play about terrorism was seen as a sign that New York was at last starting to come to terms with the trauma its citizens had experienced just over four years previously. The play was nominated for five Tony Awards.

The productions mentioned above all came within a few months of each other, but all elicited and provoked a variety of responses. In Japan, the play was seen as being about morality; in Italy, it was a playful farce; in New York it was seen as a return to normality after a terrorist atrocity. What this brief outline of the production history of McDonagh's work suggests, then, is that he should not be seen only as an Irish writer – or only a British writer – but perhaps as a global writer. In such a context, the question of what McDonagh intends becomes less important: what is more significant (and more interesting) about his work is how its meaning is seen as so different from one place to another around the world.

As we see in the chapters which follow, McDonagh's decision to move away from Ireland allowed these features of his work to emerge with even greater clarity and force.

3
WORLD PLAYS

Martin McDonagh: a world dramatist?

The title of this section might seem unsatisfactory in that, since all McDonagh's plays are set in 'the world', the designation might seem an awkward attempt to lump together two plays that share little beyond not being set in Ireland. But as we'll see, *The Pillowman* (2003) and *A Behanding in Spokane* (2010) have more in common than might at first be apparent – especially in their production histories. Yet I would also suggest that the term 'world plays' is highly appropriate, since it shows how, after *The Lieutenant of Inishmore*, McDonagh chose to move not only away from Ireland but also away from specific locations. A significant feature of both of these plays is that they are set nowhere in particular – and thus could, in a way, be set anywhere.

I've mentioned already that McDonagh's choice of location for *The Lieutenant of Inishmore* was arbitrary – in that he picked it mainly because the journey from Belfast to the Aran Islands took long enough for him to establish a number of plot points. Yet despite this apparent indifference to setting, many critics continue to assume that McDonagh is trying to reproduce a geographically and socially accurate version of the real Ireland. For instance, in a 2008 review of *The Cripple of Inishmaan*, the British critic Lyn Gardner wrote that 'I'm not alone in sometimes questioning the authenticity of Martin McDonagh's tales of small-town Irish life' – which suggests that she has deftly seen through an attempt to deceive the audience when, as I've shown, McDonagh's plays actually resist and indeed criticise the impulse to stage an 'authentic' Ireland. Like many critics of McDonagh, Gardner doesn't seem to realise that she is *supposed* to question the authenticity of what she's seeing, and thus appears unaware that she is attacking McDonagh for something he has deliberately set out to achieve.

By shifting his action to two 'non-places' – an unnamed totalitarian dictatorship in *The Pillowman*, an imaginary town somewhere in America in *Behanding* – McDonagh sidesteps the issues of accuracy and authenticity, and thus allows many other important themes to emerge. Those themes were present all along, of course; but the Irish setting of the earlier plays was clearly distracting some audience members and critics from seeing them.

McDonagh thus took pains to highlight the indeterminacy of the settings for his two non-Irish plays. Shortly before the opening of *A Behanding in Spokane*, for instance, he explained to Gordon Cox that he'd never actually been to the American city that gives his play its title – though he did pass through it while asleep on a train. Why, then, did he name the play after Spokane? 'I always liked the word,' he explains. 'That K in the middle is really nice' (Cox, 2010).

There's also a nice k-sound in the place name for the setting of *The Pillowman*: Kamenice. We don't know which country that city is located in. A number of possibilities exist, as Werner Huber has pointed out: 'Kamenice is a very common place name in the Slavonic settlement areas of East Central Europe. Thus, we find, for example, ceská Kamenice (in Bohemia, Czech Republic), and also Saska Kamenice (in Saxony, where the German form is Chemnitz)' (2005: 285). Certainly those locations can be found on a map, but that does not mean that the Kamenice or the Spokane of the plays are intended to be understood as similar to actual places with those names.

This move away from geographical specificity has had (at least) two important consequences. First, by making clear that he is not interested in staging the 'real' Kamenice or the 'real' Spokane, McDonagh encourages his viewers to stop worrying about the authenticity of his portraits of Leenane and the Aran Islands. And second, he allows us to re-read the Irish works from the perspective of the later plays: if we forget about the problem of geographical accuracy, we may find that some of the most praiseworthy features of *The Pillowman* or *Behanding* can help us better to understand *The Leenane Trilogy* or the two Aran Islands plays. Hence, we can read the treatment of authorship and power in *Pillowman* back in to *Cripple of Inishmaan* or rediscover its treatment of Christianity in *The Lonesome West*. Similarly, the consideration of race in *Behanding* is provocative and interesting in its own right, but can also revitalise and renew our understanding of the treatment of Ireland and the Irish in McDonagh's first six plays.

So, by moving beyond the vexed and vexing questions of national identity, McDonagh allows other features of his work to emerge more clearly: to show us how he is using dramatic form and how his attitude to authorial intention has developed.

'There were once upon a time two brothers':
The Pillowman

The Pillowman premiered at an important moment in McDonagh's career. From 1997 onwards, his work had enjoyed sustained international success – but that popularity had soon given rise to a critical backlash, not only from members of the English theatre community (as we've seen) but also from scholars of Irish drama. The complaint made by the latter group was that McDonagh was misrepresenting Ireland and the Irish, that he was earning lots of money by exploiting Irish stereotypes, that he was making Irish people seem violent, foolish, credulous and backward. Of particular concern to these critics was that McDonagh's Ireland might be mistaken for the real thing – that audiences who saw the plays in, say, Australia, might form the impression that Irish people are as stupid as Mairtin in *A Skull in Connemara* or Bartley in *Cripple*, as violent as Valene and Coleman in *The Lonesome West* or as barbarous in matters of politics as Padraic in *The Lieutenant of Inishmore*.

In many ways such complaints seem absurd, overestimating international audiences' awareness of and interest in Ireland, while also underestimating the discernment and intelligence of theatregoers worldwide. Yet those concerns seemed partially justified when evidence emerged that some international audiences *were* misunderstanding the plays. As noted in the last chapter, at least one production of *Cripple* told audiences that the play was representing something true about Ireland, while several productions of *The Lonesome West* characterised it as a metaphorical treatment of the Troubles. But rather than blaming the theatremakers responsible for such ill-informed choices, critics instead turned on McDonagh. He thus found himself being attacked not for what he had written, but for the misunderstanding, misinterpretation and misrepresentation of his work by others.

If McDonagh had wanted to defend himself against such accusations, *The Pillowman* would have been an ideal response. It comprehensively asserts the autonomy of the writer, arguing that although a storyteller can elicit reactions of pleasure or pity or disgust, he or she is not responsible if audiences choose to react negatively to what they read, see or hear.

If we apply the apparent theme of *The Pillowman* to McDonagh's critical reception, a clear message seems to emerge: that he is entitled to write plays however he wishes, and if a theatremaker or audience member in Ohio or Tokyo or anywhere else misinterprets his intentions, then McDonagh should not be held responsible – just as his protagonist Katurian should not be held responsible when his brother Michal is inspired to act out the murders that Katurian merely imagines in his short stories.

The play's only reference to Ireland might also be seen as an attempt by McDonagh to refute his critics. Towards the conclusion, Katurian tries to guess what a young Jewish boy might have looked like, and assumes that his hair was a 'browny-black sort of colour'. He is told, however, that the boy's 'mum was fucking Irish, and her son closely resembled a red fucking setter' (*PM*, 97). Implicit here is the view that it is foolish to make assumptions about a person based on national and ethnic identities: McDonagh shows that there are many ways to be Jewish, and thus many ways to be Irish also.

And finally, McDonagh's two police detectives – Tupolski and Ariel – exemplify the idea that there is something rather brutal about seeking always to reduce a work of fiction to one narrow set of meanings – a characterisation which might be seen as an oblique attack on some of the conventions of literary and dramatic criticism.

For these and other reasons, *The Pillowman* is often seen as presenting an attitude towards writing that contradicts the views of McDonagh's most vociferous critics; many people therefore see the play as a direct response by McDonagh *to* those critics. It is also widely believed that the artistic principles outlined in the play should be seen as representing McDonagh's own views on the primacy of art over politics.

As is so often the case with McDonagh, such opinions are entirely logical, but also entirely wrong.

The Pillowman was McDonagh's sixth produced play, but it had actually been performed publicly in a rehearsed reading in Galway in April 1997 – after *Beauty Queen* and *Cripple*, but before any of the other plays, and also before McDonagh's international reputation had been established. Tempting as it is to see *The Pillowman* as responding to events that occurred after McDonagh became famous, the reality is that his ideas about art and its reception were present from the very beginning of his career.

The basic storyline of the play was already there in 1997. A writer in a totalitarian state is interrogated by two police officers who are investigating a series of murders that appear to follow the plot of several of the writer's short stories. The problem for the writer – whose name is Katurian – is that only one other person is familiar with his work: his intellectually disabled brother Michal, who just happens to be under interrogation in the next room.

This set-up will remind some of Harold Pinter's *One for the Road* (1984), a play in which a seemingly innocent man is interrogated by a disturbed authority figure, who uses the presence of the man's wife and son in nearby rooms to intimidate his prisoner. The interrogator's repeated use of the phrase 'one for the road' (commonly used to refer to one last drink) is an example of how he uses everyday speech in a menacing fashion: the mundane quality of the language contrasts so completely with the implied threat to the prisoner's family as to undermine altogether his (and thus the audience's) sense of security. Likewise, in McDonagh's play Tupolski will attempt to 'disconcert and destabilise the prisoner with asinine nonsense' (82). Again, the proximity of a family member is used to unnerve the prisoner, for Katurian's attitude towards the interrogation changes noticeably when he becomes aware of his brother's screams from the next room. And in both plays there is a strong suggestion that interrogation can be a form of performance, that it involves a playing of roles in order to force a prisoner to reveal a truth.

Indeed, the two detectives in McDonagh's play often show an awareness that they are performing. 'Oh, I almost forgot to mention,' says Tupolski in the first scene, 'I'm the good cop, he's the bad cop' (12). 'Me and Ariel,' he continues, 'we have this funny thing, we always say "This reminds me" when the thing hasn't really reminded us of the thing we're saying it reminds us of at all. It's really funny' (14). Ariel admits to using 'fake blood' for dramatic effect (29), and encourages Michal to pretend that he's being tortured;. 'He said I did it really good,' says Michal, beaming with the pleasure of an actor who has received a positive review (38). Tupolksi, however, considers the performance inadequate and criticises Ariel for using blood that is so obviously fake.

Such role-playing is essential to both men's sense of personal identity. Late in the play, Ariel tells a story in which he imagines himself at the end of his life being thanked for the help he provided others as a police officer – which Tupolski dismissively refers to as his 'Children are gonna come up and give me sweets when I'm an old man' speech (79). Ariel has apparently imagined himself occupying such a role many times before, probably in an attempt to justify and give meaning to the brutality that he routinely inflicts upon people. He has turned himself into a character in a kind of story which Tupolski has obviously heard more than once.

So Ariel and Tupolski see themselves as actors, in a way; they also see themselves not just as *being* something, but as *meaning* something. Ariel, for instance, asserts that as a policeman he 'stands for something' (78). Similarly, Tupolski tells a story about an old man who rescues a boy, saying that 'the old man . . . represents *me* . . . [and] the little deaf retarded boy . . . represents my fellow man' (89). The roles that these characters play therefore have a symbolic significance that expresses their view of the world, their sense of morality and their understanding of how past events have shaped them. The men also show an awareness that their ability to wield power has a symbolic meaning of its own. As Tupolski says:

> We like executing writers. Dimwits we can execute any day. And we do. But you execute a writer, it sends out a signal, y'know? (*Pause.*) I don't know what signal it sends out, that's not really my area, but it sends out a signal. (*Pause.*) No, I've got it. I know what signal it sends out. It sends out the signal 'DON'T . . . GO . . . AROUND . . . KILLING . . . LITTLE . . . FUCKING . . . KIDS'. (30)

Tupolski's point is unsubtle but important. He shows that the enactment of law involves not just the punishment of the criminal but also the performance of the *act of punishment*, which is used as a way of discouraging others from committing crimes. Katurian's execution will thus have a symbolic meaning: it will be interpreted by others as a deterrent and will influence their decisions about how to act in the future.

As a result of that attitude towards meaning, both detectives insist that Katurian's stories must have a metaphorical as well as a literal meaning. As Tupolski puts it, Katurian's stories are 'saying to me, on the surface I am saying this, but underneath the surface I am saying this other thing' (5). Their role as interrogators thus begins to overlap with the role of the literary critic, who must delve below the surface meaning of a story in order to understand the truths that underlie it.

That both men see literary analysis as equivalent to policing is made clear on many occasions. Katurian tells the pair that they can 'draw their own conclusions' about his stories. 'Ariel's getting a bit aggrieved,' says Tupolski in response: 'Because "We can draw our own conclusions" is, sort of, *our* job' (11). And the pair certainly are skilled critics: Tupolski in particular displays an obsession with meaning, demanding of Katurian that he be more precise, and insisting that he use words more carefully. Hence, we find them debating the meaning of the phrase 'peripheral vision' (6), considering whether Michal is 'backward' or 'slow' (8), contemplating whether the idea that 'the world's a pile of shit' constitutes a 'world view' (85), and asking whether it is correct to say 'write quicker' or 'write more quickly' (notably, they choose the incorrect option) (73). Also notable is their correction of Katurian's description of his parents as funny people: 'For "funny" I guess read "stupid fucking idiots",' says Tupolski (8). As Pinter's interrogator in *One for the Road* points out, 'one has to be so scrupulous with language' (1995: 227).

Such precision is necessary because in many ways Katurian is (unusually for a writer) not particularly articulate or eloquent. 'I'm not one of these . . . you know?' he tells his interrogators at an early stage in the play, failing to supply the necessary description of himself, but assuming that he has been understood nevertheless (3). And he is also a terrible critic of his own work. His stories, he says, do not have a political 'what-do-ya-call-it' (7), but at least one of them is 'something-esque. What kind of "esque" is it? I can't remember' (18). Later in the play, he shows an awareness that the word 'unpaintoverable' does not exist, and seems conscious of its ugliness – but he doesn't bother trying to find an adequate replacement (66), just as earlier he had described a 'method of suicide' as 'preferred' despite being aware of that being 'the wrong word' (44). And he also seems capable of thinking about his art only on a very superficial level: when asked what a bad father in one of his stories represents, Katurian can only reply that 'He represents a bad father' (10).

It may be that Katurian's inability to answer Tupolski's questions arises because of a need to be cagey; he is being interrogated in a 'totalitarian fucking dictatorship' (23), after all, and so he must be aware that his life is under threat. Nevertheless, his lack of depth when describing his work – and his inarticulacy in general – should encourage the audience to be a little sceptical when Katurian outlines his views about art.

Katurian puts forward four artistic principles that, to many, seem to represent McDonagh's own views about writing. He expresses some of these views early in the play:

> I say if you've got a political axe to grind, if you've got a
> political what-do-ya-call-it, go write a fucking essay, I will
> know where I stand. I say keep your left-wing this, keep
> your right-wing that and tell me a fucking story! You know?
> A great man once said, 'The first duty of a storyteller is to
> tell a story,' and I believe in that wholeheartedly, 'The first
> duty of a storyteller is to tell a story.' Or was it 'The *only*
> duty of a storyteller is to tell a story'? [. . .] I can't remember,
> but anyway, that's what I do, I tell stories. No axe to grind,
> no anything to grind. No social anything whatsoever. (7)

We can derive from this statement Katurian's belief that the only duty of a storyteller is to tell a story, and that writing should aim to be apolitical. Later he adds that readers can 'draw your own conclusions' (11) because 'I'm not trying to say anything at all! That's my whole fucking thing!' (16). So he (rather like McDonagh) aims to empower his readers by insisting that they (rather than he) determine what the final meaning of each story might be. His fourth principle is expressed later in the play, when he rejects the idea that fiction must always reveal something of its author. 'I kind of hate any writing that's even vaguely autobiographical,' he says. 'I think people who only write about what they know only write about what they know because they're too fucking stupid to make anything up' (76).

However, one of the most interesting features of *The Pillowman* is that Katurian does not really live up to his own principles. For instance, the play is sometimes interpreted as providing a defence of the author's right to freedom of speech, yet Katurian offers to burn his stories more than once, saying that if there is a political element in any of them he wants his interrogators to 'show me where the bastard is. I'll take it straight out. Fucking burn it. You know?' (8). This makes Katurian very different from McDonagh: as I've discussed, *The Lieutenant of Inishmore* is a highly politicised work and far from being willing to excise any political elements from that play, McDonagh actually refused to allow himself to be censored. In contrast, Katurian deliberately censors others. In his autobiographical tale 'The Writer and the Writer's Brother', the protagonist reads a story written by his brother, describing it as 'the sweetest, gentlest thing he'd ever come across. [. . .] So he burnt [it]' (34). McDonagh shows Katurian burning the pages onstage. So while Katurian is very interested in protecting his own reputation, he is perfectly happy to destroy the work of others, especially if that work is better than his own. And it is worth bearing in mind that Katurian, rather than the police officers, is the only person who is shown destroying a story during *The Pillowman*. It seems mistaken, then, to identify Katurian too closely with McDonagh himself.

There are other reasons to be cautious about accepting Katurian's statements as entirely reliable. We might think that he is willing to give up his own life to protect his art, but he only decides to confess to the various murders in the play after he realises that his execution is inevitable. And, perhaps more admirably, he is motivated by many duties beyond simply telling a story. He kills his parents because of their mistreatment of Michal, for example, and then smothers Michal with a pillow in order to save him from a crueller execution by the police – yet, in doing so, he also guarantees his own death.

And are Katurian's stories really apolitical? The story of 'The Little Green Pig' could easily enough be read as a political allegory, since it focuses on an animal who is determined to retain its individuality at all costs, despite the pressure to conform from an oppressive and thuggish majority. This tale could be read indirectly as Katurian's celebration of his brother, who, though 'a little bit peculiar' (67), is still deserving of love. But it can also be read metaphorically as a rejection of totalitarianism, as an implicit celebration of the dignity of the individual in the face of the violence of the mob. Katurian may genuinely believe that his stories are not political, but they do reveal a world view that is subversive of the status quo.

His rejection of the idea that stories reveal something of their author must also be treated with some scepticism. He concedes that his tale 'The Writer and the Writer's Brother' is 'the only story of mine that isn't really fiction' (76). Yet almost every story told in the play reveals something about the storyteller and how he sees himself. Most of them are dramatisations of the abuse suffered by Katurian and Michal at the hands of their parents, and most of them also dramatise the desire for revenge against such parents.

For example, the story of 'The Little Apple Men' features a child who, like Katurian, tries to gain vengeance against an abusive parent – not realising that this act of revenge will ultimately lead to her own death.

Furthermore, the stories that Katurian tells often turn out to be unexpectedly relevant to the characters' lives. This can be seen in 'The Tale of the Three Gibbet Crossroads', in which we find a prisoner who has been accused of a terrible crime, but is unaware of what he did. His crime is written above the gibbet in which he finds himself: it is visible to passers-by but not to the prisoner himself. This means that the written word is used to determine his identity in ways that he cannot control or contradict. In a scene that is reminiscent of the crucifixion of Christ, he is one of three condemned prisoners – but where one of the thieves was saved in the gospel, here the prisoner dies without any sense of consolation or redemption, having been murdered by a passing highwayman:

As our man is dying he screams out, 'Just tell me what I've done?! The highwayman rides off without telling him [. . .] The last words that our man ever says are, 'Will I go to Hell?' And the last sound he ever hears is the highwayman quietly laughing. (18)

Again, the story has an identifiable autobiographical element. Katurian clearly feels a sense of guilt because his parents had tortured Michal in an effort to stimulate Katurian's imagination – and thus to make him a great writer. Katurian is not responsible for that abuse, but he obviously finds it difficult to live with the fact that he has benefited from it anyway. Indeed, his desire to ensure that his stories survive could be seen as an attempt not to protect his art, but rather to make the abuse of his brother seem meaningful in some way. So Katurian, like the prisoner in the gibbet, is guilty without having committed a crime (that he knows of). And like the prisoner, Katurian will die experiencing a desperate desire for certainty rather than survival. The prisoner does not seem to mind being killed so much as not knowing *why* he has been killed; similarly, Katurian does not seem to be bothered by his execution once he knows that his stories will certainly be preserved. The tale, then, tells us something about Katurian's past – but it also comments upon his present and in some ways anticipates his future. This shows us how stories have a capacity to reveal truths about their authors even when no such revelation is intended. It also shows how the meaning of a story can change depending on the circumstances of its telling.

The telling here also gives the audience a chance to think about their own roles as interpreters of the action. Just as McDonagh put an audience onstage in *Cripple* in order to show us how to react when we are confronted with something that claims to represent the truth, here he gives us a detailed example of the relationship between an author and his audience. Tupolski and Ariel are clearly frustrated by the lack of closure in 'The Tale of the Three Gibbet Crossroads', and are angry because (as Katurian puts it) it is a 'puzzle without a solution' (17). The demand by the police that the stories must *mean something* will soon seem oppressive and reductive; the fact that the tale unexpectedly and coincidentally speaks to Katurian's own situation shows how stories can take on multiple meanings that are unplanned and unintended. Audience members who demand that a play must convey one specific 'message' will thus find themselves identifying not with Katurian but with Ariel and Tupolski: men who are limited in their perspective, brutal in their outlook and violent in their impulse to reduce everything to one narrow 'truth'.

As well as revealing truths about his life, many of the stories also articulate Katurian's 'world view' – or, to put it slightly differently, they reveal an ethical consciousness which is clearly based on his upbringing. One example is 'The Tale of the Town on the River'. In that story, a child offers help to an adult who then chops off the child's toes. This seems like an act of terrible cruelty, but it is revealed the adult is the Pied Piper, who has come to Hamelin to steal away the townspeople's children. By disabling his victim, he ensures that the child will not be able to follow the other children from the town to their demise. This story exemplifies a philosophy that has dominated Katurian and Michal's life: that suffering can indirectly benefit its victim. So to the extent that it attempts to make sense of both men's upbringing, 'The Tale of the Town on the River' is autobiographical.

As in *The Lonesome West* and *In Bruges*, *The Pillowman* seems infused by a strong Catholic sensibility in that it is dominated by the notion that pain, suffering and the representation of both through art can inspire positive actions or outcomes. Besides the little boy whose life is saved when he is maimed by the Pied Piper, there is of course also the eponymous Pillowman, whose job is to show mercy and compassion to suffering adults by travelling back in time to persuade them to commit suicide as children (thus avoiding a lifetime of misery).

One exception to this theme might be the story of 'Little Jesus', in which a young girl is crucified onstage before being buried alive, and then dying horribly some days later. In itself, the story rejects the notion that redemption is possible through suffering – but, intriguingly, McDonagh chooses to subvert Katurian's 'fashionably downbeat ending'. The audience believed that Michal had acted out the story of Little Jesus – that he had kidnapped a girl, tortured her and buried her alive. But instead Michal had painted the girl green and left her with a group of pigs (re-enacting the story of 'The Little Green Pig'). Her unexpected arrival onstage in the play's third act is like a mock Easter Resurrection – which has the impact of reinforcing the idea that something positive can emerge from suffering.

And finally, just as McDonagh subverts the stories, so does Tupolski, executing Katurian before he has a chance to finish his last tale. In that final narrative, Katurian imagines a young boy (who obviously represents Michal) choosing to be tortured because he believes that he will like the stories that his brother will write about those terrible events. Because he dies four seconds earlier than he thought he would, Katurian never has the chance to give the tale one of his characteristic 'twists'. Tupolski's actions may ruin the story, but they are 'more in keeping with the spirit of the thing', as the play's last line has it (104). As usual, Katurian has given us a weak description in that final statement: we're never quite clear whether 'the thing' refers to the story, his life or *The Pillowman* itself. But the fact that the play is given a relatively happy ending does rather suggest that something positive may arise after a series of dreadful events.

The idea that suffering can be a good is one of several examples of how McDonagh challenges our expectations about ethics and values in *The Pillowman*. He gives us two brothers who have between them killed at least five people (their own parents, two children – and of course Katurian kills Michal). Yet we sympathise with those characters far more than we do with Tupolski and Ariel, whose job is to protect the weak and uphold the law. Similarly, the story of 'The Pillowman' is one of the most poignant in the play – yet we are being asked to sympathise with a giant, fluffy character whose job is to encourage children to kill themselves. And perhaps most strangely, we find ourselves in agreement with Michal when he refers to the murder of his parents as an example of a story with a 'happy ending' (59). The play, then, puts the audience on the side of child-killers and parricides, and allows us to be fairly comfortable with that position.

This transposition of values can be seen as arising from the play's indebtedness to fairy tales. *The Pillowman* appears to be strongly influenced by the kind of stories told by (among others) the Brothers Grimm, who collected fairy tales in Germany during the early nineteenth century. Many of their own stories are built around dualities: we often encounter tales about pairs of brothers who represent opposing traits (one might be good, the other bad; one rich, the other poor), while other stories feature brothers who band together to overcome their enemies (as in the story 'The Two Brothers', the first line of which is used as the title for this section). And a great many of the Grimms's tales feature terrible acts of violence being committed by parents against their children, in such well-known stories as 'Hansel and Gretel' (in which two children are abandoned by their parents when they can no longer afford to feed them), and in less familiar ones such as 'The Girl without Hands', in which a miller who unwittingly does a deal with the devil chops off his daughter's hands. Such stories are shocking because they take the values that we regard as unshakeable (such as the notion that parents will always protect their children), and then consider what happens when those values no longer apply.

Like the Grimms's fairy stories, *The Pillowman* sweeps away its audience's sense of moral certainty – but it does so to reinforce an ethical perspective at its conclusion. The play achieves this objective by working through a series of dualities (again, as in the fairy tales). We have the two brothers (one of whom was treated well and the other treated badly); two policeman (one who uses his intelligence while the other uses brute force); and we also have the relationship between the brothers on the one side and the two policemen on the other. That duality also functions spatially. There are the two interrogation rooms side by side, each containing one brother – just as in their house there were two bedrooms: one where Katurian slept peacefully and comfortably and another where Michal was brutalised for many years. In one of those interrogation rooms, Katurian reads out his stories, while in the other Michal pretends to be tortured.

That arrangement mirrors the structure of the play itself, in which there is a duality between the realistic action (the interrogation scenes) and the acting out of the stories as they are recited by Katurian – a duality, that is, between dramatic re-enactment and narrative account. And finally, the duality functions thematically: as we have seen above, there is a clear relationship between suffering and redemption running through the play.

One of the key dualities in the play – the one that allows McDonagh to re-assert an ethical sensibility – is between past and present or, more precisely, between cause and effect. A joke that recurs throughout the play is that many of the characters blame their actions on their 'problem childhoods'. Each of the four male characters was clearly shaped by his parents' treatment of him: Ariel was sexually assaulted by his father, Tupolski's father was a 'violent alcoholic' (80), and Katurian and Michal's parents obviously had a terrible impact on the lives of them both. What marks one man as different from another is the extent to which they allowed their parents' actions to determine the direction of their own lives. Again, we are being asked to consider whether the creator of something is responsible for his creations: just as parents should not be blamed for the actions of their children, so we should not blame an author for the consequences that arise when other people read his or her stories.

There is an interesting link, then, between authorship and paternity – both being thought of in terms of responsibility. *The Pillowman* rejects the notions either that Katurian is responsible for how others read his work, or that we can blame others for our own choices. We cannot blame authors for what they write, our parents for our 'problem childhoods', or McDonagh for our insecurities about how Irishness is seen abroad. So even if the play was not written as such, *The Pillowman* can be seen as offering a way of thinking about the author's work in its entirety. It illustrates his apparent belief that what matters most are not the views of the author, but the actions of audiences. McDonagh's challenge to audiences is – and always has been – to consider ourselves as active in the interpretation and analysis of what we see: not to receive a play passively, but instead to view ourselves as actors too, as creators of meaning and as people who have responsibilities as a result.

As we have seen throughout this book, issues of interpretation and authorial responsibility have been central to McDonagh's work from the beginning. From *The Beauty Queen* onwards he has not sought to communicate a message from author to audience, but instead to reveal to the audience the strangeness of their own presuppositions and assumptions. This strategy places the responsibility for the creation of the play's meaning upon those who are watching it: we are forced, that is, to examine afresh our own sense of how the stage scene is constituted, and to question the values that are assumed by that presentation.

In following this approach, McDonagh revealed his own goals as a playwright. Like the absence of sound made by the proverbial tree falling in a forest when no one is present to hear it, McDonagh's plays seem to declare that they are meaningful only when they are performed before an audience: he is not trying to communicate with the viewers of his work, but to inflict an experience upon them – an experience that will at least partially be determined by the needs, interests and assumptions of the individual audience members themselves. An author certainly has intentions in creating a play, McDonagh concedes – but he appears to be denying that there is a direct causal link between his own intentions, the performance of his plays and the responses of audiences to his work. Instead, his plays can be understood as stating the necessity for storytelling in everyday life, and as considering the ethical dimensions of the interpretative acts that inevitably arise when audiences encounter such stories.

So while *The Pillowman* may have been written at the same time as McDonagh's other plays, it does seem to bring his early drama to a culmination, tying together the major themes and providing a strong overview of how his work should collectively be judged.

After the play's premiere, McDonagh turned his attention to cinema – first with the short film *Six Shooter* and then with *In Bruges*. But as we'll see in the following section, the fact that *The Pillowman* resolved many of the tensions in McDonagh's drama presented him with something of a dilemma when he returned to playwriting with *A Behanding in Spokane*: where could he go next?

'Not so much a vision as . . . some other kinda thing': *A Behanding in Spokane*

A common criticism of Martin McDonagh is that he is uninterested in theatre: that he wrote plays only as a way of breaking into the movie business. There is not much evidence to support that accusation which, as discussed earlier in this book, seems to arise from a misinterpretation of a comment in an early interview about theatre being the 'least interesting' of the art forms. Nevertheless, that view of McDonagh appears to be widely held. For that reason, the news that he was returning to the theatre after the success of *In Bruges* came as a surprise to many. He announced his decision to resume playwriting in an interview with *The Galway Advertiser*, the local newspaper that had carried his first ever interview in 1996. 'I'm actually in the middle of writing a new play,' he told Charlie McBride in September 2008:

> I find writing plays easier. To make a feature film takes up so much of your life, like two years pretty much dedicated to that . . . The process itself is fun but just having to give so much time to it, I didn't like so much. So at the moment . . . I'm writing plays again and I'll be concentrating on theatre for the next year or two . . . [M]y whole thinking was to make one film and then leave it and see if it was fun or if I could do it. Now I've achieved that and I haven't been put off it as much as I thought I could be – but I'm not going to rush back to film immediately.

McBride then asked if the new plays have an Irish setting. 'Quite consciously not,' came the response. 'Their settings are more American or non-specific like in *Pillowman* . . . I will definitely do more Irish stuff but not for a while yet' (McBride, 2008).

We can be almost certain that one of the plays McDonagh had in mind when he spoke to McBride was *A Behanding in Spokane*, a dark comedy set in a motel room somewhere in 'small-town America' (*BS*, 5). This became the first of McDonagh's plays to premiere on Broadway when it opened at the Gerald Schoenfeld Theater on 4 March 2010. The success of *In Bruges* undoubtedly helped to build a sense of anticipation for the play, though its commercial success probably owed more to the casting of Christopher Walken in the lead role, as the eponymously 'behanded' psychopath, Carmichael.

As McDonagh had promised, there were no explicit references to Ireland in the play (though its director John Crowley is originally from that country). Yet *Behanding* certainly allows us to view the Irish plays from rewarding new perspectives, while its treatment (or mistreatment) of race and racism contextualises the debate about McDonagh's representation (or misrepresentation) of the Irish. But perhaps the play's most exciting quality is that it shows McDonagh attempting to find new ways of solving the problems he had encountered in his earliest works.

As we will have come to expect, *Behanding* does many of the things that the other plays do: it avoids answering all of its audiences' questions; it seems to celebrate its own ambiguity; and its allusions to films, music and other forms of popular culture allow us better to understand the play itself. But a new approach to audience expectation is evident in the play. In the past, McDonagh had always aimed to surprise his audiences, to use successive plot twists to warn them of the danger of making assumptions based on plot or character. Yet in this new work, McDonagh would not so much aim to surprise his audience as to frustrate them.

McDonagh thus gives us a play in which several exciting events happen – but all occur offstage or before the action has begun. His characters constantly imagine situations in which they do interesting things or occupy significant roles. But the fact that they can only *imagine* such actions shows how boring their ordinary lives are and how insubstantial their actual identities. McDonagh raises several questions about his characters' motivations, but in the end gives us few answers – not because those characters have hidden depths, but rather because they barely understand their own reasons for doing anything. The play thus seems like an extended exercise in provocation: teasing us, testing its audiences' tolerance of bad language (notably in its use of taboo words absent from the other plays, such as 'cunt' and 'nigger') and refusing absolutely to live up to anyone's expectations.

Even its title points us in the wrong direction. The play is not set in Spokane, but in a town called Tarlington – some indeterminate location in the middle of nowhere. And Carmichael's 'behanding' happened long before the play began. *Behanding* itself is relatively lacking in violence: despite featuring his most dangerous character, it is one of the few McDonagh plays *not* to feature a murder or a suicide, or even a particularly bad beating. And notwithstanding McDonagh's skill with plotting, it is a play in which almost nothing of importance actually happens onstage.

All this may seem to amount to a criticism of *A Behanding in Spokane* – and many of the critics who disliked the play did attack it on grounds similar to the above, assuming (in most cases) that these apparent 'flaws' were not deliberate. Yet a close examination of the script suggests that McDonagh was very deliberately testing his audiences' limitations. The play can therefore be seen as genuinely experimental: it shows McDonagh trying to find a way of telling stories while also working through his awareness of how tired the conventions of plotting and characterisation – and indeed of performance – have become. In *Behanding* he seems to be trying to find a new way forward, even though he has yet to leave behind all of his old techniques.

These features of the play can be illustrated by considering the long monologue by Carmichael about the loss of his hand:

> Twenty-seven years ago, almost to the day, a young lad of about seventeen or so, who lived in a town name of Spokane, Washington, was happily playing catch outside of his momma's house, when six hillbilly bastards he did not know drove up, and they took him and they dragged him to a beautiful mountainside outside of town, where a bunch of railroad tracks crossed over a river there, and for no reason that was ever specified, without even a word in fact, they held the boy's hand down upon those railroad tracks . . . This boy is me, I'm talking about . . . and they held him down, him screaming and hollering as any boy would, as a freight train came up from the pine trees distance, and they made him watch this train, him hoping even at this point, somewhere in his mind, that they were only kidding, but they weren't kidding, and as he watched the train's thunderous approach, and he watched as it hacked his hand clean off at the wrist. (10–11)

This passage needs to be quoted at length, because it establishes what the play is setting out to achieve. The delivery of this speech is the moment when McDonagh teaches his audience the rules of his game: he tells us what to expect (or, more correctly, what not to expect), he lays out the major themes and he establishes the ethical perspective of the play.

The first major issue to emerge from the passage is the importance of storytelling to Carmichael's sense of himself. Carmichael has certainly told this story before – and the fact that he sees it *as* a story (rather than a memory being spontaneously recalled) is evident from his decision to refer to himself in the third person, as 'a young lad of about seventeen or so', rather than using the word 'I'. As is discussed later, McDonagh suggests towards the end of the play that the entire story is an invention; and the obvious craft with which it is narrated might persuade his audience that Carmichael has indeed made the whole thing up. But it is of greater importance that McDonagh is signalling at this early stage that *all* of his characters share an impulse to imagine themselves as *acting*, as being characters in a story.

This tendency is most obvious in the presentation of Mervyn, the receptionist – though he 'wouldn't really call myself a receptionist. Yeah. I work on the reception. I wouldn't really call myself a *receptionist*' (6). Mervyn thus distinguishes between *being* and *doing*: to work on a reception does not make one a receptionist – or, as he puts it later, to 'operate sometimes' and to 'do bit of operating' does not make one an 'operator' (28). Mervyn holds that view not from any kind of Marxist-inspired refusal to identify himself solely in terms of his job, but instead because he has developed the habit of imagining himself engaging in activities that would make him a far more interesting and admirable person than he actually is:

> Maybe a prostitute would get stabbed and I'd have to go rescue her? Or some lesbians would get stabbed? I wouldn't mind that they were lesbians, I'd save 'em. You gotta look out for people, y'know, even if they're different from ya. Maybe I'd get some kind of medal from some kinda lesbian association. (21)

Mervyn is a fantasist, someone who uses imagination to distract himself from the sheer boredom and meaninglessness of his life. 'See, I've had this vision,' he tells Carmichael, 'not so much a vision as . . . some other kinda thing, that if I worked her long enough and kept my eyes open, man, something was gonna happen, you know? Something *dramatic* was gonna happen' (8). Mervyn gives us several examples of the 'something dramatic' that might happen in his motel: a group of guys in cloaks with harpoons could check in, as might a panda, as might 'some guy from Nigeria' looking to sell a rollercoaster. As Mervyn repeatedly asks, 'Where's a story like that gonna go?' (4). Storytelling for him is not just an escape or relief from everyday reality (as in *The Cripple of Inishmaan*); it appears to be an alternative to that reality – an alternative to leading a worthwhile life.

Where Mervyn refuses to identify himself with the role that he actually occupies, the pitiful small-time crooks Toby and Marilyn are attempting to play roles that they *can't* occupy – perhaps least successfully of all as con artists. 'All we'd heard was there was a guy come to town was going round looking to pay top dollar for his own . . . chopped-off hand,' explains Marilyn. So the pair decide to con Carmichael: they break into the local natural history museum and steal a hand from an aboriginal person, hoping to pass it off as the one he is looking for. 'At that stage we didn't know what [Carmichael] looked like, y'know? So when we met him we was kind hoping that he might be more, y'know, black. And if he wasn't then what we was gonna do, we was gonna kinda wing it,' says Marilyn (29).

Yet the problem the pair have is that they can't 'wing it': whenever they are faced with the need to improvise, they show themselves almost completely unable to do so, surviving through guesswork rather than guile. McDonagh underlines the fact that the duo are dangerously out of their depth by giving Toby the last words of the first scene: 'What do you think I should say?' he asks, helplessly (20). Of course, Marilyn has no answer for him.

Yet if they are unable to improvise, they are also very poor actors, showing themselves unable to perform a variety of roles, even ones that are very clearly defined. Toby, for instance, is criticised several times for not matching the stereotypes associated with his gender and ethnicity. And the couple often criticise each other for not performing the roles that expected of them: Toby attacks Marilyn for not using her sexuality to charm Carmichael, while she is scathing about him for his unwillingness to defend himself against Carmichael's racist taunts.

So Marilyn, Toby, and Mervyn's lives are all determined (and, in the play, put at risk) by their inability to engage successfully in role-playing. And, as the conclusion of the play suggests, Carmichael's own story about the behanding – the story that has determined the direction of his life for decades – is almost certainly an invention. When told the story, Mervyn declares that it 'doesn't sound very plausible' (47):

> **Mervyn** So, wait, they held your hand down, train comes up, train chops off your hand . . .
> **Carmichael** (*sighs*) Train chops off my hand, they pick up my hand . . .
> **Mervyn** After the train has gone by . . .
> **Carmichael** After the train has gone by. Obviously. They wave goodbye to me with my own hand. From a distance.
> **Mervyn** And your hand wasn't just mush?
> **Carmichael** My hand wasn't just mush, no. My hand was a perfectly normal chopped-off hand. I would not spend twenty-seven years of my life searching for a hand that was just mush.
> **Mervyn** And the rest of your arm wasn't just mush?
> **Carmichael** Does the rest of my arm look just like mush? . . .
> **Mervyn** So what were the wheels of the train made of? Razor blades? (**Carmichael** *stops and stares at him*). And the rails? Razor blades? (43)

Mervyn may be foolish, but he correctly points out that Carmichael's story does not make sense. Notwithstanding his use of such terms as 'obviously' and 'perfectly normal', there is nothing obvious or normal about Carmichael's story: even if he had survived an ordeal such as the one he describes, his hand would certainly have been reduced to 'mush' (as indeed might the hands of the 'hillbillies' who held him down while the train approached). As the play finishes, the audience is left with the strong possibility that some other explanation exists for

Carmichael's mad determination to seek out and collect dozens of severed hands as he travels across the 'decaying nation' of the United States (11). It is very likely that Carmichael, like the other three characters in the play, is trying to play a role – and by the approach of the play's conclusion his performance has lost much of its credibility.

Just as the characters define their own sense of identity by attempting to play roles, so do they constantly seek to impose roles on each other. As we have seen, there is the impulse to reduce individuals to their occupations: to describe Mervyn as 'the receptionist' or 'the operator' rather than judging him as the (certainly unique) person he is in his own right. But Mervyn himself is just as likely to form impressions of people based on appearances, jumping to the conclusion that Carmichael is 'totally' a drug-dealer, while assuming that 'the black guy' (Toby) 'looked kinda suspicious' (8). So *A Behanding in Spokane* is a play in which the characters are often judged on the basis of their appearances: the colour of their skin, the uniforms they wear at work, the extent to which their behaviour meets masculine or feminine norms, and so on.

Toby is the most frequent victim of such prejudice, being referred to as both a 'nigger' and (because he cries) as a 'fag' on multiple occasions. And while Carmichael is by far the most insulting of the characters, they all show a willingness to judge Toby based on stereotypical thinking. Even Marilyn taunts him based on his race: 'Stop crying! . . . Where's all your Black Panther shit *now*, cry-baby? Where's all your "Fight the Powers that be" now, huh? . . . Stop crying! . . . *Please*, Toby . . . Jesus! Am I the only grown-up round here?' (15). McDonagh underlines the fact that Toby is doomed to be thought of in terms of such stereotypes by ensuring that the first thing the audience sees him doing is coming out of the closet – a metaphor for revealing one's true identity which is here made profoundly literal.

When Marilyn drags Toby from the closet where he'd been hidden by Carmichael, she reveals one of the play's key tensions: that between the visible and the invisible. It is worth pointing out, for instance, that one of the most racist characters in the play – Carmichael's mother – is never actually seen or heard onstage. We make inferences about her based on reported speech or the responses to her when the characters talk to her on the phone. But we are never allowed to see or hear her for ourselves. One of Mrs Carmichael's major complaints about her son relates to visibility, to the act of looking: that is, to his viewing of pornography. She finds it objectionable that he's stashed pornographic material in their house – not because she sees porn as degrading to women, but because Carmichael owns magazines that feature pictures of black women. 'Ma,' he responds, 'It's a *magazine*, okay? Alright, yes I *do* find some black women attractive . . . That doesn't mean I'm not a racist . . . I'm standing here right now, okay, there is a black man chained to my radiator and he's covered in gasoline, now that's hardly Affirmative Action, now is it?' (38).

There's a contrast here between the invisible (but obviously white) Mrs Carmichael and the very visible black character being described (only in visual terms) by Carmichael – not to mention the black women in the magazines, who are objectified by Carmichael for sexual gratification. So the play shows us that race is not an essence, but rather a way of looking at or seeing the world – and thus of judging people in it. Toby, after all, is the only character whose race is ever named in the play: even the stage directions refer to him as a 'black guy' (11), where Carmichael is referred to only as 'mid to late forties' (5), Mervyn as 'hotel uniform, nametag, smiling' (6) and Marilyn as a 'pretty twenty-two-year old' (9). The whiteness of these characters literally goes without saying.

This returns us to Carmichael's story. One of its best crafted features is the use of contrasts to achieve pathos: the image of the boy playing catch at the start, for example, is a subtle reminder of what the loss of his hand will entail. The story's major contrast is between protagonist and antagonist – that is, between the innocent boy and his assailants. Carmichael refers to the people who maimed him only as 'hillbillies', specifying that they were white – 'You can't get black hill-billies!' he tells Mervyn (42) – but telling us nothing else about them. We don't know where they were from, what they looked like, what age they were, what their physical appearance was – even how Carmichael was able to determine that they *were* hillbillies. The epithet in itself seems to be enough to explain their actions, and the audience will probably be unlikely to need too much additional information in order to believe Carmichael's story when he first tells it. A point being made here is that the word alone seems to explain why those people assaulted Carmichael: *hillbillies*, like the rural poor in McDonagh's Irish plays, will be perceived as prone to acts of incomprehensible violence simply because they *are* hillbillies.

The audience thus finds itself in an awkward position at the end of the play: they will have spent much of the action criticising (perhaps rather complacently) Carmichael for his racism and homophobia, but they will themselves have to face the question of why they were willing to believe that *anyone* would be capable of the kinds of actions Carmichael describes. If we think this kind of behaviour is plausible because it's carried out by hillbillies, then it's possible we might have one or two prejudices of our own, McDonagh seems to suggest. So just as it takes the stupidest character in *Cripple* to point out the implausibility of Billy's screen test, so in *Behanding* does the oddest character point out the incredibility of Carmichael's story.

McDonagh thus seems to want his audience to think again about their attitudes towards race, ethnicity and other forms of personal identity. He gives us that vivid image of the hillbillies who 'waved the boy goodbye with his own hand' (8) – an image which is vivid precisely because it involves a person having something essential to himself being taken away, and then used to signify something over which he has no control, something which actually signifies his own victimisation. This is a fascinating metaphor for the process involved in racism, whereby a person's body is turned into a symbol of something *other* than the person himself or herself – and that symbolism then becomes a force for violence against the individual.

McDonagh further develops that metaphor by having Toby and Marilyn steal a hand of someone 'aboriginal', which had been on display in the local museum. This act of theft from a display case again reminds us of the way in which race is constructed in order to be *seen* and looked at; it also shows McDonagh's awareness of what it means for someone to exploit a culture that they don't belong to. Given that McDonagh was himself accused of taking an 'aboriginal' culture (that of the Irish) and putting it on display for an audience of outsiders, his treatment of race, visibility and exploitation in *Behanding* allows us to think again about the reception of his Irish plays. But more pertinently, he aims in the play itself to show what happens when people are judged in terms of their race. And he explicitly criticises the actions of those who seek to exploit the objectification and exploitation of others.

By the end of the play, then, McDonagh has made clear that the racism of Carmichael is deplorable, but he has also criticised the emptiness of his other characters' attitude towards prejudice. Marilyn's sense of self seems strongly determined by a need to seem liberal: 'It's pretty offensive you keep using the word '"nigger" all the time and that's all I'm gonna say,' she tells Carmichael (12). Yet as we have seen above, she is entirely capable of attacking Toby based on his race or masculinity – and, by complaining to Carmichael, she also takes upon herself the right to speak *about* Toby's race, something Toby seems to have little interest in doing for himself. Similarly, for all the 'nobility' of Mervyn's desire to rescue 'lesbians' because 'You gotta look out for people,' his words reveals with dismal clarity that he still sees such people as very different from himself (and indeed as being in need of rescuing). The difference between Carmichael, on the one hand, and Marilyn and Mervyn, on the other, is that Carmichael is actually aware that he is prejudiced.

One final contrast between the visible and the invisible relates to the issue of dramatic action. As mentioned earlier, the play's most dramatic moments all happen offstage. There is of course the 'behanding' itself, just as there are the bizarre phone calls of Mrs Carmichael – who may (or may not) have fallen out of a tree in pursuit of a balloon, and who claims to have broken her ankles. Amusingly, Carmichael doesn't believe his mother's story about how she received that awful injury: are his accusations against her a form of confession? McDonagh doesn't ever let us know for certain what happens to this woman, but his point is clear: we are being forced to watch a series of events in a hotel room, when there are many much more interesting and dramatic events happening somewhere else. This technique is made even more obvious in the play's second scene, when McDonagh forces the audience to sit through a long and rather pointless monologue from Mervyn which is delivered while the candle burns towards the gas can in the motel room (21). Again, he points the audience's gaze at precisely the one thing that they *don't* want to see.

We therefore frequently find ourselves in a situation of wanting to see things that are invisible to us. At the very start of the play, Carmichael fires a 'single gunshot' into the wardrobe, for instance (5), but we have to wait several minutes before finding out who his victim was (only to realise, of course, that the gunshot had harmlessly hit a wall). The play's first words are 'I did say, didn't I?' (5) – but we'll never be sure what exactly Carmichael *did* say. In the play's final moments, we'll watch Carmichael attempting to light a cigarette – in a room doused with gasoline, as sirens signal the approach of policemen who will surely want to know what he is doing with so many hands in a suitcase. He gazes at the word 'love' on his hand, but responds with the word 'fucker' (another example of the play's capacity to place contradictory messages into dialogue with each other). So, to use Mervyn's question from the start of the play, where is this story gonna end? Does Carmichael blow himself up? Does he have a stand-off with the police? Does he escape?

We don't know. What we have instead of knowledge is an awareness of our own impulse to *look*. McDonagh creates an intriguing link between audience expectation and prejudice, showing that in both cases people are making assumptions about reality based on a thoughtless assessment of surface appearance. He clearly wants to force the audience to think again about the politics of prejudice – to show that Marilyn's determination not to be racist is simply another form of racism, to show that Mervyn's desire to rescue lesbians and (as he tellingly puts it) 'women' arises not because he cares about others but because he is thinking about himself. Yet McDonagh also wants us to think about our own role as *watchers*, as viewers of the action. After all, the title *A Behanding in Spokane* refers *not* to the play we have just watched, but to a story told during the play – and we never know whether that story is true or not. What we have watched instead is a play that shows us what happens when several more interesting things are under way elsewhere.

In developing that theme, *Behanding* looks forward – but it also looks back, to the influences that were evident in some of the earlier work. We can view the play as exemplifying clearly McDonagh's use of postmodern strategies (a theme that José Lanters explores in detail later on). Furthermore, there are clear overlaps between McDonagh's new drama and Synge's *Playboy of the Western World*: both hinge on the narration of a violent story of questionable credibility and both make extensive use of reported speech rather than the dramatisation onstage of interesting events. With its treatment of two small-time crooks who are outwitted by a far more violent individual, *Behanding* will (as mentioned earlier) seem reminiscent of Tracy Letts's *Killer Joe* – but may also call to mind Quentin Tarantino's *Pulp Fiction* (1994), a movie in which a man and woman attempt to rob a diner but are overpowered by an infinitely more dangerous gangster. And, like *Pulp Fiction*, *Behanding* plays very provocatively with racist epithets, placing the explosive word 'nigger' into the mouth of a high-profile white actor (Walken in *Behanding* and Tarantino himself in *Pulp Fiction*).

There are of course also strong echoes of Pinter, who frequently gave us plays that are set either before or after considerably more dramatic events than those shown onstage. And those Pinteresque echoes lead us naturally back to Beckett: *Behanding*, like many of Beckett's plays, seems to show an impulse to surrender to the limitations of dramatic form, even as it attempts to push against those limitations. The play is in some ways a deliberate failure as drama, but it also shows a determination to fail better next time.

The question we face, then, as we leave the theatre is *what next*? McDonagh has shown a sense that he needs to find new ways of writing, that he needs to move on. So we must ask, borrowing from Mervyn, an intriguing question: where's this story gonna end?

The plays in production

Ostensibly, *The Pillowman* and *A Behanding in Spokane* are linked only by the fact that they are not set in Ireland; they might otherwise seem to occupy very different places in McDonagh's *oeuvre* and career. Certainly there are some important differences between the two, not the least of which is that *The Pillowman* was hailed from the beginning as a masterpiece, whereas *Behanding* has received a decidedly mixed response. Yet in production the two plays have intriguing similarities.

The first is that the move away from an Irish setting opened up the possibility of celebrity casting for both productions. The premiere of *The Pillowman* took place at the National Theatre in November 2003. While some of the pre-publicity was dedicated to McDonagh (who, as I've discussed, was by that time something of a celebrity himself), there was also considerable advance attention to the casting of Jim Broadbent in the role of Tupolski. Broadbent is of course a distinguished actor with a long career on the English stage, but his international profile had grown considerably due to his starring roles in the films *Moulin Rouge* (2001) and *Iris* (2001); indeed, he had won an Academy Award for his role in the latter movie (about the Anglo-Irish author Iris Murdoch). The premiere of *The Pillowman* was thus presented in some quarters not just as a new play by McDonagh but also as a return to the stage by an Oscar-winning actor. Something similar happened when the play opened on Broadway in 2005, when the role of Tupolksi was played by Jeff Goldblum, with Billy Crudup as Katurian. Both again are experienced stage actors but, particularly in the case of Goldblum, the opportunity to see a Hollywood star in the flesh was an obvious selling point for the Broadway production.

Similarly, the casting of Christopher Walken in the role of Carmichael was the major selling point for *A Behanding in Spokane*, helping to generate over $1.4 million in ticket sales before the play had even begun previews, according to Gordon Cox (2010). Walken's distinctive intonation and line delivery was singled out as a major feature of the production in almost every review – and indeed his performance was a clear reminder that one of the benefits of celebrity casting is that it (occasionally) brings extraordinarily skilled actors back to the theatre. The production's director John Crowley stated that it was Walken's ability to give emotional depth to Carmichael that made his performance so strong. 'The most surprising thing that Chris does,' Crowley told the journalist Patrick Healey, 'is that while he has this ambient, freaky, chilling quality that curls around him, he can also plug into a character's vulnerability in a split second with his face, his tone, his body'. Healey also recounts a story from Zoe Kazan, who played Marilyn, about Walken's approach during rehearsal. He was, said Kazan,

> explaining how it felt to have his hand cut off and asked if she knew what that felt like. My character says, 'Not very nice?' and suddenly Chris – who has been terrorising us onstage – softens his face and the mood of the play shifts nicely . . . Chris said to Crowley that his interior thought at that moment for Carmichael was, 'I remember a time when I thought things could be nice.' It's a lovely moment of connection between the characters, and then he went back to terrorising us. (2010)

However, an unexpectedly negative result of Walken's casting may have been that he so dominated the production as to have distracted audiences from its other features. While reviewers universally praised his performance, there was a strong tendency to be critical of the other three actors: Kazan, Anthony Mackie (who played Toby) and Sam Rockwell (who played Mervyn). Some critics were inclined to blame McDonagh himself for the perceived problems with those actors' performances: all three roles were seen as superficial and underwritten – unacceptably so. 'This funny throwaway feels a tad lazy,' wrote David Rooney in *Variety*; while in the *New York Post* Elisabeth Vincentelli thought that McDonagh 'doesn't push himself nearly enough here'. Yet after the Broadway premiere of the play, *Behanding* received several regional US productions which seem to have conceived of the play not as a star vehicle but as an ensemble piece. And in general, those productions were very well received, perhaps because audiences were better able to concentrate on the interactions between the four characters. This suggests that Walken's brilliance may inadvertently have undermined audiences' appreciation of other features of the original production.

Another overlap between *The Pillowman* and *A Behanding in Spokane* is that both were directed by the Irishman John Crowley. Crowley (whose brother Bob designed *The Cripple of Inishmaan*) has a particularly well developed ability to provide a visual counterpoint for dramatic texts – something he was praised for in his direction of

The Pillowman. In his production of that play both on Broadway and for the National Theatre in London, Crowley presented the action in a compartmentalised set, which was designed by Scott Pask. As the play began, the audience saw one room, where the interrogation was held; the rest of the stage was left in darkness. As the stories began to be narrated, Crowley then lit up other sections of the stage, representing the bedrooms of the two brothers in 'The Writer and the Writer's Brother' or the living room where the young girl is crucified in 'The Little Jesus'. Crowley directed the actors who performed the stories to use exaggerated, almost mime-like gestures; and he dressed them in gaudy clothes that were presented in striking colours. The effect was to make the stage appear like a puppet theatre and the performers like marionettes – or perhaps to make the space seem like a page in a 1950s horror comic book, with several different frames of action visible simultaneously. But the overall impact was to offer something that could not be gained merely from reading the play: the audience did not just listen to the tales as they were told by Katurian; Crowley transformed them from short stories into plays-within-the-play.

There is of course a need to leave some features of the action to the audience's imagination. Interestingly, in previews of *The Pillowman* in London, Crowley had actually placed an actor in a Pillowman costume onstage. 'I thought it would be quite spooky and scary, but it wasn't,' Crowley told Caryn James:

> For one thing, that Pillowman too closely resembled an English cartoon character called Mr Blobby. For another, people said it looked nothing like the Pillowman of their imaginations, even though the costume had faithfully reproduced Katurian's description. It was here in the conversation that Mr Crowley cited Bruno Bettelheim, who observed that imposing an interpretation on a fairy tale diminishes its enchantment. (2005)

A Behanding in Spokane is, of course, not as fantastic as *The Pillowman*, but Crowley again showed an intense awareness of the visual impact of the play. As Hilton Als describes:

> As the play begins, the theatre's ratty-looking curtain is drawn, not raised, thereby alerting us both to the production's old-fashioned style (footlights, some of them broken, line the front of the stage) and to our own voyeurism: we're peeking through the window of a large, dark room in a crummy hotel where Carmichael . . . a drifter and a sociopath, has holed up. (2010)

Als astutely points out that the design of the plot aimed to implicate the audience as voyeurs, as in a relationship with the play that is not unlike Carmichael's relationship with pornographic images of black women. This forced us to think about the issue of *looking* which (as discussed earlier) is one of the play's key themes. So, again, Crowley used the design to highlight the play's artificiality, and thus to remind audiences that they needed to be prepared to *think* about what they were seeing.

That said, not everyone was happy with what they saw. For Hilton Als the production's presentation of race was utterly unacceptable. 'I don't know a single self-respecting black actor who wouldn't feel shame and fury while sitting through Martin McDonagh's new play,' he wrote.

> Nor do I know one who would have the luxury of turning the show down, once the inevitable tours and revivals get under way. The play is engineered for success, and McDonagh's stereotypical view of black maleness is a significant part of that engineering. Still, one wonders how compromised the thirty-one-year-old Anthony Mackie must feel, playing Toby, a black prole whose misadventures are central to this four-character show . . . The sad fact is that, in order to cross over, most black actors of Mackie's generation must act black before they're allowed to act human. (2010)

Als's response is extraordinarily harsh: he is accusing the production of the kind of exploitation which the play itself seems to be attacking. Eamonn Jordan considers Als's response further, but here we find again an echo of the reception of previous McDonagh plays: if we substitute the word 'Irish' for 'black' in Als's statement, we could easily be reading one of the critical attacks on *The Leenane Trilogy*. It could be argued that Als, like so many of the Irish critics, had missed the point: that if McDonagh is putting stereotypical characters onstage, it is because he wants to reveal such characterisation *as* stereotypical and not as reality. But again we are dealing with the ethics of authorial intention and reception: if an African American actor (or critic) feels 'shame and rage' at McDonagh's presentation of race, is McDonagh culpable?

That such questions are raised by *Behanding* shows that although McDonagh is moving away from specifically Irish settings, the provocative and controversial elements of his work remain undiluted. The play was itself not especially well received; leaving aside the accusation of racism, it is seen by many as a lesser work than McDonagh's earlier plays. *The Pillowman*, then, is probably McDonagh's most respected play, while *A Behanding in Spokane* could well be his least admired. Yet we find in both a crystallising of many of the themes that were overlooked in the Irish plays – and which, as we shall see, would emerge with new force in McDonagh's first two films.

4
THE FILMS

Martin McDonagh as filmmaker

In his first press interviews McDonagh seemed to speak more often about cinema than theatre. He rarely acknowledged being influenced by other playwrights – occasionally mentioning Pinter and Mamet, and referring directly to Joe Orton as a major presence in *The Lieutenant of Inishmore*, but otherwise avoiding detailed reference to most other dramatists. But he spoke constantly about filmmakers who had inspired him: Martin Scorsese, Terrence Malick, Sam Peckinpah and many others. It therefore always seemed likely that McDonagh would make a movie.

It took him almost a decade to do so, however. His twenty-eight minute short *Six Shooter* was completed in 2004 and released the following year (nine years after *Beauty Queen* had premiered); and his first full-length feature *In Bruges* followed in 2008. As had happened with his playwriting career, he then experienced an amazing and un-precedented series of successes, winning one Academy Award for *Six Shooter* and being nominated for another for *In Bruges*, which also earned Colin Farrell a Golden Globe for Best Actor. McDonagh was understandably very proud of his Oscar, but realised he still had much to learn about filmmaking. 'That was just luck,' he told the *New York Times* when asked about the award.

That statement might seem like an example of (possibly false) modesty, but in fact McDonagh has spoken often of his belief that he didn't do as good a job with *Six Shooter* as he might have done. 'I didn't take control over many of the aspects of filmmaking,' he told Ed Caesar:

> I didn't get involved with the director of photography, or the costume designers, or the production people . . . All of those things I really needed to do. If your name is on it as the writer/director, you need to make sure it's your statement. So I didn't learn as much as I should have done. (2008)

These comments should not be interpreted as a dismissal of the film: 'There's lots about it I like, and I think the Oscar makes me like it even more,' he stated. That said, even Brendan Gleeson acknowledged that McDonagh didn't know much about filmmaking when he shot *Six Shooter*. 'He's such a genius he won an Oscar without having a clue!' the delighted actor told the *New York Times*.

McDonagh has explained that the experience of *Six Shooter* made him nervous about the prospect of a full-length film. Perhaps in response to that fear, he drew on his theatre experience, deciding to spend three weeks working through the script with Farrell and Gleeson before shooting began. 'That felt more like what I was used to,' said McDonagh, 'analysing a script, people talking about character and getting at the truth of something' (Caesar, 2008).

Yet if the film required McDonagh to draw on his experiences in the rehearsal room, it also marks a distinct departure from his plays. As we have seen, the Leenane and Aran Islands of his plays bear little resemblance to the real places of the same name; his Kamenice could be anywhere in central Europe; and although he mentions Spokane in the title of his 2010 play, the action does not actually take place in that city. Yet *In Bruges* is very deliberately rooted in that specific location. 'If I hadn't been able to shoot in Bruges, I would have scrapped the whole thing,' McDonagh told Ed Caesar. 'Every single location that was written into the script had an effect on what was happening in each scene. Every bench had to be that bench, at that canal, by that statue. It had to be Bruges.' That city thus becomes a fourth character, and there is an obvious desire to treat the place respectfully (despite the remarks made by Ray at the beginning about it being a 'shithole').

Yet there is also a continuity with that earlier work. Where McDonagh had often seemed uncomfortable with having his plays related to the Irish dramatic tradition, he seemed keen to describe *In Bruges* as an Irish film. 'The writer and director - i.e., me – is Irish,' he told Patricia Danaher. He elaborated as follows:

> The two leads, Colin [Farrell] and Brendan [Gleeson], are Irish, as is Ciaran Hinds [who plays the priest]. I don't think Ireland has ever made a really great film yet, and I'm not saying my film is it either. But I think it's a few baby steps towards it, and towards not caring about the American market –

saying, you know, in an Irish anarchistic way, 'I don't care about government or nationalism,' splurging with a kind of Pogues-like anger, using then subverting the form.

It remains to be seen how McDonagh's career as a filmmaker will progress, but his statement about using the form in order to subvert it helps to explain his work to date. And it is notable that the Belgian setting of his film allowed him to acknowledge openly that he sees his work's iconoclastic tone as distinctly Irish, though the reference to the Pogues suggests that it might be more precise to see that attitude as exemplifying the attitude of second-generation Irish artists – a point I return to in the conclusion of this book. Also interesting is that the move to film allowed McDonagh to acknowledge much more openly his indebtedness to Pinter and Beckett.

So there are obvious and important differences between the plays and the films. Yet we can also identify some resemblances, especially in terms of theme and (as McDonagh says himself) form and tone. We'll see in the films a preoccupation with issues of responsibility and guilt – so that (for example) the treatment of religion in *In Bruges* clarifies the way he used that theme in some of the earlier plays, just as the exploration of the ethics of watching in *Six Shooter* speaks to the treatment of violence in *Lieutenant of Inishmore* and *The Pillowman*.

McDonagh's film career is still in its infancy – and indeed (as suggested in the discussion of *A Behanding in Spokane*), his career as a dramatist obviously will continue to develop in new ways too. What is exciting, however, is how the work in one medium is starting to inform and speak back to the work in the other. We'll find resemblances and differences, then – but perhaps of greatest interest is that an investigation of how McDonagh's film and drama interact allows us to form a clearer understanding of the major features and achievements of his work as a whole.

'Today was the last straw': *Six Shooter*

One of the hardest things about the death of a loved one is that, although something essential has vanished from one's life, the world seems to carry on as if nothing has changed. Faced with a bereavement – especially a sudden one – we expect everything to come to a halt; we imagine that nothing will ever be the same again. Yet all around us people continue to go about their business and the ordinary bustle of everyday life persists uninterrupted. The world thus feels both familiar and strange – and the combination is terribly disorientating.

Martin McDonagh's first film is only twenty-eight minutes long, and in many ways it is his most playful and least substantial work. Yet it somehow manages to capture the sad confusion that arises after the loss of a family member, by giving us a vision of the world as it's seen by a man whose wife has just died. The man (Donnelly is his name, and in the film he's played by Brendan Gleeson) tries to maintain his grasp on the ordinary by engaging in everyday activities. He shares a chat with a stranger; he watches the world pass by through a train window; he eats and drinks; he shows concern for and interest in the people around him. In one way, then, he's living through a day like any other – a day that any of us can (at least initially) recognise as familiar.

But there's something oddly out of kilter about Donnelly's view of the world: as we watch the movie, we form a sense that although things *seem* normal, they are gradually becoming more unrecognisable. For Donnelly's journey does not just take him away from the hospital where his wife lies dead, it also strips from him everything else that he values: his faith in God, his belief that life has meaning and that life is even worth living. He therefore moves from a world that seems familiar to one that seems alien and unpredictable – and we are forced to go along with him.

Six Shooter, then, is a film about looking, about how our ways of seeing the world are determined by what we feel. The audience finds itself watching the film through Donnelly's eyes: we see what he sees, especially as he gazes through the train window. He initially observes a scene that we'd expect to find within any Irish frame – lush green fields, a cinematic icon of Irishness. But as the journey continues, that frame starts to be filled with sights that are more and more incongruous. First, there is a dog standing on a wall barking, then there's the decapitated head of a woman and finally there is a gang of armed policemen. The train window thus becomes a kind of cinema screen, with images associated with Irishness gradually being replaced by scenes from other movies, culminating in a *Bonny and Clyde*-like showdown between a criminal and the police. We start with a kind of pastoral but end with a particularly violent Western, as if *Man of Aran* has been intercut with Peckinpah's *The Wild Bunch* (1969).

It would be easy to dismiss that combination as a playful pastiche, and to leave it at that. But if we think back to the plays' treatment of the ethics of watching (especially in *The Pillowman* and *Behanding*), we may form a conviction that McDonagh is pointing out that images do not just *represent* reality, but can actually *construct* reality for us. Hence, the film appears to suggest that the mediated image can sometimes seem more real than reality. The accidental tearing of a photograph of a baby, for instance, seems almost as tragic as the death of the child himself. Similarly, as we move towards the conclusion of the film, we see Donnelly placing a picture of Jesus face down just before he attempts suicide. The act is illogical, yet it makes sense emotionally that he would treat the image of Jesus as if it had the power to witness real life. In *Six Shooter,* images appear to have an agency: it's as if their function is to see instead of being seen.

If the film emphasises the power of the visual image, it also seems to convey an anxiety about the value of the spoken word. Donnelly tells his wife (or, strictly speaking, his wife's remains) that he doesn't know where she is any more. 'I don't know what to say to you, babe,' he tells her several times. And indeed Donnelly's spoken words seem to misfire frequently in the first minutes of the film. When he learns that a woman has been shot in the head, he asks if she survived, but the doctor who's speaking to him appears surprised by such a strange question. 'She's dead,' says the doctor. 'She had no head left on her, like' (a joke that appears in a slightly different form in the opening scene of *The Lieutenant of Inishmore*). And as Donnelly boards the train, he asks a young man (referred to as 'the Kid' in the credits) a 'perfectly simple question': whether there is anyone sitting in the empty seat opposite him. 'Oh aye,' says the Kid, 'hundreds of fellas, like.' Donnelly's first few attempts at communication, then, seem to be met with confusion, surprise and sarcasm.

Also sitting in the carriage is a couple: a man and woman, apparently married and obviously distressed. It's revealed that they have suffered the death of a child. In an interesting twist, the man is called Pato; the woman with him is called Mrs Dooley. The use of these names is an obvious nod to the character of Pato Dooley in *Beauty Queen*; as we'll remember from the end of that play, Pato had emigrated to Boston, where he became engaged to Dolores Hooley (or was it Healey? – we never found out). It is not clear whether McDonagh intends that the Pato in *Six Shooter* should be seen as the same character who appears in *Beauty Queen*. If so, poor Pato's life takes a rather unfortunate turn after his departure from Leenane, since, in addition to losing a child, he will lose his wife too when she throws herself from the train.

The difficulty that we have in determining whether *Six Shooter*'s Pato is the one who appears in *Beauty Queen* is another example of the tendency in the film towards incongruity, towards a resistance of the simple identification of one thing with another. There are many other examples of that tendency. There is, for instance, the young man who runs the train's snack trolley but refuses to be judged on the basis of his profession, saying that it's not what he would have wanted for himself: like Mervyn in *Behanding*, he obviously believes that a person's job should not be used to determine his or her identity. Likewise, the Kid at one stage confuses Rod Steiger and Tony Curtis – two very different actors. Even the use of the word 'like' in the film is slightly misleading: the word *should* mean that one thing is similar to another, but instead it seems repeatedly to refer back to itself (becoming the grammatical equivalent of a hall of mirrors), most amusingly when the Kid complains about his failure to kill anyone in the movie's shoot-out. 'I didn't hit one of them . . . Fucking woeful. Do you know what I mean like, like, like . . . Just fucking woeful,' he says.

The Kid himself is something of an enigma. As played by Rúaidhrí Conroy (who had originated the role of Billy in *The Cripple of*

Inishmaan), he is very obviously a psychopath. We learn that he had murdered his mother; he also drives Mrs Dooley to suicide, telling himself afterwards that 'I think you might have gone a bit overboard there now fella.' As he says himself, 'I'm a rotten kid.' Yet there is something oddly likeable about the character, and Donnelly seems to respond positively to him, even if the most complimentary thing he says about the Kid is that he's probably not 'retarded' since he knows what dressage is.

It also seems likely that the Kid is trying to be someone he's not. When the police finally corner him, he makes no effort to escape, or indeed to protect himself: he simply stands up and begins shooting wildly with his two revolvers. He is striking a pose, then, rather like Padraic in *The Lieutenant*. But he's not as successful in playing the role as is Padraic: as we've seen, the Kid manages to miss every person he shoots at.

The death of Conroy's character greatly upsets Donnelly, who had tried to intervene to save the younger man's life. Donnelly had clearly felt some kind of connection with him, and perhaps as a result of that connection felt a moment of comfort and consolation after his wife's death. This apparent (and short-lived) improvement in Donnelly's mood had arisen when the Kid tells him a story about a childhood visit to a cattle mart with his father, where they encountered a cow with trapped wind.

As we'd expect from McDonagh, it's a tale with many surprises along the way. A short farmer with a beard stabs the cow several times with a screwdriver, but what seems like an act of terrible sadism is actually beneficial, releasing the gas from the cow and thus saving its life. Becoming aware that he's gained the admiration of an audience, he proceeds to begin a performance: he 'tells his life story' and then ignites the gas coming out of the cow with a cigarette lighter. But he becomes so engrossed in this performance, that he doesn't notice the flame disappearing into the cow – which explodes, covering everyone with blood and gore. That, says the Kid, was the best day of his life.

The story appears to cheer Donnelly up, perhaps because it seems to show that even when dreadful things happen it's possible to maintain a positive outlook – or perhaps because it's just such a strange tale. 'Good luck to you.' says Donnelly to the Kid, getting up to leave. 'Fella,' comes the reply, 'I'm sorry to hear about your dead missus and all.'

The subsequent shoot-out and the death of the Kid appear to shake Donnelly's faith again, and so he returns home to commit suicide. We then have an apparent allusion to the final moments of *Waiting for Godot*, when Beckett's two tramps contemplate suicide: one removes the string from around his waist to hang himself, but because of his doing so his trousers fall down. Beckett's play thus appears to suggest that life is never funnier than when things seem most desperate. The film reaches a similar conclusion. Donnelly intends to use the final two bullets in the revolver to kill himself and his pet rabbit David. He shoots the rabbit; then he goes to shoot himself – but the gun misfires, leaving him with a decapitated rabbit in his lap, and with no way of ending his life. 'What a fucking day!' says Donnelly, as we shift into the credits and the song 'St James Infirmary Blues' as played by the White Stripes.

Donnelly's last words are somewhat ambiguous. They capture perfectly his frustration with his life – his sense of despair at the loss of everything that he cares about. Yet there is implicit in his outburst an awareness that these are the events of *just* one day: that there will be another day tomorrow when things may not be quite so bad – since they cannot possibly get any worse.

This ending looks back to McDonagh's plays, many of which end inconclusively. And indeed, there are s number of echoes of the earlier dramas, from the reference to Pato to jokes about Tayto crisps and shooting people with two guns. But *Six Shooter* also anticipates *In Bruges*. Both films feature attempted suicides that fail unexpectedly. Both ask what happens when guilt and grief coalesce. And, as we'll see, both are about the process of *looking*: about how our emotional state determines the ways in which we view the world.

'A matter of honour': *In Bruges*

In an interview for the DVD edition of his first full-length film, Martin McDonagh gives a typically self-effacing account of how he came up with the idea for *In Bruges*:

> I went on a little weekend away . . . to Bruges, not really knowing anything about the town . . . So I booked into a hotel, started walking around, and was surprised and stunned by how beautiful it was. At the same time, after two or three hours I started to get bored. So it's like two sides of my brain were arguing with me: one finding this place so stunningly attractive, and the other . . . being bored out of my head.

McDonagh took those two perspectives and turns them into two characters: the unfortunate Dublin hitmen Ray and Ken. 'Then,' said McDonagh, 'I thought why would two guys who didn't want to be there *have* to be there. So that's where the original germ of the story came from.' Thus McDonagh developed the idea of Ray and Ken being sent to Bruges by their boss, Harry, after Ray's assassination of a priest has led to the accidental death of a child who was waiting to have his confession heard.

The revelation that McDonagh based his two protagonists on different aspects of his own personality allows us to think of the film in relation to his plays. We've seen many times how he creates pairs of characters who, between them, just about manage to form one functional human personality – from Valene and Coleman in *The Lonesome West*, to Donny and Davey in *The Lieutenant of Inishmore*, to Katurian and Michal in *The Pillowman*. In fact, there are strong links between *In Bruges* and the last of those plays. Both stories are initiated by the murder of children: Michal's first victims in *The Pillowman* and the penitent little boy who is accidentally killed by Ray in *In Bruges*. And both stories end with the revelation that what had looked like the murder of another child was actually something else. In *The Pillowman*, the mute girl who had (we believed) been crucified and buried alive turns out to have been merely splattered with green paint, while in the film an apparently dead schoolchild turns out to be Jimmy, a dwarf dressed in a school uniform as part of a film shoot. In both cases, the arc of the story – from an actual murder to the revelation that an apparent murder must be reinterpreted as something else – is used to develop the themes of guilt and redemption, especially as they are mediated through art. Perhaps in an attempt to underline the resemblance between the film and the play, McDonagh's shooting script has Ken reading a book called *The Death of Capone* – written by one K.K. Katurian (12).

The film will also remind some viewers of *The Cripple of Inishmaan*. Like that play, *In Bruges* tells a story that is set on the fringes of a film set – which here involves the making of a movie that seems partially based on *Don't Look Now*, the 1973 thriller about a couple who travel to Venice after the death of their child. It's not clear precisely what the relationship is between the new film and the source material. Ray's love interest Chloe calls the movie 'a pastiche of . . . *Don't Look Now*,' but then corrects herself. 'Not a pastiche, but a . . . "homage" is too strong. A "nod of the head" ' (14). Jimmy describes the film rather more bluntly (but somewhat less helpfully) as a 'jumped up Eurotrash piece of rip-off fucking bullshit' (45). Nevertheless, with its focus on the need to come to terms with the death of a child – and with its use of imagery from the paintings of Bosch – the film-within-the film seems uncannily to mirror Ray's point of view.

But, as he did with *Cripple of Inishmaan*, McDonagh is also using the presence of the film crew to reveal how his own story is constructed: he is not just giving us a representation of reality, but showing us how that representation is made, how it is put together. By placing within his own frame the technology of filmmaking, by reminding us that roles in films are played by actors – and that actors often differ strongly from their characters – McDonagh is gesturing towards the artificiality of his own creation. He is, as usual, encouraging us to avoid treating his story as a copy of the real world which we must passively accept. As always, we need to be on our guard, and prepared to respond to what we see with a critical outlook.

Another link between *Cripple* and *In Bruges* is that both equate the gaze of the filmmaker with the expectations of tourists. In the play,

McDonagh showed how the reputation of Ireland internationally was shaped not by reality but by films like *Man of Aran*. Similarly, *In Bruges* uses film to reveal the beauty of its location while also criticising the way in which tourism turns that beauty into a consumable commodity. Ray may be the 'worst tourist in the whole world' (7), but that might not seem quite so negative a description when we consider the tourists who do actually appear in the film: the obese Americans, the anti-smoking Canadians – and of course Harry, who thought of Bruges as a 'fairytale' place. McDonagh's film, then, constantly risks deconstructing itself: like the two sides of McDonagh's reaction to Bruges, the movie is both dazzled by the location and sceptical about its commodification.

The film also (again like *Cripple*) displays an uneasiness with tourism generally: with the desire many people have to consume a location as if it's a product, to see it as 'authentic', and thus to miss out on the day-to-day existence of ordinary people living there. McDonagh therefore creates a tension between a tourist version of Bruges and a real one. At the start of his script, he describes the town as 'otherworldly', adding that 'we could be in any period of the last five hundred years'. As we've seen in the discussion of *Cripple* and *Man of Aran*, the impulse to see a place as timeless is very common, but also tends to result in the misrepresentation of the lives of real people. Hence, McDonagh goes to some trouble to root *In Bruges* in a specific time, with his references to football teams and movies emphasising the contemporary setting. He also contrasts the idealised Bruges with a seedier image: it is no coincidence that the local characters are all criminals, with both Chloe and her partner Eirik making a living by stealing from tourists.

Ray's lack of interest in seeing the sights of Bruges is very funny, as is his description of history as 'just a load of stuff that's already happened' (13). We might think that we're supposed to simply reject Ray's attitude, but for McDonagh, what is necessary (as always) is balance: as Ken proposes, a 'balance between culture and fun' (19) or, to put it slightly differently, a balance between enjoyment of the past and living in the present. Similarly, McDonagh tries to hold in balance the competing needs to represent the beauty of Bruges as a tourist site against its more mundane (but also more alive) qualities. As such, he does for Bruges what the contrast between *Man of Aran* and *Cripple* achieves for Inishmaan.

But perhaps the most important link between the film and the plays is that *In Bruges* makes explicit something that is only hinted at in the earlier works: McDonagh's indebtedness to Harold Pinter. A major influence on the film is Pinter's 1960 play *The Dumb Waiter*. In that work, two hit men, Ben and Gus, are hiding out in a room together, waiting for their next job. They are in Birmingham – which is not their home town, and they seem uneasy in their new surroundings. One of the hit men – Gus – nevertheless seems curious about his environment: 'I like to get a look at the scenery,' he says. 'You never get the chance in this job' (1996: 118), a statement that is somewhat similar to Ken's delight in having the chance to see the sights of Bruges. And just as Ken will be told to kill Ray, so in Pinter's play it seems that one of the hitmen has been hired to kill the other.

There are other resemblances. One of the most revealing moments in Pinter's work is when the two hit men talk about football, discussing a hotly contested game between Aston Villa and Tottenham Hotspur that had taken place some years earlier. That match was settled by a disputed penalty decision. 'Talk about drama,' says Gus. 'He [a Tottenham player] went down just inside the area. Then they said he was just acting' (121). The use of the words 'acting' and 'drama' to describe something that happens offstage tells us a great deal about Pinter's approach to dramaturgy: the use of those words shows us how he does not *reveal* action but instead will hint at it, will force us to anticipate it without ever having the dramatic moment (namely, the murder of one hit man by the other) performed onstage.

McDonagh does something similar with the only mention in the film of a football team – which is (of course) Tottenham Hotspur. Ray uses that team to explain the representation of purgatory in visual art: it is a place to go if 'you weren't really shit, but you weren't all that great either' – like Tottenham (24). Just as Pinter uses Spurs to refer to an offstage drama that contrasts with his own art, so McDonagh uses the same team to describe the work of Bosch and other great artists. In both cases, the contrast between the football team and high art is used to undermine an audience's expectations about the author's own work.

These resemblances may seem incidental or indeed coincidental, but McDonagh makes the indebtedness clear when Ray and Ken check in to the hotel in Bruges. The pseudonyms they give are Cranham and Blakely. And the actors who played Gus and Ben in the 1985 BBC version of *The Dumb Waiter* were Kenneth Cranham and Colin Blakely. We may choose to see *In Bruges* as a 'pastiche' of *The Dumb Waiter*, as an 'homage', or as a 'nod of the head' – but certainly the influence is there, and McDonagh seems willing to celebrate it.

But does that influence actually mean anything? Throughout this book I have argued that one of the most important features of McDonagh's work is its ambiguity; another is his ability to show how apparently everyday speech can not only obscure violence but also convey the threat of violence. Both of those features – which, of course, dominate Pinter's work – are important for an understanding of *In Bruges* as well. McDonagh's film is ultimately very different from *The Dumb Waiter*, but his willingness to celebrate the ambiguity of meaning and his desire to show how ordinary speech can mask appalling violence must be seen as arising from his reading of Pinter's work.

Where McDonagh departs slightly from Pinter, however, is that he uses ambiguity – both in terms of his characters' meanings and his own intentions – as a way of exploring specific forms of morality. The tagline used in pre-publicity for the movie was 'Shoot first. Sightsee later.' That is an eye-catching blurb that neatly captures McDonagh's blend of tourism with gangsterism (as was also evident in the poster's representation of Colin Farrell, who is shown holding a pistol and an ice cream). But that image and phrasing might suggest that the violence in the film is thoughtless: that it is arbitrary and trivial. In fact, one of the curious things about *In Bruges* is that almost all the characters seem to believe that their acts of cruelty and violence are justified on moral grounds. This is because much of the film's dramatic energy (and its humour) arises from a clash between three competing forms of morality.

There is first the morality of 'honour among thieves', which defines the actions of both Ken and Harry. Ken, we learn, works for

Harry because of a sense of personal debt. The story that he tells is that his wife was murdered in 1976, and Harry appears to have taken revenge on the murderers on Ken's behalf. As a result, Ken has spent the subsequent thirty or so years acting as a paid assassin for Harry. The language Ken uses to describe this relationship reveals much about his sense of the ethical. 'Harry,' he says, 'I am totally in your debt. The things that's gone between us in the past, I love you unreservedly for all that. For your integrity, for your honour. I love you' (73). Ken sees Harry's act of vengeance as an act of 'honour' – one which deserves love. And as a result of that love, Ken has (to use his own words) to reconcile his desire to lead a good life with 'the fact that, yes, I have killed people. Not many people. And most of them were not very nice people' (26). The murder of Ken's wife set in train a cycle of violence that is broken only at the film's conclusion (when both Ken and Harry die), and this cycle is spoken of in terms of love and honour.

Such words are also used by Harry, who sees the decision to kill Ray as a 'matter of honour' (62). For him, morality is a simple matter of cause and effect. 'Listen,' he says to Harry. 'I liked Ray. He was a good bloke, but when it all comes down to it, y'know, he blew the head off a little fucking kid. And you brought him in, Ken. So if the buck don't step with him, where does it stop?' (40). The consequences here are obvious: if Ken doesn't kill Ray, Harry will kill both of them – using the death of the child as his reason for taking vengeance on them. Harry explains that his thinking comes from a deep-rooted sense of principle. 'If I'd killed a little kid, accidentally or otherwise, I wouldn't've thought twice, I'd've killed myself on the fucking spot!' he claims (67). And, as we see at the end of the film, Harry commits suicide precisely because he is led to believe that he has killed a child. So both men act from a thoroughly skewed attitude to morality. They believe that 'honour' compels them to do things, that they have no choice but to act in particular ways. One mistake – Ray's accidental murder of a child – cannot be forgiven, but must be atoned for with Ray's death.

Yet Ken shows an awareness that Ray deserves a chance to change – a very sad statement for him to make, since it suggests that he thinks that change is no longer possible for himself; Ken's preference for 'culture' over 'fun' thus shows that his interests lie in what has passed (and so cannot change) rather than the present (which is in a constant state of change). Harry, on the other hand, seems relatively unperturbed by the many deaths he has caused, by the misery he has inflicted upon people. As so often happens with McDonagh, the character who talks most about morality is in many ways the most amoral – because his morality allows for no ambiguity, no nuance, no personal interpretation of events and their consequences. Once again McDonagh shows a thorough distrust of people who only see the world from one rigid perspective.

The second form of morality – which in some ways relates to the first – is the morality of religion, and specifically the difference between the Old Testament morality of 'an eye for an eye', as compared with the Christian ethic of forgiveness and redemption. As with *The Pillowman*, a great deal of Catholic symbolism is employed to develop those themes. There is, for instance, the fact that the film takes place close to Christmas, and features a pregnant woman called Marie – who gives others room at her hotel, rather than being turned away from an inn as her namesake was in the Gospels. Ray achieves something like redemption by 'saving the next child' when he persuades Harry not to risk Marie being shot in a crossfire (another example of the 'honour among thieves' motif), and although the Christmas-time birth of that child is not shown during the film, its imminence does seem to suggest some sort of atonement for Ray's accidental killing of the boy in the church.

That murder happens during another Catholic ritual – one that, as we've seen, dominates *The Lonesome West*: confession. Ray had been hired to kill a Catholic priest, who is named Father McHenry in the script. Despite the occasion being Ray's 'first time' as a hired killer, he shows an unusual presence of mind in his interactions with the priest.

Ray Murder, Father.
McHenry Murder? Why did you murder someone, Raymond?
Ray For money, Father.
McHenry For money? You murdered someone for money?

> **Ray**   Yes, Father. Not out of anger, not out of nothing. For money.
> **McHenry**   And who did you murder for money, Raymond?
> **Ray** *clears his throat.*
> **Ray**   You, Father. [. . .] Harry Waters says 'Hello'.
> **Ray** *shoots him point blank.* (22–3)

The assassination is an excellent example of McDonagh's ability to build tension through the use of repeated vocabulary – and to release that tension with an act of violence. But the shock experienced by the audience may cause them to overlook what this scene tells us about Ray. He shows first that he is familiar with the sacrament of confession. Like Ken, he was almost certainly 'brought up Catholic, which I've more or less rejected most of . . . But the things you're taught as a child, they never really leave you, do they?' (25). Ray's 'confession' of the crime he is about to commit initially appears callous, but in fact it reveals his capacity for guilt – it shows, that is, that even if he has left Catholicism behind, it 'never really leaves you'.

But if Ray's familiarity with confession explains why he feels so guilty – and is the real reason for his intolerance of all the 'holy shit' in Bruges – it also explains his belief that redemption might be possible. Also interesting about this scene is that the priest appears to know Ray: he calls him by his name several times, which goes against the custom that the penitent is treated as anonymous. It seems possible that Ray is killing someone whom he knows, and that too might worsen his sense of guilt.

McHenry's last words are 'the little boy' (23). Given that his concern in the final moments of his life is for another person, the priest may be a thoroughly decent man; in fact, a deleted scene from the movie suggests that he was killed only because he was blocking one of Harry's property developments. But even if we discount that scene, those final words strongly imply that the priest's death is unjust and undeserved. Even leaving aside the death of the boy, Ray *ought* to feel guilty.

We then see one of the film's most upsetting images: the piece of paper upon which the boy had written down his 'sins' prior to confession. As the filmscript tells us, 'it reads "1. Being moody. 2. Being bad at maths. 3. Being sad" ' (23). Of course, none of those faults can reasonably be considered a 'sin' – and the fact that a boy seeking forgiveness actually ends up being killed suggests that we are seeing a world from which morality, fairness and justice are utterly absent.

In one of the film's cleverest moves, McDonagh shifts directly from the image of the dead child and priest to the Groeninge Museum, where we see three paintings: 'The Judgement of Cambyses' by Gerard David, 'De gierigaard en de Dood' by Jan Provoost and 'The Last Judgement' by Hieronymus Bosch – all of which are from the late fifteenth and early sixteenth centuries, and all of which are still on display in Bruges. McDonagh's decision to cut from the scene of confession to these paintings proves revelatory. All three images directly link judgement with violence. David's painting gives us a prone figure who is being skinned alive; Provoost's displays a 'skeletal death come to collect his due' (24); and Bosch's terrifying image shows dozens of people being dragged away to hell, some of them being eaten alive by demonic figures. By choosing to show us these images, McDonagh reminds us of how the presentation of religion in art often sought to provoke terror rather than to console. The God of Bosch is a vengeful one; and so too is the God who allowed the penitent child to be killed by Ray's stray bullet.

What separates *In Bruges* from such works is that McDonagh seeks to find a way for Ray to redeem himself. That such redemption is possible is hinted at early on. We are told that one of Ken's few regrets is that he once killed 'Danny Ailband's brother . . . He was just trying to protect his brother. Like you or I would. He was just a lollipop man. But he came at me with a bottle. What are you going to do? I shot him down' (26). Ray seems to approve of this action: 'a bottle, that can kill ya. That's a case of "it's you or him". If he'd come at you with his bare hands, that'd be different. That wouldn't've been fair' (26). By using the word 'fair', Ray shows that (like Ken and Harry) he applies unshakeable moral principles to immoral acts: his belief that murder is acceptable once the conditions under which it is carried out are 'fair' is very similar to the outlook of the other two men. Yet minutes later, Ray actually has the opportunity to test this principle when a disgruntled tourist comes at him with a wine bottle. As the script tells us,

'Ray hits her in the chin . . . and she collapses' (32). We know that Ray has no gun, but he has shown through his actions that Ken had options other than murder when he found himself in a similar situation. Indeed, as mentioned above, Ken seems aware that Ray can do things that are no longer possible for him. 'The boy has the capacity to change,' he tells Harry. 'The boy has the capacity to do something decent with his life' (67).

What we find in the characterisation of Ken, Ray and Harry are two competing moralities. The first, as represented by Harry, is rigid and uncompromising: if someone kills a child, they have no option but to take their own life, he believes. This is a morality founded on vengeance and executed through violence. On the other side, there is a morality of redemption, one that appears to allow for the possibility of change. We don't know if Ray really will change. But we do know that Ray decides not to commit suicide because he appears to believe in the possibility of change. And it is also important that Ken sacrifices himself to give Ray that possibility, offering up his life to redeem someone else's – a fundamental Christian motif, of course.

A third form of morality evident in the film might be termed 'political correctness'. In common with McDonagh's other works, the film pushes against taboos, exploring various forms of racism and other kinds of discrimination. It also shows how the language associated with such attitudes can shape identities. In the interview mentioned earlier, McDonagh relates this theme to the characterisation of Ray. 'There's something quite childlike about the Ray character,' says McDonagh. 'He's dangerous but he's got a beautiful spirit as well. He's just a very sad and mixed-up guy who doesn't adhere to any of the P.C. notions that we might – not because he's trying to attack anything, but just because that's the way he is.' So Ray is decidedly un-P.C: he insults tourists who are overweight, and holds two Americans responsible for 'the Vietnamese' and 'John Lennon' (32). What is funny here, of course, is that the people being attacked are actually Canadian (like the Belgians and the Irish, Canadians are a people long used to being mistaken for their larger neighbours). It's unlikely that Ray learns the lesson, but his mistake shows how national stereotypes can only ever lead people to wrong conclusions.

Ray's inability to speak sensitively about others is exemplified in his interactions with Jimmy, whom he gleefully calls a 'midget' despite knowing that Jimmy prefers the term 'dwarf' (15). But, again confounding his audiences' expectations, McDonagh shows that, far from being a victim of the prejudices of others, Jimmy is in fact the film's most prejudiced character:

> There's gonna be a war, man, I can see it. There's gonna be
> a war between the blacks and between the whites. You ain't
> even gonna need a uniform no more. This ain't gonna be a
> war where your pick your side, man. Your side's already
> picked for ya [. . .] You don't know how much shit I've
> had to take off-a black midgets, man. (49–50)

Jimmy's outlook returns us to the issues of choice and the possibility of change. Jimmy argues that 'your side's already picked for ya' (50) – that our role in the forthcoming battle will be determined by our ethnic identity rather than by our will, our beliefs, our principles. Opting out is certainly not a possibility. Race thus becomes a kind of 'original sin', something that dooms us to certain inevitabilities before we are even born.

Yet it is Ken rather than Ray who rejects the idea that his fate is predetermined. 'My wife was black,' he says. 'And I loved her *very* much. And in 1976 she got murdered by a white man. So where the fuck am I supposed to stand in all this blood and carnage?' (51). Jimmy's response is telling: 'I think you need to weigh up all your options and let your conscience decide, Ken' (51). This option clearly depresses Ken, who likes his morality to be (to use the appropriate cliché) black and white; evidently, he has no wish to think for himself. But again we are faced with a contrast here: between a world view that tells us what to think (as both political correctness and racism do) and a morality that demands that we react to circumstances as they occur around us.

The film draws these ideas together in its ambiguous conclusion. Its final lines are spoken by Ray in voice-over: 'I really really hoped I wouldn't die,' he says. There may be a 'nod' to *The Dumb Waiter* here, which also concludes by leaving one of the protagonists' survival in some doubt. But this approach is consistent with McDonagh's plays, most of which refuse to give audiences any sense of closure. There is a lovely mix of verbal tenses in that final line: 'I hoped' says Ray (referring to something that happened in the past – implying that he lived) 'that I wouldn't die' (as if referring to something that might happen in the future). This disruption of time brings us back to the first lines of the script, which celebrate Bruges because 'we could be in any period of the last five hundred years', but it is notable that the shift from beginning to end is from the timelessness of the city (as consumed object) to the indeterminacy of the individual's fate (placing the emphasis on the audience's interpretation). We have moved, then, from being passive recipients of an image to being forced to continue the story for ourselves. The simple act of trying to understand Ray's last words will guarantee that we have taken over the role of authorship from McDonagh.

So, as with *The Pillowman*, there is a link being made between authorship and morality. The film aims to criticise those who are imprisoned by a morality that predetermines their actions – a morality that allows psychopaths to use the apparently ethical language of honour to justify horrendous actions. The film calls instead for balance: that we reject the rigidity of Harry and the apathy of Ray, and perhaps take up the position adopted by Ken, a man who ultimately does the right thing, sacrificing himself for someone else. It thus argues that morality is an act of interpretation rather than a series of rules to be followed. The moral person must thus treat life like the audience at McDonagh's film: we observe, we assess, we imagine – and then, we act.

5

PERFORMANCE AND CRITICAL PERSPECTIVES

'Monstrous children': Garry Hynes in conversation

Garry Hynes is Ireland's leading director, and has been influentially involved in the development of Martin McDonagh's theatrical career. She premiered his first play, *The Beauty Queen of Leenane*, in 1996, later bringing that production to Broadway, where it won four Tony Awards. One of those awards was for Best Director, making Hynes the first woman ever to receive that honour. She also directed the premieres of *A Skull in Connemara* and *The Lonesome West*, which joined with *Beauty Queen* in 1997 to become *The Leenane Trilogy*. Those plays were seen throughout Ireland and toured to London's West End and Australia; *The Lonesome West* was staged on Broadway in 1999, where it was nominated for four Tony Awards. Hynes has also directed *The Cripple of Inishmaan*, which went on a major tour of Ireland, the UK and the United States between 2008 and 2010. Her company Druid Theatre also staged a reading of an early draft of *The Pillowman* in April 1997.

As a director Hynes is particularly admired for her commitment to ensemble work; she is also noted for major reinterpretations of numerous Irish writers, such as John B. Keane, M.J. Molloy and (in particular) John Millington Synge. And she has been very influential in the development of new Irish writing. In addition to directing the premiere production of *The Leenane Trilogy*, she has also been responsible for the first productions of many Irish plays, including Tom Murphy's *Bailegangaire* (1985), John McGahern's *The Power of Darkness* (1991), Marina Carr's *Portia Coughlan* (1996) and *On Raftery's Hill* (2000), and Mark O'Rowe's *Crestfall* (2003).

She co-founded Druid Theatre in Galway in 1975 with the actors Marie Mullen and Mick Lally, both of whom appeared in *The Leenane Trilogy* – Mullen playing the role of Maureen in *The Beauty Queen* and Lally playing Mick Dowd in *Skull*. Their company is now known as one of the leading theatre groups in the world, and, according to its website, in 2009 alone Druid toured to 'Australia, Canada, the UK and the USA, presenting 364 performances in 26 venues'. Hynes was also Artistic Director of the Abbey Theatre, Ireland's national theatre, from 1991 to 1993.

I met with Hynes in August 2011 to discuss her discovery of McDonagh and the subsequent development of *The Leenane Trilogy*. Her relationship with McDonagh began after the conclusion of her contract with the Abbey when having taken a year's break from directing, she returned to resume the position of Druid's Artistic Director in early 1995. Druid was then (as now) particularly admired for its commitment to new writing, and it therefore receives a huge number of unsolicited scripts every year. 'When I got back to Druid, I asked to see what was coming in,' explains Hynes, who soon came across the play that eventually became *A Skull in Connemara*. 'I just couldn't believe how funny it was,' she states. 'Straight away I asked, "Who is this guy?"' The staff at Druid had had some dealings with McDonagh but didn't know much about him: he lived in London and, since sending in the first drafts of his plays, had acquired an agent. So Hynes asked to read the other works that the company had received from him – *Beauty Queen* and a prototype of what eventually became *The Lonesome West*. 'And within a few weeks of reading the plays I arranged to meet him,' says Hynes.

When she met McDonagh, Hynes quickly agreed with him that Druid would definitely produce one of the works he had submitted. 'I told him that we were going to do one of these plays and option all three,' she said, explaining to him that they might not actually stage all three. This agreement immediately gave rise to the issue of which play to stage first. 'The first question was which was the best play to introduce this writer to the world,' Hynes explains – but other considerations also had an impact. Hynes knew, for instance, that the play she chose would be the opening production at the Town Hall Theatre in Galway, a brand new municipal theatre for that city – 'So I needed to get a play that could stand up to that occasion.' And then the final and perhaps most important consideration was casting: 'Marie Mullen was available at that time [February 1996], and that was why we finally decided to do *Beauty Queen*.' Casting, Hynes states, is almost always the crucial factor in her decisions about which productions she can do.

Another major casting decision was to include Anna Manahan in the role of Mag. Manahan (who died in 2009) was one of the most popular Irish actors of her generation, appearing in many important productions. One of her earliest roles was as Serafina in a 1957 Dublin staging of *The Rose Tattoo*, for instance – a production which, notoriously, was shut down by the Irish police, who prosecuted its director Alan Simpson for obscenity (probably upon the insistence of the Catholic Archbishop of Dublin, Charles McQuaid). She was also well known for her roles in popular comedies, and in the works of John B. Keane. McDonagh's plays are often compared to Keane's: both writers analyse how community functions in rural Ireland (paying particular attention to the plight of people who are isolated due to their sensitivity or intelligence), and both make use of techniques of melodrama (such as using the plot device of letters going missing). Yet there are clear differences between the two writers, and it's also important to note that in the mid-1990s Keane's reputation as a serious dramatist had somewhat declined: at that time his work was often produced in a style that emphasised coarse humour and cheap pathos over the plays' more demanding (but more satisfying) elements. I asked Hynes if she'd been worried that, by casting Manahan, she ran the risk of creating too strong an association between *The Beauty Queen* and the work of Keane. 'That was part of the whole cheat,' she replies. 'We *wanted* them to think they were seeing a John B. Keane play.' Part of the strategy in staging *The Beauty Queen*, she explains, was to persuade audiences that they were seeing something familiar – something just like earlier Druid productions. 'The curtain goes up, there is a daughter of forty, there's a possible suitor; and so the audience thinks "we know where we are",' she explained. 'They'll think it's a John B. Keane play they haven't seen before. But half an hour later they're watching something completely different.' The impact of staging *Beauty Queen* for Druid was thus to signal both continuity and a change of direction: the group were still operating in the territory explored in their earlier productions of plays by Tom Murphy, Synge, Molloy and others, but there was also something very obviously – and perhaps unsettlingly – new. Hynes agreed: 'It was our territory, but strategically flipped around.'

It's often stated that Druid 'discovered' McDonagh, the implication being that he might not have been produced by anyone if Hynes hadn't read that draft of *Skull* in 1995. It is difficult to say whether this is true, but the assertion tends to obscure the way in which McDonagh benefited Druid, just as Druid benefited McDonagh. 'Fintan O'Toole once wrote that if Martin McDonagh hadn't existed, Druid would have had to invent him,' says Hynes. 'I think that's really true. Our meeting was serendipitous. It was serendipitous for us, but it was serendipitous for him too.' Druid's productions of McDonagh signalled new ways forward for Irish drama – allowing audiences in that country to look again at earlier work, especially by writers such as Synge and Keane. And the production of *The Leenane Trilogy*, which allowed audiences to see all three plays in one day, emphatically revealed the benefits of staging works in cycles. Druid would later build on that achievement when they staged all of Synge's plays in a single production called *DruidSynge*, which started at one o'clock in the afternoon and finished close to eleven the same night. The premiere of *Beauty Queen* in February 1996 was thus momentous in many ways.

The play is now produced frequently throughout the world and is one of McDonagh's most popular works – but when it was first in rehearsal it wasn't clear that it would work. Of course, the rehearsal of any new play is likely to involve anxiety, but there was no way of knowing whether McDonagh's use of techniques that seemed very old-fashioned would be successful. 'You find yourself being pretty insecure about things like the letter,' admits Hynes, referring to the play's fifth scene, in which Pato writes to Maureen. 'Originally we were seeing Pato writing the letter, spelling out each word, but it wasn't working,' she says. Hynes worked intensively on the problem with Briain O'Byrne – the actor who originated the role of Pato, and who would later play Valene and Thomas in *Lonesome West* and *Skull* respectively. Eventually, they decided that Pato would speak the letter out to the audience. That decision to break through the fourth wall proved tremendously successful: in most productions, it has the impact of heightening the audience's connection with the action while also allowing us to empathise much more with the character – and thus to understand better how much Maureen has to lose.

Other important decisions had to be made. The audience may initially have allowed their familiarity with Anna Manahan's reputation to convince them that they were watching a melodrama – but those associations needed to be quickly dispensed with. Hynes therefore considers it essential that anyone playing Mag needs to restrain themselves as much possible. 'I kept Anna in the chair as much as I could,' she explains, a decision that allowed Manahan to focus most of her performance on the use of her face, hands and upper body. That said, there were times when it was dramatically useful to have Mag moving around the stage. 'There's the scene with the potty,' Hynes recalls (referring to the beginning of the play's fourth scene, when Mag pours a potty full of her own urine down the sink). 'I had Anna take the longest possible route to get to the sink, walking from the door at the side of the stage, right up front and then around to the other side, so that the audience will spend the whole time thinking "Oh my God, she's not going to pour it down the sink" – and then she does.'

That scene is very funny in performance, but Hynes states clearly that the audience must understand that Mag is 'literally evil and dangerous'. 'Think about how the play opens,' she says: 'Maureen arrives in and she's soaking wet, her clothes dripping with rain. And Mag says "Wet, Maureen?" And it's clear that all she ever does is torment her daughter.' The performance by Mag thus helps determine an audience's ability to identify with Maureen. 'They have to think, when they're watching the play, "In the same situation that's exactly what I would have done." If you don't have that feeling, the play just doesn't work.'

I asked Hynes about the ending of the play, referring to those productions that imply that Maureen leaves Leenane like Nora in *A Doll's House* – not necessarily heading off to a better new life, but liberated from a restrictive old one. 'That interpretation makes no sense at all to me,' states Hynes, who is convinced that Maureen stays in Leenane. 'I remember the way Marie played it: just looking at her eyes, you could see how much Maureen is like an animal trapped in the headlights. I always imagined – and we talked about this in rehearsal – that what happened with Maureen is that she wouldn't have been seen around Leenane for a while and someone like Ray would call up to see what happened to her – and she'd be found dead in her bed. That's just my interpretation, but that's the way I'd see it.'

Having made the decision to open *Beauty Queen* in Galway, Hynes then approached London's Royal Court Theatre about a possible co-production. 'I wanted the production to have an English element because of Martin's background,' she explains. 'A lot of the play is very Irish, but there are fragments of English speech too – an English presence because that's where he grew up. So I contacted Stephen Daldry who was in charge at the Royal Court at the time; I was an Associate Director there too, so there was a good relationship. We opened at the Royal Court Upstairs in early 1996.' Was there any difference between the responses of English and Irish audiences? 'No,' says Hynes. 'From the first preview onwards it was exactly the same.' This, she suggests, is because the play makes sense in much the same way in any country where there are the remnants of a peasant culture. 'It could be the Czech Republic or Poland or Oklahoma – in many ways, the Leenane in *Beauty Queen* is an Irish version of *Deliverance* country.'

As discussed earlier, *Beauty Queen* was enormously successful. So the discussion at Druid soon turned to which of the remaining two plays they would stage next. 'And I said: "Why do we have to pick one?"' Hynes states. 'Why not do all three together?' *Skull* and *Beauty Queen* both had four characters; *The Lonesome West* had originally had three (the two brothers and a woman), but McDonagh had been redrafting the play to include Father Welsh and Girleen – so now that too had four characters. The case for staging all three together was even more compelling.

As for the Leenane setting, that was not initially the strongest link between the plays. 'It was in the title of *Beauty Queen*, but that was because Martin just liked the sound of it – that echo between "queen" and "Leenane".' I put it to Hynes that there is an evident moving outwards in the plays – from Leenane to Connemara to 'the west'. She agrees, but notes that the plays are 'quite different in their own ways'. '*Lonesome West* is probably my favourite,' she says, expressing regret that, despite mostly positive reviews, it was not as successful in New York as *Beauty Queen*.

I wondered if the relative popularity of *The Lonesome West* in Ireland (where it remains one of McDonagh's most popular plays – so much so that it is now taught on the Irish post-primary school curriculum) arose due to its treatment of the Catholic Church: that it literally showed Irish Catholicism in meltdown at a time when that institution was collapsing. 'I agree that was relevant,' says Hynes. 'But it wasn't intentional. That [Catholicism] is definitely part of Martin's landscape as a writer, but he'd never set out to be relevant deliberately or intentionally – if anything, he'd be quite against that.'

Indeed, a major problem with performing *The Lonesome West* is (again) that it could easily lapse into melodrama or perhaps even farce. 'When I was re-rehearsing *The Cripple of Inishmaan* in 2009, I needed to explain to the cast how we were doing it,' Hynes replies. 'And on the first day I said to them, "If I was writing a book about Martin McDonagh, I'd call it *Monstrous Children*." If you think about Valene and Coleman: if they were aged seven, everything they do with each other would make complete sense.' This approach doesn't mean, however, that the production can be infantile or absurd. 'All the plays have to be rooted in reality,' says Hynes, 'otherwise, you don't have permission for the craziness.'

To date, Hynes has directed four of McDonagh's plays, and hopes to work again with him in the future. I wondered if *A Behanding in Spokane* might ever be produced in Ireland. 'Well, one of the things Martin does in his plays is to take tropes from American film and put them in an Irish setting – we talked about *Deliverance* and *Beauty Queen* earlier. So would the same tropes work when they're put back in an American setting before an Irish audience?' That remains to be seen. She speaks warmly of *The Pillowman*, which Druid presented as a reading in 1997: that play also has never been produced in Ireland.

A crucial feature of Druid's work with McDonagh has been touring, both throughout Ireland and internationally. Hynes states that touring is essential to everything that Druid does. 'Productions are shaped by audiences, by small communities throughout Ireland. When we revived *The Cripple of Inishmaan* in 2009, we played in [rural Irish venues] where there was an audience with no expectations at all: so you really have to really sell it to people, to make it work.' The need to achieve excellence throughout a tour has a major impact on the development of the production itself.

What about the reception of the Irish plays when they tour abroad? Druid's production of *The Cripple of Inishmaan*, for instance, toured the United States as part of an Irish government-funded project called 'Imagine Ireland', one aim of which was to use the arts to promote Ireland internationally – and to restore the country's tattered reputation after the collapse of its economy in 2008. In one sense, *Cripple* is an ideal vehicle for such a project, since it questions seriously the notion of Ireland presenting an idealised version of itself before international (and especially American) audiences. Druid's production of the play thus helps us to consider the consequences that can arise when government agencies use the arts to brand the nation. Hynes states that she's fully aware of the risks of art being turned into a commodity, but points out that *Cripple* shows that there's no such thing as a 'real' version of Ireland: 'All you get is another version of Ireland that's just as inauthentic as what came before.' What, though, of the risk of misrepresentation – of the accusation that Martin McDonagh's plays are making the Irish look like a nation of 'feckin eejits'? Hynes's response is a powerful one: 'There isn't the slightest responsibility on the artist to be authentic. Representing the real Ireland is not what theatre is about, or what it's for. As artists, we only have one responsibility – the responsibility of artistic quality, to do the best work we possibly can.'

As we concluded the interview with these remarks, it seemed to me that Hynes's statement encapsulated clearly why the relationship between Druid and McDonagh has been so important for both. There is in each case a strong commitment to performing the work before an audience, to working tirelessly to ensure that the experience for each audience is as rich as possible. Yet there is also a clear prioritising of the same principles. If McDonagh was expressing his own views in *The Pillowman* when he wrote that 'the first duty of a storyteller is to tell a story', there's a clear overlap with Hynes's views: that an artist is not responsible to the nation, or obliged to tell the truth or to represent the real – but, rather, to be consistently excellent.

'Like Tottenham': Martin McDonagh's postmodern morality tales

José Lanters

When Martin McDonagh contended in an interview that he is 'not into any kind of . . . -ism, politically, socially, religiously, all that stuff' (O'Toole, 1997: 1), and when he maintained that all he wants to do 'is to tell stories', to leave 'little things behind that nobody else could' (quoted in Feeney, 1998: 27), he expressed a postmodern position, at least in terms of Jean-François Lyotard's definition of the postmodern as 'incredulity toward metanarratives' (1984: xxiv). Postmodernism rejects totalizing (religious, political, philosophical) theories – the -isms of McDonagh's statement; it replaces the so-called 'grand narrative' with the situational and preliminary 'little narrative' that 'remains the quintessential form of imaginative invention' (Lyotard, 60). Fredric Jameson has defined (and been critical of) some of the most important aesthetic characteristics of postmodernism, particularly the displacement of norms by codes – a displacement which has led to an image-driven culture of depthlessness, eclecticism and fragmentation, in which postmodern artists operate as recyclers of previous works and styles. Postmodern art typically takes the form of pastiche, which results in the erasure of a sense of the past 'because of the continual promulgation of a diversity of linguistic and aesthetic styles that are taken out of their historical context and presented as currently available' (Constable, 2004: 49).

If grand narratives are no longer credible, the question presents itself, 'Where . . . can legitimacy reside?' (Lyotard, xxv). Indeed, '[c]ritics hostile to postmodern thought believe that its support for multiplicity endorses an "anything goes" approach that . . . ends in unrestrained moral relativism' (Kilian, 1998: 17).

Critics who dislike the postmodernist aspects of McDonagh's work have called his plots and characters shallow and empty, and have condemned their author for having 'a disturbingly defective moral sense' (Taylor, 2003: 16). To them, McDonagh is the poster-boy for a postmodernist stance that represents a nihilistic relativism in its rejection of traditional values and forms of knowledge. The question is whether this is a fair assessment of a body of work that seems preoccupied with questions of truth and falsehood; love and hate; good and evil; guilt, sin, punishment and redemption. Rather than dismiss McDonagh as a facile postmodernist *bricoleur* lacking in responsibility and seriousness, it might be more accurate to consider him a writer whose 'dilemma lies in trying to reconcile the post-modern and the moralistic' (Dean, 2009: 169).

McDonagh's *oeuvre* embodies the postmodern concept of art as the recycling of culture, abounding as it does in references to and borrowings from sources both trivial and profound, ranging from stage plays and movies to American and Australian television series, to cartoons and comic books. Audiences might recognise the titles of *The Lonesome West* and *A Skull in Connemara* as quotations from, respectively, J.M. Synge's *The Playboy of the Western World* and Samuel Beckett's *Waiting for Godot*. The Dutch movie being shot in *In Bruges* is described by Chloe, who sells drugs on the set, as 'a pastiche of Nicolas Roeg's *Don't Look Now*. Not a pastiche, but a . . . "homage" is too strong . . . A "nod of the head"' (14), while it is dismissed as 'a jumped-up Eurotrash piece of rip-off fucking bullshit' (45) by Jimmy, a dwarf actor who has a part in the film. Depending on one's attitude towards McDonagh's art, one might equally apply one of those two descriptions to *In Bruges* itself.

As for the premise of *A Behanding in Spokane*: while McDonagh was filming *In Bruges* in Belgium he may have come across the statue of Brabo in the centre of Antwerp. According to the Flemish legend, Brabo slew Druon Antigoon, a giant notorious for 'behanding' his victims, and the statue shows him about to fling Druon's own severed hand into the river Scheldt, an apocryphal act of *hand-werpen* (hand throwing) that would give the city (Flemish 'Antwerpen') its name. On the other hand, McDonagh may have Googled his intended sub-ject and, like Mervyn in the play, consulted a ' "chopped-off hands" website' (44) for inspiration.

Postmodern culture is defined by images; indeed, as Jean Baudrillard argues, 'the image *precedes* the reality it is supposed to represent. Or to put it another way, reality has become a pale reflection of the image' (2). Many of McDonagh's characters can only make sense of reality by comparing it to what they have seen on television or in the movies. In *The Beauty Queen of Leenane*, Maureen is sure she remembers saying goodbye to Pato at the train station 'like they do in films' (51), even though his brother Ray later claims that Pato left by taxi. In *In Bruges*, Harry Waters berates Ken for refusing to fight him, not by comparing his attitude to that of Jesus, but by accusing him of standing about like 'Robert fucking Powell out of *Jesus of* fucking *Nazareth*' (74). In the culture of the simulacrum it is no longer clear what is reality and what imagination.

Postmodern culture's attention to the play of surfaces, images and signifiers leads to a language crisis that turns meaningful communication into a struggle. McDonagh's characters frequently state the obvious and are prone to repetition, which may itself become a self-conscious trick. When Kate in *The Cripple of Inishmaan* laments the fact that Billy has sent 'Not a word. (*Pause.*) Not a word, not a word, not a word, not a word, not a word, not a word, not a word. (*Pause.*) Not a word', Eileen retorts that she is 'allowed to say "Not a word", but one or two times and not ten times' (37–8). Words may easily turn into treacherous surfaces. In *A Skull in Connemara*, when Mick asks Mairtin if he is 'finished', the latter replies, confused, 'Am I Finnish?' (61). The instability of meaning also means that characters feel the need to keep qualifying their utterances, as when, in *In Bruges,* Ray agonises that because of him, 'a little boy isn't here any more', and continues, 'And he'll never be here again. . . .] Y'know, I mean here in the world. Not here in Belgium. [. . .] Well, he'll never be here in Belgium either, will he?' (27). In *The Pillowman*, Katurian maintains that his little stories are all surface: that what you see is what you get. Nevertheless, he also argues that they will allow you to 'draw your own conclusions' (11), an interpretive paradox that amounts to a linguistic 'puzzle without a solution' (17).

Lyotard argues that language in postmodern culture constitutes a game in which 'every utterance should be thought of as a "move"' (10) within a set of rules defining the game. McDonagh's characters often privilege conversational gaming conventions over the meaning of the message. In *A Skull in Connemara*, for example, Thomas explains: 'Now, Mick, you've insulted poor wee Mairtin there, you've insulted family, such as it is, so now I have to go and say something insulting back to you. That is the way that these things operate' (35). 'Don't be stupid. This is the shoot-out,' Harry replies when, towards the end of *In Bruges*, Marie suggests he and Ray put down their guns and go home (82). The 'great oul game' (53) of apologising and forgiving played by Coleman and Valene in *The Lonesome West* serves as a particularly extreme and graphic example of 'an agonistics of language' in which the 'social bond' between individuals is entirely composed of 'language "moves"' (Lyotard: 10–11). As Jameson puts it, 'utterances are now seen less as a process of the transmission of information or messages . . . than as . . . the trumping of a communicational adversary, an essentially conflictual relationship between tricksters' (1984: xi).

Because postmodern culture is suspicious of hierarchies and classifications, boundaries between categories and genres are destabilised by means of 'all manner of ambiguities, ruptures, and displacements' (Hassan, 1987: 168). In McDonagh's work, fragmentation abounds: families are divided against themselves, political entities are splinter groups, bodies are chopped up and 'behanded', and objects smashed. Markers of categories such as gender are destabilised: in *The Lieutenant of Inishmore*, Mairead may either be 'a boy with lipstick' or 'a girl with no boobs' (51). Yet precisely because McDonagh's characters are lost in a choppy ocean of signification, they tend to latch on to linguistic markers of (racial, sexual, national, physical) difference – coloured, gay, Norwegian, crippled – that appear to serve as solid signifying anchors in an irrational world. In *In Bruges*, when Ray tells Ken he was once beaten up for no reason whatsoever by 'this big fat retarded black girl', and Ken asks, 'What has her being black have anything to do with it?', Ray does not understand the question: 'Well, she was black' (19–20). Material objects similarly function as stable points in a minefield of meaning. In *The Lonesome West*, Valene has trouble concentrating on Father Welsh's moral instruction, but he is 'sure to be getting into heaven' because he owns forty-six holy figurines (43).

In Kantian thought, morality is 'never a matter of an individual's specific self-interest, and any moral act must be universally applicable.

What is more, morality is a matter of universal duty rather than individual choice' (Kilian, 1998: 129). In postmodern thought, the 'dismantling of hierarchies results in an equalisation of value, in the sense that there is nothing which can legitimately be said to have *intrinsically* more value than something else' (Kilian: 140). This means that postmodern theory tends to avoid addressing the issue of morality, 'not because it tacitly supports nonmorality or amorality, but because it is not possible to talk about morality without resorting to metanarratives' (Kilian: 138). What is sometimes seen as Martin McDonagh's 'defective' moral vision should be reconsidered in light of this conundrum, and can instead be seen as his way of expressing a morality of contingent truth embedded in textual play rather than one based in the idea of universal, absolute Truth.

Truth claims in McDonagh should always be approached with the question Katurian asks his brother in *The Pillowman*: 'Which particular truth?' (51). The lies routinely told by McDonagh's characters constitute a gaming strategy that is often, but not always, fuelled by self-interest. In *The Cripple of Inishmaan* the lies Johnnypateen tells Billy about his parents drowning themselves so that their insurance money might pay for their son's medical bills are spun to spare Billy's feelings, when in 'reality', such as it is, Billy himself 'would still be at the bottom of the sea to this day, if it hadn't been for Johnnypateen swimming out to save him' – a selfless deed morally complicated, however, by Johnny's 'stealing his mammy's hundred pounds then to pay for Billy's hospital treatment' (80).

Sometimes characters lie to make a rhetorical point that may also serve a moral purpose. In *In Bruges*, Ken responds to Jimmy's racist prediction that there will be a war between the blacks and the whites by telling him, 'My wife was black. And I loved her very much. And in 1976 she got murdered by a white man. So where the fuck am I supposed to stand in all this blood and carnage?' (51). Ken is making the point that Jimmy's black-and-white thinking is flawed, but in a flashback scene depicting the murder (deleted from the movie's final cut), his wife is white.

McDonagh's plot structures often take the form of a string of moves and counter-moves that eventually plays itself out in a rhetorically satisfying finale or an ironic moment of ambiguity. Like McDonagh himself, Katurian in *The Pillowman* likes to write postmodern parables with 'a twist' designed to call into question the apparent moral preceding it in the story. 'The Little Jesus' turns into a tale of horror when the little girl who wants to be like Jesus is made to suffer the real torments of Christ to the point where, as she points out, she *is* Jesus (71). In its twisted logic the story exposes the hypocrisy of traditional morality (in which children are encouraged to be 'like Jesus'), and of an either–or mentality in which absolute adherence to absolute standards inevitably leads to absolute brutality. In the parable 'The Three Gibbet Crossroads', a man locked in a cage can see two other caged men, whose crimes are listed as 'rape' and 'murder'. He cannot remember his own crime or see what the sign on his cage says, and nobody who reads it is willing to tell him what it is that horrifies them so. Eventually the man is killed without having discovered the answer. Katurian maintains that there is no answer, 'because there *is* nothing worse, is there? Than the two things it says' (17). Turning such rhetorical questions into open questions is what the parable, like the play that contains it, is designed to do. In what sense is one atrocity worse than another? Is there nothing worse than rape and murder? How guilty is a man who does not know what he has done, and how just is it to execute someone in that position?

The Pillowman ends in a convoluted series of unprincipled choices, surprises and ambiguities that reflect the 'fuzzy' postmodern principle of being unprincipled. After finding out that three children have likely been killed by Michal (whose torture-induced brain damage may have diminished his responsibility), Katurian smothers him with a pillow and takes the blame upon himself. He may be guilty by association – it was his stories that inspired the killings – but Katurian's false confession seems as much motivated by self-interest (his stories will be kept in the police file for a long time) as the desire to save his brother from more torture at the hands of the ruthless investigators. The third child, however, is found alive: Michal apparently lied about making her the Little Jesus and instead placed her in his favourite story about the little green pig that enjoyed being a little strange, its plot being a celebration of difference and uniqueness over collectivism. Whether this story is 'better' than the others or changes our judgement of Michal seems less important than the emphasis on difference, uniqueness and strangeness embodied by the plot twist itself.

Postmodernism's belief in the constructed, multiple subject which 'cannot possess an essential Self that acts as a moral agent within a unified reality' means that 'the subject's conscience – the 'traditional' locus of morality – no longer originates from the subject, but is itself a textual inscription' (Kilian, 149). If morality is contingent and a question of writerly choice, of privileging one plot line over another, this means that stories – McDonagh's and those told by his characters – can be endlessly rewritten. After Katurian is executed by Tupolski at the end of *The Pillowman*, his ghost rises and explains that, seconds before being shot, Katurian made up a final story, in which Michal knowingly submits himself to a childhood of torture so that his brother Katurian may write the stories that he will end up liking very much. The 'fashionably downbeat' ending Katurian has in mind for the parable – the burning of his stories by 'a bulldog of a policeman', which renders Michal's sacrifice null and void – is aborted when Tupolski shoots Katurian 'two seconds too soon'. Instead, at the end of *The Pillowman*, the policeman, 'for reasons only known to himself', saves the stories from the flames and places them in Katurian's file (103). If this ending is 'somehow . . . more in keeping with the spirit of the thing' (104), it is because the final action is random and un-explained, and the policeman's apparently 'doing the right thing' a function of plot rather than character motivation. As in the case of the third child, however, the 'rightness' of that final thing is qualified by the events preceding the final twist in the plot.

Random plot twists also dominate *A Behanding in Spokane*, in which Carmichael's single-minded quest to retrieve his lost left hand (which he knows will be of no use to him, but which he nevertheless insists is rightfully his) leads him into the path of Toby and Marilyn, opportunistic but bungling scam artists who claim to have the missing body part for sale. Carmichael's right hand has the word 'love' tattooed on it, while the knuckles of the missing left hand spell 'hate' – a binary view of good and evil the play sets out to complicate. Both in spite of and because of the missing signifier, Carmichael has plenty of hate to go around, in the form of gratuitous racism and homophobia aimed at Toby, who is black and whose demeanour is not particularly macho. While the obsessive hand-quest is motivated by a personal grievance, the universal certainty of Carmichael's black-and-white view of the world is not based in any logical premise, for the hillbillies who – he claims – removed his hand twenty-seven years ago by forcing his wrist down in front of an oncoming train were not black; indeed, as Carmichael himself points out about the stereotype, 'You can't *get* black hillbillies' (47). Carmichael's right hand does not know what the left hand is up to: his focused quest to retrieve what rightfully belongs to him has apparently led to some serious irrational wrongdoing, seeing that his trunk is full of severed hands of all colours and sizes, including '*the sad small hands of little children*' (19).

The tattoos on Carmichael's hands are a reference not only to Charles Laughton's film *The Night of the Hunter* (1955), in which the knuckles of the psychopathic and obsessive preacher sport the same binary message, but also to Spike Lee's nod to that movie in *Do the Right Thing* (1989), where Radio Raheem's 'brass-knuckle' rings also spell the words 'love' and 'hate'. In Raheem's narrative, ' "good" is not only identifiable and absolute, but ultimately more powerful than "evil", which, correspondingly, is equally pure and clear' (McKelly, 1998: 218). Just as Lee undercuts Raheem's message in his film, McDonagh undercuts Carmichael's absolutism by placing him opposite the hotel clerk Mervyn who, throughout the play, behaves in an apparently unfocused and erratic fashion. Toby and Marilyn, the half-hearted con artists held prisoner by Carmichael, serve as foils, as they try to figure out the rules of the different games their two adversaries play with them and each other.

In the long monologue that opens scene two of *A Behanding in Spokane*, Mervyn fantasises about a life of action in which he would be a hero, always doing the right thing no matter who was in danger: 'Maybe a prostitute would get stabbed and I'd have to rescue her? Or some lesbians would get stabbed? I wouldn't mind they were lesbians, I'd save 'em' (21). Yet throughout the play Mervyn's behaviour seems to contradict his would-be persona, as when he uses a personal past contretemps with Toby over a drugs deal as an excuse not to rescue the two petty thieves from what he knows is a dangerous madman. In the end, however, it turns out that Mervyn has inexplicably 'done the right thing' after all and called the police. In the meantime, Carmichael has unexpectedly abandoned his intention to kill Toby and Marilyn for deceiving him about his hand, his contrary mood having been brought on by a telephone conversation in which he has been scolded by his racist mother for secretly enjoying pornographic magazines featuring black women.

After Toby and Marilyn have been released, Mervyn confronts Carmichael with the inconsistencies in his story about the hillbillies and the train, hinting at an alternative plot line in which Carmichael cut off his own left hand, a self-mutilation that can be read in any number of ways: as the irrational act of a madman; as an expression of self-hatred, or the desire to eradicate hatred; or as a metaphor for the self-destructive nature of hatred, or the restrictive nature of binary thinking. Mervyn's scenario finds corroboration in the fact that one of the severed left hands in Carmichael's trunk has the word 'hate' tattooed on it. The discovery unsettles Carmichael's absolute belief in his own story and robs him of the fanaticism that has been driving him for the past twenty-seven years. Alone in his room, after he and Mervyn have wished each other the best, Carmichael picks up the hand. '*He checks how it looks against his left wrist. It's not a bad match, but not perfect. He shakes his head dismissively.*' Robbed of certainty, hate and the motivation for his quest, Carmichael has no further *raison d'être*. Knowing that the hotel room is soaked in petrol, he 'artfully' takes out a cigarette and produces a lighter which, even after repeated attempts, does not ignite. As the play ends, Carmichael puts '*his chin in his hand, the word "love" clearly visible*', and resignedly utters the word, 'fucker' (52). Once again the plot's finale is 'in keeping with the spirit of the thing': everyone in *A Behanding in Spokane*, including the playwright, has ended up 'doing the right thing', not by obeying rules but by being arbitrary, selfish and inconsistent. The suggestion of love's victory at the end can therefore only be self-consciously double-edged.

In *In Bruges*, McDonagh also uses a triangular character structure (Harry Waters and the two hit men, Ken and Ray, who work for him) to tease out questions about guilt and sin in a postmodern world. Ray is all surface and instant gratification: to him, Bruges is a boring 'shithole' full of 'old buildings and that' (10), representing history that is 'all just a load of stuff that's already happened' (13). For the violent and cold-blooded Harry Waters, on the other hand, Bruges, which he nostalgically compares to 'a fairy tale' (37), is an obsession; his other sentimental passion is little children, who provide the basis for his only absolute principle, that anyone who harms a child must die. (Harry's two passions may be secretly – and paradoxically – related: although he claims that his visit to Bruges at the age of seven was the 'last happy holiday I fucking had' (36), an outtake from the movie shows him in Bruges as a boy of about seven in the company of a man dressed in civilian clothes whose identity remains obscure, although he wears the same ring we see on the finger of the priest killed by Ray.)

Ken occupies the middle ground between Ray and Harry: he is indebted to the latter for avenging the murder of his wife many years ago, but also protective towards the younger and less intelligent Ray. Ken is interested in history and art, although he seems at a loss to understand why these things are important to him: when he queues up in the Basilica to touch the phial with Jesus's blood he does so because that 'is what you do' (21). Ken is able to explain to Ray the concept of the Last Judgement, but also confesses that he has rejected most of his childhood Catholic beliefs, even though 'the things you're taught as a child, they never really leave you, do they?' (25). Between Ray's cultural and moral amnesia and Harry's unbreakable, purely personal code of one moral principle for one particular kind of event, Ken is trying to work out what 'trying to lead a good life' (26) amounts to, in a post-Christian world where the cultural memory of traditional values lingers on in ritual patterns, museums and churches.

In *In Bruges* the child, also evoked by the Christmas setting and the peaceful images of Marie, the pregnant owner of the hotel where Ken and Ray are staying, functions as a nostalgic icon of innocence. The little boy accidentally shot by Ray during the contract killing of a priest is poignantly shown, in a flashback scene, waiting to confess the 'sins' he has pathetically written on a crib note: '1. Being moody. 2. Being bad at maths. 3. Being sad' (23). The death of the innocent child is a nostalgic and sentimental stand-in for the loss of an idealised past, and the use of the trope in conjunction with the facetious tone often adopted by the film's characters and the violence in which they casually indulge is indicative of 'the very real and very uneasy tension between postmodern irony and nostalgia today' (Hutcheon, 1998: 1).

It is indeed ironic that the shooting of the priest on Harry's orders, perhaps in retaliation for abusing him as a little boy, has led to the accidental killing of a little boy by Ray, whose murder Harry then orders Ken to arrange. When Ken refuses, Harry takes matters into his own hands, but before he departs for Bruges to engage in some serious violence, he tenderly kisses his own three young children goodbye. In the postmodern,

> nostalgia itself is both called up, exploited, *and* ironised. This is a complicated (and postmodernly paradoxical) move that is both an ironising of nostalgia itself, of the very urge to look backward for authenticity, and, at the same moment, a some-times shameless invoking of the visceral power that attends the fulfilment of that urge. (Hutcheon: 6–7).

Ray sentimentalises children in much the same way Harry does. Although he has no sense of history, the killing of the little boy in his recent personal past has left him on the verge of a nervous break-down – a sign, in the absence of deeply felt authentic emotions, that 'you do think about things, and take them to heart', as Pato tells Maureen in *The Beauty Queen of Leenane* (30). At the same time, Ray is capable of gratuitous violence against people he does not know, and feels no compunction about having shot the priest, even though he does not know why Harry ordered the killing. Moreover, when he is not crying on Ken's shoulder about the little boy, he can joke about the incident without batting an eyelid. On his first date with Chloe, Ray tells her that he shoots people for money – 'Priests, children. Y'know, the usual' – in a tone that suggests he is being ironic. To her question whether there is money to be made in that line of business, he responds, 'There is in priests. There isn't in children', and when he asks her, 'Do I look like I shoot people?', she answers, 'No. Just children' (28–9). Chloe laughs, but Ray does not and changes the subject, whether because the irony has worn off or because the language game he initiated has been won by Chloe is unclear. The complex relationship between truth and falsehood is highlighted by the ambiguity of the conversation, in which the extent to which each character believes that the other is being ironic is left intentionally unresolved.

The main difference between Harry and Ray is that, whereas Harry operates from a position of complete certainty, Ray walks around lost and confused, evoking, in his apparently unironised moments of self-accusation, an association with the little boy he killed, whose childish 'sins' are not unlike Ray's own: being moody, being bad at maths (killing two people instead of one), and being sad. If the audience sympathises with Ray rather than Harry, it is because the movie exploits the audience's own penchant for the sentimental and the nostalgic, fostered by Ray's wide-eyed expression of distress. His feelings of remorse and Harry's sense of retribution in the wake of the little boy's killing lead them to the same conclusion, springing from their fetishising of childhood innocence: Ray must die. The two sentiments coincide when Ray puts a gun to his own temple at the very same moment that Ken, on Harry's orders, also points a gun at his head. Neither pulls the trigger: Ray's suicide attempt prevents Ken from murdering him, and Ken's murder attempt saves Ray from killing himself.

The paradox leads Ken to the realisation that patterns need not always be followed, that plots can be redirected and that not every killing has to be followed by an act of revenge. Ken's own refusal to fight Harry – a game of cheek-turning Harry does not want to play – and his subsequent self-sacrifice to warn Ray of Harry's murderous presence are cases in point. The misguided nature of Harry's absolutism is underscored by means of a pattern in which tragedy repeats itself as farce: when Harry shoots Ray, he also accidentally kills Jimmy the dwarf, and, led into thinking he has killed a little boy by Jimmy's wearing a school uniform, commits suicide on the spot. As a pastiche of Ray's accidental crime and aborted suicide, the scene suggests the absurdity of Harry's 'principled' attitude as well as the inauthenticity of his nostalgic idealisation of childhood innocence that led to this moment in the first place.

Because of Harry's principles about the sanctity of childhood, his own three children are now without their doting father, and there is, as Ray's voice-over points out at the film's end, 'a Christmas tree somewhere in London, with a bunch of presents underneath it that'll never be opened . . .' (86). Coming on the heels of the bloody shooting that has left Harry and Jimmy dead and Ray critically wounded, the calculated sentimentality of that image is a postmodern use of nostalgia, in that 'an inadequate present and an idealized past' are brought together for a complex purpose: the saccharine image of the perfect family Christmas is 'invoked but, at the same time, undercut, put into perspective, seen for exactly what it is – a comment on the present as much as on the past' (Hutcheon: 7).

To underline the uneasy and complex interplay of the nostalgic and the ironic in his film, McDonagh ends *In Bruges* with images of Ray in the 'present' being stretchered into an ambulance while his voice comments in the past tense on what he was thinking at the time: 'And I thought, if I survive all this . . . ' (86). Given that conditional 'if', it is unclear from what (future) vantage point Ray's voice-over is emanating. If Ray *did not* survive his injuries, he might be in hell or purgatory, a place he had earlier described in football terms as being 'kind of like the inbetweeny one. "You weren't *really* shit, but you weren't all that great, either." Like Tottenham' (24). If Ray *did* survive, is he in prison? In Bruges? In Tottenham even? But perhaps the entire plot of *In Bruges* is meant to be seen as a dream sequence, like the Dutch movie being shot in Bruges in the course of *In Bruges*. After all, Ken mentions twice that Ray had told him, 'I know I'm awake, but I feel like I'm in a dream' (39, 40). Maybe *In Bruges* is, like Bruges itself, a kind of postmodern fairy tale. These are not either–or questions; the ambiguous ending makes you 'wonder what the solution is, but the truth is there is no solution' (*PM*, 17).

In the voice-over, Ray claims that when he was put into the ambulance he resolved, should he survive, to accept whatever punishment Harry's widow should impose on him, be it prison or death. He immediately and self-servingly goes on, 'Cos at least in prison, and at least in death . . . I wouldn't be in fucking Bruges,' until it strikes him that hell might be 'the rest of eternity spent in fucking Bruges', whereupon he adds, again with self-interest, 'I really hoped I wouldn't die' (87). When, after a pause, the screen cuts to black, it is unclear whether this signifies that Ray has died, or simply indicates that the movie has ended; the question as to what punishment Ray deserves or receives also remains unanswered. In terms of McDonagh's cinematic text, however, Ray, as a character in *In Bruges*, will for ever be in Bruges, and hence in hell, if Bruges is hell, or if hell is Bruges. In that sense his punishment exists as a textual gambit, a move that illustrates the extent to which postmodern morality 'is a function of discourse and not . . . an extradiscursive regulator of a discursive practice or reality' (Kilian: 149).

Postmodernism rejects certainty and closure; its 'refusal to cling to a particular point of view for the sake of consistency means that there can be no "genuinely true" answers to "serious questions" of . . . morality' (Kilian: 17). McDonagh's refusal in his work of closure, consistency and absolutism in favour of ambiguity, multiplicity and contradiction is in itself a postmodern ethical stance in which 'nothing can be affirmed aside from the importance of the question one cannot (and must not) answer' (Kilian: 139). Merit can be found in vacillation, doubt, confusion and continual searching. McDonagh evokes traditional religious and legal concepts and systems of morality only to treat them ironically even as he approaches them nostalgically, and simultaneously makes us question whether what seemed like nostalgia was really meant to be taken as irony or what seemed to be ironic was really meant to be taken seriously.

'Do you believe in . . . [t]he Last Judgement and the afterlife and . . . guilt and . . . sins and . . . Hell and . . . all that . . . ?', Ray asks. 'Um . . . Oh. Um . . .', Ken replies (24–5). That postmodernist wisdom also eloquently captures the moral of Martin McDonagh's little stories.

A symbiotic relationship: the works of Martin McDonagh and ecocriticism

Karen O'Brien

From the early 1990s, ecocriticism began to address the issue of the environmental crisis, operating in a context created by concern over the weakening of the ozone layer, the first widespread reports on what was then known as 'the greenhouse effect' and a number of other very public environmental catastrophes. Today, there is no shortage of environmental problems: climate change, endangered species protection, offshore drilling regulation, the need to create solar energy projects that will avoid harming wildlife, habitats and ecosystems, and so on. Whether or not they are environmental activists, ecocritics aim to explore and analyse the implications of such developments, and to consider the relationship between human culture and the natural environment generally. Ecocriticism thus offers a critical lens for understanding the dynamics of human–nature interconnectivity.

In this essay I offer a brief account of ecocriticism's (relatively limited) interventions in theatre scholarship, and a demonstration of the potential applicability both of theatre to ecocriticism and of ecocriticism to theatre, in the form of a description of several potentially rich sites of analysis offered by Martin McDonagh's work. I follow this with an ecocritical reading of *The Cripple of Inishmaan*, a play that – viewed through an ecocritical lens – reveals the negative consequences that result from too simple an understanding of the relationship between nature and the human.

Lawrence Buell, whose *The Environmental Imagination* (1995) largely influenced the development of ecocriticism in America, defines ecocriticism broadly as

> an umbrella term . . . used to refer to the environmentally oriented study of literature and (less often) the arts more generally, and to the theories that underlie such critical prac- tice. [It] also has the intrinsic advantage of implying the

> tendency of such work for thinking ecologically in the meta-
> phorical as well as scientific sense of focusing on how artistic
> representation envisages human and nonhuman webs of
> interrelation. (2005: 138)

The plays and films of McDonagh offer fruitful examples of how (in Buell's words), 'artistic representation envisages human and nonhuman webs of interrelation'. McDonagh's work generates awareness and understanding of ecological ideas through his representations of the environment – something that he achieves through setting, character-isation, action, theme, subtext, allusion, metaphoric imagery and plot.

The field of ecocriticism has grown rapidly since the early 1990s. Prior to its establishment, scholars who wrote on the relationship between the environment and literature published individual studies outside a definable scholarly community: as Cheryl Glotfelty states, 'Each critic was inventing an environmental approach to literature in isolation. Each was a single voice howling in the wilderness' (1996: xvii). Emerging as a self-aware force in the early 1990s, ecocriticism initially served as a literary methodology and critical theory that focused on nature and nature writing. Ecocritics soon began seeking the 'formation of a diversity caucus' (Wallace and Armbruster, 2001: 3), which would bring more inclusivity in the theory and practice of eco-criticism. Of particular interest in this context was the development of the concept that nature and culture are not a 'dualistic construct' but are in fact 'interwoven', as Wallace and Armbruster put it (4). They go on to argue that 'Understanding how nature and culture constantly influence and construct each other is essential to an informed eco-criticism' (4). This expanded approach, which examines nature and culture as interwoven and in some ways inseparable concepts, enabled interdisciplinary study on the relationship between human and other-than-human life.

Ecological thinking may take many investigative forms, but the most influential texts have focused primarily on literary and cultural analysis. Greg Garrard's *Ecocriticism* (2004) is an excellent example of such work. Garrard identifies rhetorical strategies that engage with ecological and socio-political concerns – strategies which he sees as perceptible through literary devices such as metaphor, structure, imagery and allusion. Garrard writes that:

> As ecocritics seek to offer a truly transformative discourse, enabling us to analyse and criticise the world in which we live, attention is increasingly given to the broad range of cultural processes and products in which, and through which, the complex negotiations of nature and culture take place. (2004: 4)

A 'discourse' such as the one described by Garrard seems implicitly incapable of limiting itself to one discipline or form of cultural production, since the 'complex negotiations of nature and culture' are taking place not only in books (let alone books of so-called 'nature writing'), but also in film, visual art, architecture, design – and of course theatre.

While ecocriticism began primarily as a literary mode, new directions and advances have enhanced its purpose and interdisciplinary potential. Buell prefers the terms 'environmental criticism' or 'literary-environmental studies' because they more clearly capture the 'heterogeneous foci' of ecocriticism as well as its wide interdisciplinary range (2005: viii, 11–12). As a branch of literary and cultural studies, ecocriticism is valued for the flexibility of it boundaries, which allows for a provocative engagement with a range of subjects. As Timothy Clark writes, 'The limitations as well as the excitement of ecocritical work to date may reflect the fact that environmental questions are not just a matter of aesthetics, politics, poetics or ethics, but can affect certain ground rules as to what these things mean' (2011: 202). Ecocriticism today is used by a wide range of participants with an equally broad span of concerns, theories, disciplines and possibilities. Rather than a single school of criticism, it has become an intellectual tendency practised within many disciplines and schools.

Ecocriticism facilitates a versatile interdisciplinary approach in which various critical methods and theories may be employed to engage human culture with an ecological consciousness. How then might ecocriticism contribute to an interdisciplinary study of drama, theatre or performance studies? Buell notes that these arts are studied less often in ecocriticism, and Patrick Murphy observes an absence of such critical approaches in drama in particular (2000: 230). That said, scholars such as Una Chaudhuri, Baz Kershaw and Theresa J. May have published formative work in these areas.

Una Chaudhuri problematises the use of nature as metaphor, advocating the theatre as a site of ecological consciousness (1994: 28). Chaudhuri states that:

> The theater's complicity with the anti-ecological humanist tradition has to be of critical concern to us, but we should not overlook the same theater's own self-reflexive stagings of this complicity. The theater, that is to say, cannot escape the liabilities of its status as a cultural institution producing cultural artifacts; but it can avoid misrecognizing that status as something natural. (28)

The practice of theatre, however, has not hurried to embrace 'materialist-ecological theater' (24), to explore ecological meaning, or to acknowledge the divide (or the 'rupture', as Chaudhuri terms it), between the human and the natural.

Problematising the idea of the natural world, Baz Kershaw asks, 'How can we write about the natural world (whatever that is?) – and the relationship of performance to it – when the 'natural world', being a cultural construct, makes nature more inaccessible?' (2002: 119). He examines the paradoxes and counter-productivity of eco-activism in order to identify 'an ecology of performance that will make its inevitable paradoxes productive in the struggle for environmental sanity' (2002: 120).

Kershaw views Chaudhuri's idea of rupture differently. As is pointed out above, the very idea of a nature–culture 'rupture' is cited by some ecocritics as part of the ugly legacy of the same humanism that Chaudhuri disputes. Kershaw discusses Chaudhuri's preference for play in the paradox of rupture as a site of eco-consciousness, but Kershaw aims to avoid paradoxes and to deal with 'the crucial matters that an ecology of performance must address' (1999: 214). Kershaw argues that 'effective ecologies of performance are much more likely to be found in performance beyond theatre than within the bastions of theatre buildings' (2002: 128).

Following Chaudhuri, Theresa J. May calls for a materialist-based practice of eco-theatre and a 'material–ecological discourse' in scholarship to bring attention to the implications of cultural performance on environment (2007: 96). In support of the potential of eco-consciousness in theatre, Kurt Heinlein's full-length study promotes 'Green Theatre', a merging of theatrical practice and environmental philosophy to 're-orient Western society toward more ecologically sound socio-environmental behaviours' (2007: 219). 'Theatre studies,' May states, 'is positioned opportunistically between the literary and the performative, and as such can function as a bridge between discourses' (96). Downing Cless also works to bridge the discourses in his full-length text on ecology in European drama, in which he professes that he 'must deconstruct nature as the author writes it, first through close reading and then by collaboration with a production team . . . Quite simply, nature then and there in the text becomes nature now and here on the stage' (2010: 11). The overarching concerns of scholars and practitioners are with unifying our definitive conceptions of humanity and of the natural, and with recognising the environmental implications of socio-cultural problems.

While activists have sought to reform current environmental problems and to restore the environment, scholars have engaged critically with ideas and principles to promote an understanding of the implications of human ethics and cultural consumption and production for the function of the ecosystem. 'More than through acts of pedagogical or activist outreach,' Buell argues, there is a need to establish a broad sense of environmental stewardship in order to 'instill and reinforce public concern about the fate of the earth, about humankind's responsibility to act on that awareness, about the shame of environmental injustice, and about the importance of vision and imagination in changing minds, lives and policy as well as composing words, poems, and books' (2005: 133).

An ecocritical lens provides an understanding of the interconnectedness between sociocultural and biospheric/natural processes. The intention is to put 'the human' and 'the natural' in conversation rather than in opposition and thus to consider how we act in relation to nature.

What is at stake in the tensions and interactions between nature and culture in McDonagh's works? McDonagh's works depict both a lack of sensitivity to nature and dramatic encounters with it – so could the plays and films teach us about the interconnectedness between literature and nature? My suggestion here is that an ecocritical analysis of McDonagh's works can reveal the intricate and reciprocal relationship between human and other-than-human life. The plays and films yield insights into the cultural, historical and sociopolitical human relationship with the environment.

McDonagh's depiction of animals and his characters' relationships to forms of non-human life seem to raise ecological issues. Characters exhibit extreme behaviour in both their exploitative and violent treatment of animals, on the one hand, and their capacity for close connections to animals, on the other. In *The Cripple of Inishmaan* cows are merely entertainment for the bored Billy. Animal abnormalities and abuses, additionally, provide 'news' for Johnnypateenmike to report. Significant to *Six Shooter* is a story of a cow that has exploded, literally being blown into pieces. McDonagh's recurrent topic of the abused cow surfaces in *The Skull of Connemara* as well. In *The Lieutenant of Inishmore*, the characters show compassion for Wee Thomas (the cat) but are exceptionally cruel towards each other. In *A Behanding in Spokane,* the characters intimately identify with a variety of animals but demonstrate limited knowledge of specific animal and marine mammal types, behaviours and adaptations. In his speech about 'cleaning up the environment', for example, Toby mistakes a seal for a sea lion (only the latter can clap). The tale of 'The Little Green Pig' in *The Pillowman* or the snipping of the ears of a dog in *The Lonesome West* may offer a clear start for an ecocritical examination of the use of animals. In all these plays, McDonagh seems to raise the possibility that the extremes both of exploitation and of identification stem from the same humanist assimilation of animals to human schemes of valuation.

The function of food is another area of ecocritical investigation. The lack of nourishment in the Irish home in *The Beauty Queen of*

Leenane raises questions about the nature–culture divide. Kieran Keohane and Carmen Kuhling note the destructive excess of the mother and daughter, who eat

> [s]ickening fast food deadening the life process, clogged arteries, obesity, sluggishness. Their diet is Irish fast food: Complan, tea and fancy biscuits – fats and sugar. The house reeks of the mother's urine. She deliberately neglects her infection to annoy her daughter by reminding her of infirmity, decrepitude and death. Her cruelty is reciprocated: boiling fat from the chip pan is used to torture and eventually murder the domineering mother. (2004: 189)

The women neglect their bodies, living unhealthily in a stagnant state of imbalance and misfortune.

Food functions in McDonagh's *The Cripple of Inishmaan* to reflect how removed the characters are from the natural world. Instead of the healthy diet obtainable from the environment, the characters survive – except for the occasional leg of lamb or egg – primarily on canned peas, sweeties and poteen. The aunts have stocked the shelves of their store only with canned peas. The peas represent a product of the global ecosystem which uses methods in canning, packaging and transportation that reduce nutrients to mere calories. Slippy Helen, in addition, consistently breaks eggs, diminishing the food supply.

'Environment', 'nature' and 'landscape' are three often contested, generally difficult to define and sometimes interchangeable terms. Environment is inclusive of all locales, whether densely or sparsely populated or polluted or preserved. As Clark notes, 'The "environment", after all, is ultimately, "everything"' (2011: 203). Ecocritical studies of environment adopt an inclusive approach towards notions of nature and landscape but also stretch to consider the impact of culture, and sometimes to question the conceptual separation between nature and culture. Wallace and Armbruster state that 'Environment need not only refer to "natural" or "wilderness" areas . . . Environment also includes cultivated and built landscapes, the natural elements and aspects of those landscapes, and cultural interactions with those natural elements' (2001: 4). In drama, the conceptualisation of landscape, nature and environment provides new perspectives in the writing and practice of theatre that bring awareness to ecological thinking.

McDonagh's works often transcend their literal setting and engage with a culturally imagined sense of environment. Such use of place surely does not serve to preserve historical or cultural memory; nor does it intend misleadingly to distort a legitimate image of a community. They show various ways in which the environment shapes and is shaped by human interaction with the natural world. Whether characters encourage collaborative ecology or, in contrast, portray humans as heroic masters of the universe, the concept of environment is useful to explore the human place in and participation with larger ecosystems. From an ecocritical perspective, environment in McDonagh's plays and films performs as a sort of character that reinforces the importance of the dynamic relationship between nature and culture.

Six Shooter is set in rural Ireland (shot on location in Rosslare, Waterford and Wicklow). The juxtaposition of the countryside with human life in the film highlights the experiences of loss and the lack of human compassion. McDonagh's world is not one in which people are consoled and nurtured in a developmental way. Donnelly, for instance, shoots the head off his pet rabbit as a mercy killing before he attempts to take his own life, only to be deprived of the last bullet in the gun when it slips from his hand and misfires.

Ecocritical analysis of interactions between culture and nature are significant to the study of Irish literature as a result not only of Ireland's unique physical landscape but also the increasing impact of global environmental crisis on contemporary Irish life. Gerry Smyth promotes an ecocriticism that explores usages of the local physical environment and its entanglement with ideology in wider contexts, stating that:

> In terms of both natural and built environments, an ecocritical perspective reveals the extent to which Irish literary expression has from its beginnings been thoroughly infused with environmental and spatial concerns. These concerns, moreover, persist into the present, so that it is possible to

analyse modern Irish literature in terms of its engagement
with a range of discourses the roots of which lie in the island's
unique spatial and ecological history. (95)

The ideas of environment, landscape and nature gain complexity when
grounded in a specific locale. The west of Ireland in particular has
been romanticised in art and literature and tied to notions of Irish
identity. The idea of the landscape in paintings, for instance, has been
intermingled with Irish mythology and employed to both engage with
and resist national identity. Likewise, McDonagh's representations of
the western landscape are remarkably connected to while simultaneously disruptive of a sense of Irishness

The landscape of the west of Ireland is central to his Irish plays.
Through depictions of the west, McDonagh's dramas encourage us to
examine notions of romanticisation. In *The Leenane Trilogy* the characters' immorality and degeneracy connect to the locale of Leenane,
which serves almost as an additional character that negatively impacts
upon the human community. The representation of the shared locale
in the three *Leenane* plays is not meant to parody the village. While the
setting does not capture the natural beauty of the Galway region, it
provides a mode to explore human depravity. The setting of the Aran
Islands plays, like that of *The Leenane Trilogy*, does not attempt to
depict the real place authentically. The Aran Islands, like Leenane,
represent distinctive qualities that shape the community.

The landscape of the west serves as a common thread between the
Irish plays. The locale works to expose romantic notions and mythical
ideals of environment. Eamonn Wall states, 'Plays such as *The Lieutenant of Inishmore* set out to perpetuate myths rather than interrogate
them, and, ultimately, they do little more than dress them up in new
clothes' (138). The 'unchanging' mythic images of the west of Ireland
and America collide, however, in *The Cripple of Inishmaan* to disrupt
the romanticised timelessness of place.

In the remainder of this essay, I wish to argue that *The Cripple of
Inishmaan* may be used to explore constructions of environment and
the concealed dramaturgies that expose the sociocultural imagination
and its ecological implications. *The Cripple of Inishmaan* provides an

understanding of how human perception and imagination shape and are shaped by sociocultural and natural environments. The complexities of collaborative ecology identified in McDonagh's narrative reveal the ways in which the play problematises the romanticising of landscape and Irishness.

Set in the 1930s on the Aran island of Inishmaan, the play is spun around the filming of Robert Flaherty's *Man of Aran*, which is being shot on the adjacent island of Inishmore. The island of Inishmaan, which is located between the larger Inishmore and smaller Inisheer, is the most remote of the three islands. It presented the biggest obstacle to visits by boat through the early twentieth century and, therefore, was the least influenced by outsiders. The community thus maintained its use of the Irish language, its traditions and its customs more than was the case on the other islands. It is thus significant that McDonagh chose the site of Inishmaan, which supposedly comprises the greatest concentration of Irish 'authenticity', to illustrate the constructedness of Irish identity, and the way in which an equally contrived idea of the Irish landscape supports this other construction. A fictionalised 'nature' forms the backdrop for a fictionalised 'culture'. Through his contemporary lens, 1930s Inishmaan embodies dark, eccentric personalities that reflect the decay of tradition as well as the ruin of the physical Aran terrain. The deformed Irish body of Cripple Billy suggests an additional diminished sense of Irishness.

McDonagh's depiction of life on Inishmaan contradicts the documentary's representation of community and environment on the Aran Islands. The characters in the play do not identify with the images of Aran life presented in the film, even though Flaherty is a highly regarded and influential director famed for inventing the modern nature documentary in such films as *Man of Aran* and *Nanook of the North* (1922). In one scene, for instance, Flaherty's idealised vision of the Aran Islands as a pristine landscape incites mockery from the Aran residents. The community screens the newly released documentary at the local church hall, where the tension between physical realities and desired imaginings is intensified.

The documentary shows the lead character, Man of Aran, and other fishermen in a *curragh*, intent on harpooning basking sharks. As is mentioned elsewhere in this book, the inhabitants of the Aran Islands had abandoned shark-hunting long before Flaherty's arrival there. Helen, who tried to earn a part in his film, now hurls eggs at the screen. She says, 'Ah they're never going to be catching this fecking shark. A fecking hour they've been at it now, it seems like . . . One good clobber and we could all go home' (79). *The Cripple of Inishmaan* works to show the limits of representation in the documentary, as well as its tendency to falsify and fictionalise nature, ironically, in the act of 'capturing' it.

Pat Mullen, Flaherty's assistant director and a native of Aran, wrote a memoir, which was also entitled *Man of Aran* (1935), about the filming experience. Mullen tells how he sought out the only fisherman alive who could explain how to harpoon a shark. The film's crew worked diligently and at great risk to re-enact the lost tradition on a powerful sea that at any time might have erupted into a storm. Mullen calls harpooning an 'art'. He writes, '[T]he art of killing [the basking sharks] is lost' (105). During the filming, the 'social actors', who are actual island residents, frequently risk the dangers of drowning to ensure that the community is shown in its 'true light' (82). Mullen seems to confuse reality with fiction when he writes (quoting himself), ' "[L]ives lost or not, the *Man of Aran* ought to be made the real thing or nothing" ' (149).

The men value human-centredness at the expense of marine life, unnecessarily killing the generally non-carnivorous basking sharks. In the nineteenth century, the basking shark was hunted for its liver, which produced oil for lamplight. During the process of filming in the 1930s, however, an indefinite number of sharks were harpooned and killed, not for their livers, or for the industrial and economic usefulness of the oil they produced, but for the sake of a picturesque film sequence that offers cultivated non-Irish viewers a chance to enjoy the 'primitive' – figured as less cultured, more natural – life of Aran. Mullen's memoir specifically recounts twelve episodes of harpooning sharks and records the occurrence of four certain killings but states, 'We killed many more and had some exciting times . . . Luckily, before they disappeared [for the season] Mr Flaherty had taken enough pictures to finish the basking shark sequence for the film' (239). In the chapter entitled 'Exciting Days', Mullen describes 'the most thrilling sight', which is watching a harpoon being driven full force into a shark and its responsive thrash in the water (223). When Flaherty failed to capture the harpooning on film, the harpooners sunk the slain basking shark 'by tying heavy stones to [them]' (117).

Even though Mullen does not recognise his own human-centredness, interestingly he shows awareness of how outlanders have plundered the Aran environment. He describes how in the 1930s fishing boats from other areas ruined local spawning zones, thereby eliminating many breeds of fish: 'Nowadays we catch only mackerel or herring; there are practically no other fish because foreign trawlers have swept them away and also ruined the spawning grounds' (33).

In another scene, Man of Aran perseveres in the slow, laborious process of creating artificial soil out of crushed rock, seaweed and sand, in addition to small amounts of soil meticulously excavated from crevices in the land. Yet this practice of nurturing farmland was already fading from tradition in the 1930s. Flaherty captures the process on film in order to convey the ideology of mastery over the environment. The narrative portrays Man of Aran as a hero, overcoming a landscape that does not provide the basic ingredients for survival. Culture is clearly separate from nature in this portrayal, conquering, completing and supplementing it.

While the documentary depicts man's vanquishing of the environment, McDonagh's play exhibits a marked disconnection between human and other-than-human life, a conflict with no winner. *The Cripple of Inishmaan* presents the physically challenged Billy as the anti-hero of an impotent landscape. Absent, additionally, is the industrious and healthful Irish father-figure of *Man of Aran* who makes fertile the unsullied rock foundation. Conversely, watching cows to relieve boredom is Billy's closest communion with nature. Violence is commonly enacted on animals and humans alike in McDonagh's depiction of Aran life. The family unit and work ethic, furthermore, have disintegrated in *The Cripple of Inishmaan*. The characters do not relate to the assiduousness of the film's maternal figure, who tirelessly hauls heavy loads of water-soaked seaweed up the cliffs in order to cultivate a small patch of crops. Nor do the images invoke a desire to imitate.

In *The Cripple of Inishmaan* mothers are absent or close to being non-existent. Kate, one of Billy's surrogate aunts, fills the role of the absent mother, but she exhibits a decaying of the psyche through her compulsion to talk to rocks when she is overcome by anxiety. In a twisted sort of role-reversal, Johnny feeds his mother, Mammy, bottles of alcohol. The characters' gazes upon their supposed selves at the screening of *Man of Aran*, contrarily, become gapes upon the constructed 'other'. The characters of *The Cripple of Inishmaan* resist being absorbed into Flaherty's ideological landscape. Instead of identifying with the documentary, Helen expresses her lack of fulfilment at the film's end. She says, 'Oh thank Christ the fecker's over. A pile of fecking shite' (85). The responses fracture and displace the film's narrative.

The juxtaposition of the two contrasting representations of the islands problematises the notion of a definable Irishness in relation to the unique Aran landscape. While McDonagh's dramatic representation is clearly fictive, the documentary claims authenticity in its representation of actual island residents. It ultimately offers a romantic vision of the Aran Islands as a pristine landscape, and the grand narrative depicts man as the master of the environment. McDonagh refuses to claim such 'authenticity' for his own depiction, and even invites us, by including the scene of villagers reacting critically to their own representation in Flaherty's film, to enact a further scene in our imaginations, in which contemporary Aran dwellers react to *The Cripple of Inishmaan* itself. Indeed, Druid Theatre ended the tour of its production of *The Cripple of Inishmaan* with performances on Inishmaan in July 2011. The President of Ireland Mary McAleese and McDonagh himself attended one of the performances on the island. Aran residents reportedly reacted favourably to the production. The excitement surrounding the event and the spectators' perceptions amplified the ever-present connection between people and place.

Flaherty's ahistorical representation and idealising of the west of Ireland influences perceptions of the nature–culture interaction, in a way that has ecological implications for the relationship between the human and non-human environment. His attempt to convey the authenticity of Ireland's culture may confuse more than capture reality. Garrard states, '[R]esponsible humans have an implicit duty to let things disclose themselves in their own inimitable way, rather than forcing them into meanings and identities that suit their own instrumental values' (2005: 31). Flaherty's claim of authenticity, which is clearly contested in *The Cripple of Inishmaan*, raises the question of whose desire is being fulfilled in the documentary. While Man of Aran ensures his own survival and through the documentary image secures a sort of immortality, Billy, who embodies an entirely antithetical site of knowledge and production, faces a sure death. McDonagh's play in the contemporary moment exposes an impoverished cultural space. It also raises questions about the adequacy of Flaherty's culture conquering nature parable for those who would preserve the possibilities for life – all life, including human – on Aran.

The symbiotic relationship between ecocriticism and McDonagh's works provides insight into how literature and culture reflect and even shape our perceptions and understanding of the environment. Ecocriticism, however, has a broad, interdisciplinary scope and may be influential in studies of works of all genres and periods, even those in which nature is explicitly absent. As Wallace and Armbruster point out, 'If ecocriticism limits itself to the study of one genre . . . or one physical landscape . . . it risks seriously misrepresenting the significance of multiple natural and built environments to writers with other ethnic, national and racial affiliations' (2001: 7). Ecocritical interpretation can bring interesting critical insights and analyses that may improve awareness and understanding of community building, the interconnectivity of nature and humanity, and responsible engagement with all forms of life.

McDonagh and postcolonial theory: practices, perpetuations, divisions and legacies

Eamonn Jordan

Much has been written about Martin McDonagh's plays since the premiere of *The Beauty Queen of Leenane* in 1996. Some theatre scholars have utilised postcolonial theory to consider the dramaturgical values and codifications, as well as the imperatives, strategies, resistances and legacies of colonisation, in relation to Irish theatre. More particularly, these theories have been heavily applied to issues of representation in McDonagh's work.

Plays are written to be performed, and many of the productions of McDonagh's works are produced without consideration of any sort of theory, postcolonial or otherwise. Nevertheless, the first five of his plays to be performed are populated by Irish characters and rely on Irish locations, namely Leenane and the Aran Islands. *Six Shooter* is set in Ireland and *In Bruges* has two London-based, Dublin criminals lying low in Belgium. These aspects ensure that ideas of Ireland and Irishness arise implicitly or explicitly when production decisions have to be made about approaches to characterisation and accents, casting, stage and lighting design. Thus, the various *mises en scène* are informed in one way or another by notions of Ireland and sensibilities of Irishness. Similarly, for plays with Irish locations generally, each audience member will bring his or her own expectations, experiences, understandings, perceptions and attitudes to the theatrical event – all of which will shape how performances are received.

It is thus vital to remember that there is often a huge gap between what a playwright may intend with his or her writing and what he or she unconsciously creates; there is also a massive variation between the author's intentions and a production's realisation of the script. So a theatre text must be evaluated not only in terms of its substance as a written script but also in relation to the performances it inspires.

Globally, the most significant perception of Ireland, apart from its natural beauty, is that it has been shaped fundamentally by its colonial history. The ideas of rural or pastoral Ireland depicted in many novels, films and advertisements perpetuate a romantic evocation of rural living – but they also bring to mind the challenges of being close to nature, often under conditions of subsistence living. Furthermore, such images regularly evoke a period of time that is often long past or that is passing away quickly in a globalised world. Related to that vision of environment is the notion of the Irish themselves: the fighting, drunken, religiously superstitious, slovenly, feckless but pleasantly humoured and good-natured Irish – a stereotype that continues to be propagated across different forms of popular culture.

Apart from delving into the origins of such images, there is an imperative to look at how the Irish themselves both exploit and perpetuate those stereotypical associations. Commonly, characters in 'Irish' works often display stereotypical traits, and thus invite the typical responses associated with those stereotypes. Concomitantly, from the early 1990s, globally and within American popular culture specifically, Diane Negra notes now Irishness is represented as not only 'reliably' and 'invariably, a form of whiteness', but more than that a form of 'enriched whiteness' (2006: 1), thereby losing some of its colonial negativity.

While those stereotypes generally remain pejorative in their orientation, even when they might be regarded as softly sentimental, the point has to be made that many of these associations and dispositions have precedents in history, especially during the period when Ireland was a colony of Britain. Both Ireland and Irish identities are, in part, the constructions and consequences of the experiences of conquest and colonisation.

Generally when people discuss colonisation, they are likely to be emphasising European colonisation in Asia, Africa, Australia and the Americas from the sixteenth century forward. There are different types of colonial projects, ranging from civic, bureaucratic, military and political control of a territory, to substantial settler situations where individuals from the mother country are settled on native lands, often by killing, removing or quarantining the locals and taking over lands and accommodations. Ania Loomba puts it simply by placing at the core of her definition of colonialism the 'conquest and control of other people's land and goods' (1997:2).

The impact of colonisation depends on many variables. These include the length of the contact time and the nature of the contact; the impact of colonisation on labour and religious practices, local rituals, and communal structures; and the extent of political and military power that is used to enforce the colonial project. Similarly, the levels and the types of resistances to the colonial encounter also vary and differ widely.

Ireland's close physical proximity to Britain makes it very different from most other nations discussed under the rubric of postcolonial theory – for many reasons. The plantations of Irish lands by British settlers impacted far more substantially on Ireland than almost anywhere else in the world, given that the indigenous population at the time of the initial contact was substantial. A second difference is that religious persecution became part of the colonial strategy, which was not just an Irish–British, indigenous–settler or Catholic–Protestant conflict, but was also more indicative of a pan-European battle for power and dominance. Significant trading patterns and human mobility existed between both countries; and relationships and marriages between locals and settlers also had an impact. Furthermore, the ethnicity of the Irish made them less easily distinguishable from the British, so that accent and dress were the codes by which distinctions were calibrated. Finally, the division of Ireland into the Free State of Ireland and Northern Ireland in 1922 is one of the major legacies of colonisation. For some, the partition was achieved to contrive artificially a Unionist majority in the North, while for others it was both a political and just solution for those Loyalist communities caught in an anomalous situation. The division of the island not only caused the sectarian conflict that persisted for many years in Northern Ireland; it also led to policy decisions that resulted in gross socio-economic injustices; and it was the context for subsequent military and paramilitary actions, ranging from intimidation to wilful injury to murder. The Troubles left over three thousand dead, and many more wounded and psychologically scarred. And it is this legacy to which I will return in relation to McDonagh's play *The Lieutenant of Inishmore*.

Historically, under British colonial rule, aspects of the law, education, governance and industrial development were substantially determined outside Ireland, and were structured to serve the interests of the British state and not the Irish population generally. The near exclusion of the Irish from the ownership of lands, the attacks on the Catholic religion and the outlawing of the freedom to practise that faith, and later the subversive if more subtle attack on the native Gaelic language all suggest that colonisation was not simply the sum of military, economic and political actions. The lack of significant industrial development in Ireland was never offset by the fact that at times Ireland was, as Declan Kiberd has noted, used as a laboratory to test new British developments in educational policy and pedagogy, postal services or railroad systems.

Colonial discourse studies, as one part of postcolonial analysis, have shown, according to Loomba, 'how stereotypes, images, and "knowledge" of colonial subjects and cultures tie in with institutions of economic, administrative, judicial and bio-medial control' (54). Such practices, Loomba continues, are evident in 'a wide range of cultural texts and practices such as art works, atlases, cinema, scientific systems, museums, educational institutions, advertisements, psychiatric and other medical practices, geology, patterns of clothing, ideas on beauty' (47–8). In addition, she suggests, 'newspaper stories, government records and reports, memoirs, journals, historical tracts or political writings are also open to an analysis of their rhetorical strategies, their narrative devices', for their biased reflections on colonial practices, and indigenous populations (81). These texts predominantly affirm the justness of the imperial action, and in many instances they reveal views on the inferiority of local populations. They also helped to disseminate fear, suspicion, anxiety and negative stereotypes – using notionally the objectivity of science and superior insights on custom, food and cultural practices, to justify prejudicial articulations about the colonial subjects themselves. But as with all assertions and observations, such writings tend to be infused by subtext, transference, anxieties and prejudices.

In addition, native populations found it increasingly difficult to maintain their own values; indigenous communities began to eschew their own sense of self, until they, in effect, internalised many of the negative qualities that had been projected onto them. Consequently,

colonial violence is understood as a threat and as a form of impris-
onment, but it also includes an 'epistemic' aspect: that is, an attack on
the culture, ideas and value systems of the colonized people' (Spivak,
1990: 226.)

Loomba highlights the transnational consistency of such practices:

> Thus laziness, aggression, violence, greed, sexual promiscuity,
> bestiality, primitivism, innocence and irrationality are attrib-
> uted (often contradictorily and inconsistently) by the English,
> French, Dutch, Spanish and Portuguese colonists to Turks,
> African, Native Americans, Jews, Indians, the Irish and
> others. It is worth noting that some of these descriptions were
> used for working-class populations or women within Europe.
> (107)

Loomba's analysis is correct in linking the oppressive stereotyping of
the colonised on the one hand, with that of women and the working
classes on the other.

Declan Kiberd, whose work is prompted by Franz Fanon's ideas
and Edward Said's groundbreaking book *Orientalism*, suggests that
Ireland had been effectively 'patented as not-England' (2005: 9). To
make this point resonate, he utilises the writings of the poet Edmund
Spenser in the late sixteenth century, who regarded the Irish as 'wild',
'hot-headed, rude and nomadic, the perfect foil to set off their own
[English] virtues' (9–10). Kiberd goes on to suggest that Ireland
effectively functioned as England's 'unconscious' (17), where all that
is disavowed, repressed, disliked or abject is accommodated. While
here I am emphasising the stereotyping of the Irish on the material and
discursive levels, it must be remembered that, as Loomba has pointed
out, it was more substantially a global colonial strategy in its intensity
and purpose, with some local variations. However, that strategy was
seldom if ever used for the good, and it was always enacted to affirm
the superiority of the 'mother' country and thus to uphold the sub-
jugation of the indigenous populace.

So if the focus of power and coercive practices is to maintain
control and domination, how can resistance be recognised, fostered,

articulated and managed? And how might it be surreptitiously fostered by colonial powers to give a voice of opposition and dissent to indigenous populations? If there is a force bent on rejecting colonisation, how might revolution occur?

Many critics identify the difficulty that local populations have in finding a position of subjectivity. This subjectivity holds often internalised and contaminated versions of colonial ideological practices; as such, negative internalisations often lead to a self-destructive, self-defeating, passive-aggressive engagement with the socio-political environment rather than a more positive assertive disposition. There is a good deal of debate around the notion that colonial rule can only be confronted by distorted mirror-image activities of itself. Anti-colonisation resistance to such imperial domination and control can be political, military and textual. Ireland's long and problematic cycle of hope, rebellion, failure, capitulation and the eventual re-energising of resistance is a part of that process.

As Loomba argues, the prefix 'post' in postcolonialism implies an aftermath, in terms of time, as in coming after, but also as 'ideological, as in supplanting' (7). As she continues, 'If the inequities of colonial rule have not been erased, it is perhaps premature to proclaim the demise.' Generally, independence should be followed by a period of decolonisation or decontamination, which really involves adjusting to a new order and attempting to inscribe new values constitutionally. But the reality of southern Ireland was not unique, in that after independence in 1922 there was little substantial change: power was exchanged from one elite to another. What took the place of colonialism was therefore a neo-colonialism, as Victor Merriman suggests (1999).

Far from representing a break from the past, neo-colonial societies merely duplicate the power dynamics of previous administrations, perpetuating gender, class, racial and ethnic inequalities. Effectively, the policies of successive Irish governments ensured that economic, social and educational disadvantages were maintained. Crucial to this maintenance of power was the economic retrenchment under the de Valera government, which pursued an isolationist economic policy from the 1930s until the late 1950s.

After the Second World War, the sheer poverty of the country and the absence of work opportunities meant that many of its citizens were forced to emigrate. McDonagh's parents joined a significant portion of the population in heading off the island and to London. According to Fintan O'Toole, 'McDonagh's father, a construction worker, and his mother, a cleaner and part-time housekeeper, met and married in the nineteen sixties, in London, where they had moved from Ireland in search of better wages' (2006). And if poor economic conditions and entrenchment constitute the negative side of the equation, the more positive side is of course that Irish citizens could move freely to Britain, in a way that created options for themselves.

For many of that generation of the Irish abroad, the issues of how they transacted, worked, schooled, communicated and socialised were shaped by a longing to return home. There was a yearning then to regain the space from which they had been banished, due to social, religious, family, economic or sexual reasons. While a small minority deliberately chose to leave Ireland, most felt they had no option but to leave. Some left to make their fortunes, some to disappear. The work that many acquired was often menial, and it is well documented that the Irish faced a vast range of prejudices in Britain from the 1950s right up to the late 1990s.

For most migrants, returning home was as much an obsession as it was an ambition. McDonagh himself holidayed regularly in Ireland, and eventually found success, and an authorial voice when, in order to evade the influences of David Mamet and Harold Pinter, he set his plays in the west of Ireland, using the Hiberno-English of his family's relations for his characters' speech. Hence, one response to the plays and the films with Irish content is to build an argument around the fact that McDonagh is a second-generation Anglo-Irish diasporic writer who in part accidentally happened on to Irish scenarios for his work. Further, hailing from a diasporic community that has the cultural, emotional and psychological relationship with the country of his parents' births, he has access to a complex tradition, and also a great deal of socio-cultural awareness. But this awareness is complicated by the fact that he has an equally complex relationship with the city, country and society into which he was born.

The characters in his *Leenane Trilogy* and in the two Aran Islands plays are marginalised and dispossessed in a variety of ways. They share some of the characteristics of stereotypical Irishness, and this has prompted many critics to accuse the work of perpetuating racist stereotypes. This is an accusation that also greeted *A Behanding in Spokane* (2010) as a result of McDonagh's characterisation of Toby, the African-American character in the play. As mentioned elsewhere in this book, Hilton Als harshly criticised McDonagh's treatment of race, which was seen not as attacking stereotypes but as perpetuating them. In his review, Als does not adequately address the fact that the characters' negative remarks about race were always undermined by later comments; furthermore, the performance of Walken in effect placed his racist comments in quotation marks, holding them up high in order to illustrate and undermine the racism of the character. In some ways it could be argued that a depleted form of 'blackness' (which I will later clarify in terms of a depleted 'Irishness') is used in this instance not to align blackness with something inferior, but to challenge the propensity of politically correct culture to mobilise a type of optimism and suppression that is painfully uptight.

This situation is not unlike the one that faces the characters across *The Leenane Trilogy*. With their self-obsession and lack of empathy for others, they seem to have internalised a very negative, ambivalent and contradictory sense of self, which (as we have seen) is consistent with colonial projections. Their sense of dispossession is seldom if ever met with resistance, positive talk or self-reflection. They are often not only numb to each other but have little relationship with their broader society. Their views are built around a combination of ignorance, spite, bitterness, intimidation and petty hurts, inspiring fantasies of revenge. They have almost no sense of agency or purpose and no capacity to be intimate; they seem incapable of negotiation, and are seemingly best motivated to destroy. So Maureen kills her mother in *Beauty Queen*; in *Lonesome West* Coleman slays his father over a small insult about his hairstyle; and in *Skull* Mick Dowd's drink driving has led to his wife's death, though if the rumours are to be believed she may have been fatally wounded before the accident.

The apparent equation of marginalised Irish characters with decrepitude and with varied forms of violence (from physical and mental violence to emotional blackmail and verbal abuse) is used by critics like Victor Merriman to build an arguments against McDonagh. In an article about Marina Carr's Midland plays and McDonagh's *Leenane Trilogy*, Merriman sees these works as 'a kind of voyeuristic aperture on the antics of white trash whose reference point is more closely aligned to the barbarous conjurings of Jerry Springer than to the continuities of an indigenous tradition of dramatic writing' (1999: 312). Merriman thus sees the work as offering no more than a recycling of the worst colonial stereotypes. He adds in another article that McDonagh, again alongside Marina Carr, perpetuates 'gross caricatures with no purchase on the experience of today's audiences[;] their appeal to the new consumer-Irish consensus lies in their appearance as ludicrous Manichaen opposites – the colonial simian reborn' (2004: 253).

Perhaps the most useful way of considering these complex issues is to extend such arguments to McDonagh's notorious play *The Lieutenant of Inishmore*. This work includes a great deal of violence, which seems to confirm the colonial view of the Irish as destructive, uncivilised and barbaric. Yet the play also purports to deal with paramilitary Republican violence, a decision which McDonagh claims was prompted in part by his rejection of Republicanism and his disgust with the murders carried out by the IRA, most notably their bombing of Warrington in 1993, which led to the death of two children.

Since the partition of Ireland in 1922, the significant Catholic minority in Northern Ireland faced well-documented social and political injustices, in terms of voting constraints (gerrymandering), educational and employment disadvantages, and poor access to housing and other social services. One of the major incidents of the Troubles occurred on Bloody Sunday – 28 January 1972 – when a civil rights march was met by military violence, leaving thirteen dead (a fourteenth died later). That event was a major turning point for many members of the Nationalist community, who now felt that civil protest was no longer the only way of protesting against injustice and the occupation of Northern Ireland by the British. In the aftermath of Bloody Sunday, many joined or supported the IRA. Internment without trial and increasing Loyalist paramilitary activities only added to the problems. Many in the Catholic minority thus saw the illegal Republican paramilitaries as defenders of their community, at least initially. Hence, Republicans from the 'physical force' tradition claim that theirs was a violence of last resort.

However, when Republicans brought their bombing campaigns to England, not only to army barracks but to public places, many atrocities occurred and many innocent people were murdered. One such bombing was the already mentioned attack on Warrington on 20 March 1993, which led to the deaths of Jonathan Ball (aged three) and Tim Parry (aged twelve). While the IRA admitted planting the bomb, the group claimed that the fundamental responsibility for the deaths 'lies squarely at the door of those in the British authorities who deliberately failed to act on precise and adequate warnings', as Richard English reports (2005: 280).

McDonagh has expressed a serious objection to such violent acts, saying 'hang on, this is being done in my name [and] I just feel like exploding in rage' (quoted in Spencer, 2002: 2). McDonagh tells of writing the play 'from a position of what you might call pacifist rage. I mean, it's a violent play that is wholeheartedly anti-violence' (quoted in O'Hagan, 2001: 32). However, although set on the Aran island of Inishmore, and although including characters with paramilitary allegiances, the play is not an authentic portrayal of the Northern Ireland Troubles, since it does not attempt to address historical colonial or postcolonial conditions, or to consider Loyalist or state terrorism. Therefore, it is in no way a balanced or objective representation of the political situation. What it offers instead is a certain sort of anarchy, coupled with direct and indirect criticisms of paramilitarism. As a result of its limited perspective, this hugely successful play evoked numerous controversial responses, many of them objecting to the play on grounds similar to those laid out by Merriman: that is, that it seriously misrepresented Ireland and the Irish.

The play tells of the revenge actions of three paramilitary members of the Irish National Liberation Army (INLA), a group with the same political aspirations as the IRA, but driven by a more fanatical Marxist ethos. Christy, Joey and Brendan lure their ex-colleague, Mad Padraic, into a trap by intending to kill his cat, Wee Thomas, for whom he has colossal and misplaced affection. Padraic is rescued from this death squad by the teenage girl Mairead, who wounds the three men with air rifle pellets. What follows is a gruesome shoot-out which leaves the three would-be assassins dead, and later these bodies are gruesomely, if grotesquely and comically dismembered on stage, by Padraic's father Donny and Mairead's brother Davey. Padraic falls in love with his rescuer, only to die at Mairead's hands when she discovers that he has killed her precious cat, named after the national hero Sir Roger (Casement). It needs to be emphasised that there is no attempt at realism in these scenes, which are farcical in construction and outcome.

Yet Mary Luckhurst objects to the play on a variety of grounds, arguing firstly that '[b]roadly, the play depicts an orgy of random violence, and individuals fuelled by a mixture of puritanism, sentimentality and mindless fanaticism, whose political aims have long been subsumed by a desire to terrorise for its own sake' (36). Luckhurst is picking up on the duplication and recycling of the 'colonial simian' in the play. By using that image, the argument suggests, McDonagh ensures that 'political substance' is all 'but air-brushed away' (37). Luckhurst further argues that the play as it was premiered in England by the Royal Shakespeare Company does nothing other than reinforce the hegemonic status of England over Ireland, or in Merriman's terms rich over poor; the 'little Englander' is Luckhurst's target, 'Little Irelander' is Merriman's.

Tom Maguire's response to the play is built in part around Patrick Magee's 'survey of the representation of Republicans in prose fiction', in order to confirm that '[t]he representation of the composite Republican was to reach its nadir' in *The Lieutenant of Inishmore* (2006: 33–4). Magee's position is that 'the composite Irish Republican to materialise was a Mother-Ireland fixated psycho-killer, aka a Provo-Godfather, readily discernible with recourse to an identikit indebted to Tenniel's 'Irish Frankenstein' and other images from *Punch* redolent of Victorian racism' (2001: 2). For Maguire and Magee, such misrepresentations need to be confronted.

Maguire utilises Seamus Deane's contentions from 1985 that 'the language of politics in Ireland and England is still dominated by the putative division between barbarism and civilisation' (39). Deane has suggested that for centuries there were powerful attempts to force the Irish into adopting British norms, in business, politics, religion, law and so on. Those who remained outside the law were deemed barbaric, uncivilised and undisciplined – and effectively criminalised, suffering 'the condition of *homo criminalis*' (39), a position from which 'the quaint Paddy or the simian terrorist . . . arise quite naturally from the conviction that there are criminal types, politically as well as socially identifiable to the state and to all decent citizens' (39). Such a division is still perpetuated in the cultural representation of terrorism in Northern Ireland, whereby the military wing of Republican movements are framed as terrorists and so are seen as uncivilised, barbaric criminals. That characterisation in turn legitimises the actions of the state, which can, according to Deane, 'kill with impunity, because they represent, they embody the Law' and civilisation (40).

Although Deane offers a sophisticated argument about binaries and the historical manipulation by colonial powers of those who protest or strike by using physical force, the play's emphasis on the connections between paramilitarism and drug dealing, or the gaining of profit from such deals, makes the case for Republican purity more difficult to promote. Spokespersons for the Republican movement have always denied being connected with organised crime, and claim their heavy involvement in anti-drug campaigns as proof of their integrity. For many this is simply untrue.

But it is the connection between paramilitarism and punishment beatings raised by the play that is the most formidable criticism of a paramilitary form of policing in Nationalist/Republican areas. While these areas may have been more secure for their inhabitants, who in any case had a complete lack of faith in the Royal Ulster Constabulary, there is no getting away from the ruthlessness of the summary punishments, the gruesomeness of the injuries they caused or the denials of any right to a fair trial for those who had had accusations made against them. Often youths involved in joyriding or other anti-social behaviour were 'punished' by physical beatings with bats and sticks, or by so-called 'punishment shootings' which involved kneecapping and the destruction of joints. According to Kevin Rafter, 'There were over 1,200 so-called punishment attacks in the post-1995 period which were attributed to the IRA. These brutal attacks – which underlined the IRA's self-adopted role as judge, jury and near executioner – frequently left people crippled or limbless' (27). Scene Two of *The Lieutenant* has Padraic torturing James for selling drugs to Republican youths; thus issues of drug dealing and punishment beatings are brought together in the play.

Equally, through his deconstruction of a soft, sentimental, unrefined, unfocused and contradictory ideology that is not shared by any of the paramilitaries, McDonagh challenges some of the touchstones of Republican rhetoric. He does so by undermining the justifications that his characters have for their actions, and thus completely tarnishes the traditional notion of blood sacrifice, which is often deemed sacrosanct to Republicanism. For instance, the contradictions, confusions and sheer ignorance of Christy, Brendan and Joey contradict the suggestion that such people are motivated by a depth of political understanding. For McDonagh, the actions of these men cannot be justified, and so the statement 'the ends justify the means' in the hands of the INLA gang becomes comedic but also explosively undermining.

McDonagh's play fails the test of re-evaluating the motivations of paramilitaries, particularly in its refusal to question whether there is a historical and colonial legitimacy to their actions. In denying his Republican 'freedom fighters' any purity of tradition, McDonagh sees his mission to reject, undermine, deface and take his anarchic revenge upon Republican paramilitarism. But clearly he does not set out to represent it authentically: as in all wars, truth is the first casualty. Fundamentally, McDonagh not so much denies context as makes any notional context incoherent; and yet by using real incidents of murder, he insensitively blurs things that should not be blurred. While McDonagh does not challenge the legitimacy of Republican aspirations, what he does challenge is their tactics. It is not so much that he surrenders to the stereotypes but that he refuses to validate violence. The play's remit seems to be to expose the conspiracy of tacit approval or ambivalence that many, including key public commentators in the media, academia and the Irish diaspora, had for paramilitary actions.

And yet the above discussions and accusations need to be balanced by a consideration of the play's form as farce. The dark issues are offset by the play's maniacal, farcical energy, and by the comedic exchanges, whether the opening dialogue between Donny and Davey diagnosing the health of a murdered cat, Davey's pathetic attempt to use polish to make an orange cat look black, the curious love between Mairead and Padraic, or the homophobia of the paramilitaries. While Luckhurst accepts that *Inishmore* is 'composed as black farce', she maintains that farce does not 'inevitably contain characters who are hopelessly dumb, out-and-out psychopaths' (35).

However, in contrast, John Lahr, in his review for the *New Yorker* of the Atlantic Theater Company's production, regards the text as 'a sort of cautionary fairy tale for our toxic times. In its horror and hilarity, it works as an act of both revenge and repair, turning the tables on grief and goonery, and forcing the audience to think about the unthinkable' (2006). For him, 'The louts and lunatics who inhabit the play are just such gruesome and unforgettable figures; as all gargoyles do, they inspire an almost childish terror and elation in the audience.' By framing the characters as 'gargoyle' figures, Lahr displaces any fundamental connection to the real and his analysis also can be seen to impact indirectly on the modes of analysis deployed by both Merriman and Luckhurst. The anarchic approach to Republicanism owes much to Joe Orton's work; and Quentin Tarantino's recent *Inglourious Basterds* (2009) and Chris Morris's *Four Lions* (2010) are later examples of the complexities of blending incongruity, naivety, violence, revenge and farce. In some ways, it is by looking backwards from these two movies that we can begin to understand McDonagh's work better.

This essay began by tracing the practices and impacts of colonisation generally on countries throughout the world, noting strategies and patterns of colonial domination and control, noting particularly some of the variables that shaped Irish and British relationships, and then showing how political freedom for part of the island did not directly lead to a rise in living standards or greater forms of democracy, but instead to persistent poverty for most and emigration for a significant portion of the population. Partition also left the country divided politically, with the Troubles a direct consequence of the colonial practices that shaped life on the island.

Clearly, the work of McDonagh can be approached from a variety of different methodologies and critical frames, but these approaches can never be exclusive. For instance, considerations of gender feed into any postcolonial reading, in part due to the feminisation of indigenous populations, and also to the feminine symbolisation of resistance – but finally as a result of the notion of woman as doubly colonised, by patriarchy first and colonisation second. Similarly, the relationship between a postcolonial framing and a postmodern one are not as clear cut as one might wish, since many of the strategies of postcolonial writing are duplicated or mimicked by postmodern writing. The attributes of a text or performance tested by a postmodern critic can be very similar to those used by critics who take a postcolonial viewpoint.

But a postcolonial approach allows the incorporation of the historic relationship between Ireland and Britain, and thus the materiality and discourses of colonisation. It offers a way of taking a view on the perpetuation of Irish stereotypes today in popular culture and, most significantly, in relation to McDonagh's work, it allows for a consideration of the significant legacy of colonisation on socio-economic developments, including emigration. Diasporic communities, particularly in Britain, have had to deal with displacement, ideas of and longings for home, and with the hostilities and discriminations they suffered abroad. Most of all, in relation to Northern Ireland, in terms of both illegitimate state practices and paramilitary actions, these diasporic communities have had to deal with the continuities of colonialism in their everyday lives, and from the state in which they now lived. For instance, the Irish in London were at times held responsible for the bombing atrocities that befell Britain throughout the Troubles – a period which coincided with McDonagh's formative years.

In a different way, some would argue that the complexities of diasporic identities ensure that there will always be fundamental contradictions in any representations of Ireland. Some will have a need to represent ironically, others wilfully to subvert the birthplace and the values of one's parents' home. Still others seem to think that by both embracing and perpetuating outmoded representations, they may gain a hold over the past. Somehow, in such transactions there is the potential for the sort of betrayal that affirms a colonial consciousness, where all that is irrational and uncouth and dispossessed is made *other*.

It seems to me that McDonagh is not guilty of such betrayals, but instead offers a depleted rather than 'enriched' form of Irish identity, while also contesting deeper stereotyping through subversion. One might say that McDonagh is denying the legitimacy of Republicanism by undermining its rationale – something that imperialist powers have always done to revolutionary groups, including paramilitary ones. But on the other hand it is possible for a writer to accept the legitimacy of a cause without accepting that violence is a necessary form of protest and resistance, even as a last resort. The darkness of McDonagh's vision, the outrageous nature of his dramatic scenarios and the artifice of the work combine to create a consciousness or a sensibility that is dark and depleted, but more importantly *playful*. A sense of playful darkness both obscures stereotypical Irishness, and equally centralises McDonagh's Anglo-Irish diasporic identity and ambivalences.

Fundamentally, it was the discovery of an Irish disposition or idiom which both liberated the young writer from the more urban influences of Pinter and Mamet, and afforded him the chance to consider his Irish background and influences. This was neither a quest for authenticity nor a way of locating his work with universal, if unfashionably pastoral values. It was more that the artificial and performative qualities of Irishness allowed McDonagh to evade the traditionally restrictive binaries and more assertively to accommodate hyphenated identities, Anglo-Irish or otherwise.

To his detractors, McDonagh perpetuates many of the colonial representations of the Irish as immoral, uncivilised, barbaric and murderous. Those who support the work champion the right of someone to reject armed struggle, and defend the freedom to frame that rejection within a dramaturgy shaped by anarchic farce, even when there is considerable irony, in using extreme if playful violence to give expression to a 'pacifist rage'. It is possible to argue that one can accept the legitimacy of claims for a united Ireland without accepting the legitimacy of armed struggle, and that such a dialectical conflict has been central to almost every global challenge to colonisation.

McDonagh's gender troubles

Joan FitzPatrickDean

The construction of gender through performative choices reiterated and refined over time, famously explored in Judith Butler's *Gender Trouble* (1990), allows individuals to assert their own agency. In Martin McDonagh's works the construction of gender is most evident in the late adolescents who figure in all his Irish plays. Mairead, who will stake a claim to be the eponymous *Lieutenant of Inishmore* by that play's conclusion, first appears carrying an air rifle and wearing '*army trousers, white T-shirt, sunglasses*' (17). At sixteen, Mairead is notorious for her marksmanship, honed over years of target practice on the eyes of livestock. Although she claims to have begun blinding cows as a protest against 'the fecking meat trade' (18), she has developed impressive skills with a rifle and carefully staged her self-presentation to attract Padraic.

Her seventeen-year-old brother Davey has made no less surprising choices. He first appears riding his mother's pink bicycle and sporting what Donny calls a 'girl's mop o' hair' (4). Davey is fully aware of the disapproval his long mane provokes. He tells his sister: 'Sure, I have as much concern for the cats of this world as you do, only I don't go around saying it, because if I went around saying it they'd call me an outright gayboy, and they do enough of that with me hairstyle' (18). Like his sister and Padraic, Davey professes to love one thing above all others, but it isn't a cat: 'I love my mam. Love her more than anything. Love her more than anything' (26).

That both Mairead and Davey invert gender expectations is not a momentary oddity but the result of a careful construction of them-selves over many years. When Padraic cuts off his hair, Davey protests that he has been growing his hair long for eight years (48): that is, since he was nine years old. Similarly, Mairead has been developing her skills as a sniper since she was eleven. Mairead and Davey, moreover, are not the only inhabitants of Inishmore known for their performance of an unconventional gender identity. Of Padraic, Davey recalls: 'Didn't he outright cripple the poor fella laughed at that girly scarf he used to wear, and that was when he was twelve?!' (7). Indeed, Padraic performs his role as a terrorist with some surprisingly delicate nuances. He politely asks the victim he has trussed upside-down: 'Will you hang on there a minute, James . . . ?' (13) and later apologetically says, 'I'll be with you in a minute now, James' (14). More central to the plot is Padraic's obsessive sentimentality over his cat, Wee Thomas.

Mairtin, the seventeen-year-old in *A Skull in Connemara* who is still negotiating a gender identity, endures a torrent of abuse about his incipient manhood: to Mick, he is 'a wussy oul pussy' (17); to his brother Thomas, a 'babby' (37), 'thick as five thick fellas' (30). Even his own grandmother sees him as 'a wee get with nothing but cheek' (19). In the cemetery when '*he idles around with the skulls, placing them against his chest as if they're breasts at one point, kissing them together at another*', Mick says he's behaving 'like an oul school girl' (25). Too old for the church choir, Mairtin's forays to the Carraroe disco have brought mockery, rejection and a bottle fight. He is as confused as he is frustrated in his romantic endeavours: ' "Lesbos". Y'know, like Mona McGhee in me school with the beard. (*Pause.*) Five times I've asked that bitch out and she still won't go' (63). His refusal to seek medical attention for a concussion, 'hospitals are for poofs, sure . . . For poofs and for lesbos who can't take a middling dig' (62–3), suggests that homophobia is not conducive to good health.

In *The Beauty Queen*, the twenty-year-old Ray, Mairtin's companion at the Carraroe disco, faces comparable choices and anxieties. Ray would like to buy Father Welsh's used car, but he says, 'I'd look a poof buying a car off a priest' (9). Ray and Mairtin are eager to display their knowledge of gender and sexuality, but they show themselves more anxious than experienced.

The audience learns far less about the Kid in *Six Shooter*. The Kid just has killed his mother, likely in the same manner as Padraic's preferred means of execution in *The Lieutenant*: two revolvers fired at point-blank range to the head ('her son shot the poor head off her,' as the doctor tells Donnelly). The Kid is obnoxious, heartless and aggressive. After telling a bereaved mother that her ugly baby would only disgrace her – an insult which triggers the woman's suicide and which appears to be a crude displacement of the Kid's own feelings about himself – the other side of his childishness can be seen when he says to himself: 'I think you might have gone a bit overboard there fella.' He is desperate to tell his story of the exploding cow, which recalls 'the happiest day of my whole fucking life'. The Kid would like to go out in a blaze of deadly gunfire, but he also carries a toy, a stuffed monkey that resembles the Kid. Standing between childhood and manhood, he dies bemoaning his 'woeful' marksmanship.

While the construction of a distinct gender identity clearly is available to McDonagh's characters, self-realisation through a career, at least in Ireland, is not. Salaried employment is associated almost exclusively with emigration, specifically for Pato and Maureen who find only menial labour, and then only outside Ireland, and for Billy, who travels to Hollywood. While hardly salaried, Padraic leaves Inishmore to pursue his career as a terrorist. The two characters who do have regular employment, even professions, in Ireland – Father Welsh as a priest and Tom Hanlon as a policeman – commit suicide, not least because of failure in their work.

More often than not, it is McDonagh's women characters rather than his men who are associated with gainful work. In *In Bruges* Chloe sells drugs to film crews and robs tourists, while the Amsterdam prostitute moved to Bruges to 'get a better price for [her] pussy' (48). In *The Cripple of Inishmaan*, Kate and Eileen run a shop that is anything but customer-friendly, not least because Eileen wolfs down many of the 'sweeties'. Slippy Helen delivers eggs, although her nickname is owing to her probably breaking more eggs than she delivers. Girleen Kelleher regularly calls at the Coleman household to sell her father's illegal poteen. Their work offers a path out of the domestic sphere and provides both mobility and a measure of independence.

Like Synge, McDonagh creates young women who reject the confinement of the domestic spaces, especially the Irish country cottage. In discussing nineteenth-century painting, Barbara O'Connor describes the Irish colleen and her environment:

> The representational positioning of the colleen as rural, therefore, is not accidental but plays an important role in colonial

and Romantic discourses . . . Images of the colleen battling against the elements serve to construct her as hard working and industrious, which, again, is in stark contrast to representations of men as lazy and feckless. (2009)

McDonagh's subversion and inversion of this widely circulated stereotype are most evident in a remarkable trio of young women, all aged between sixteen and eighteen: Mairead in *The Lieutenant*, Helen in *The Cripple* and Girleen in *The Lonesome West*. Unlike the young men of their age, they are witty, ambitious and clever, a pattern that conforms to popular gender representations reaching back into the nineteenth century. If the under-twelves girl football squad in *The Lonesome West* is representative of the coming generation, Mairead, Helen and Girleen are hardly atypical of women in the west of Ireland. Father Welsh, the team's coach, laments: 'Ten red cards in four games, Coleman. That's a world's record in girls' football. That'd be a record in boys' football. One of the lasses from St Angela's she's still in hospital after meeting us' (9). Father Welsh has not encouraged bloodthirsty tactics on the pitch but is powerless to moderate the girls' aggression, which is greatly admired by the Connor brothers and the community at large.

Whereas the adolescent boys in McDonagh's Irish plays seem gormless and dim-witted, their female counterparts are characteristically ruthless and determined. McDonagh's young women, however, depart from the nineteenth-century stereotype in their penchant for violence, foul language and aggression. Although Girleen is ultimately exposed as kind-hearted, Mairead's violence is responsible for the deaths of half the characters in *Lieutenant*. In her stand-off with Padraic in Scene Three, when he points both his pistols at her head, she is '*poised, disgusted and superior*' (35) as she levels her rifle at his eye. In *The Cripple*, Helen's violence is non-lethal, but more sadistic. Helen not only uses eggs as weapons, but also pokes Billy's bandaged head '*hard*' (82). Both Helen and Mairead torment, humiliate and terrify their brothers.

No less shocking are the vanity and promiscuity that Girleen and Helen claim for themselves. Helen offers lively accounts of how she pegged eggs at Father Brennan for attempting to molest her. She says that she'll pay Babbybobby in kisses for taking her to the filming of *Man of Aran*, although he clarifies that the kisses were at Helen's, not his, insistence. She tells everyone who will listen that she can charm her way to Hollywood: 'Sure, look at as pretty as I am. If I'm pretty enough to get clergymen groping me arse, it won't be too hard to wrap film fellas round me fingers' (14).

Girleen's preferred name uses the Irish diminutive and suggests her youth and innocence, but she regales Father Welsh and the recently bereaved Connor brothers with her sex appeal:

> **Girleen**   That postman fancies me, d'you know? I think he'd like to be getting into me knickers, in fact I'm sure of it.
> **Coleman**   Him and the rest of Galway, Girleen.
> **Welsh** *puts his head in his hands at this talk.*
> **Girleen**   Galway minimum. The EC more like. (9)

Girleen consciously performs her tough, shocking behaviour both as a defence mechanism to cope with the Connor brothers and as a subterfuge for her hopeless schoolgirl crush on the only decent man she knows: Father Welsh. She says whatever she thinks will scandalise him, including announcing her pregnancy. When she speaks alone with Father Welsh or only with the Connor brothers, however, her sexual banter vanishes.

Girleen consciously rejects her given name, Mary, 'the name of the mammy of Our Lord' as Father Welsh reminds her (36). Of an earlier age, Susan Cannon Harris in *Gender in Modern Irish Drama* asserts that 'representations of sex, gender and sacrifice are the way they are because Catholic dogma and iconography have made Christ and the Virgin Mary the only culturally acceptable role models available to Irish men and women' (2002: 4). By the end of the twentieth century, a flood of international imports – Hollywood films, American detective series, Australian soap operas and the long-denounced English press – have bedazzled and then bored McDonagh's Irish characters. The power and, no less importantly, the reputation of the Catholic Church in Ireland declined sharply, a reality that resonates in Father

Welsh's suicide. Girleen rejects her baptismal name because 'It's the reason she never got anywhere for herself. Fecking Mary' (37).

Father Welsh describes Girleen as 'a morbid oul tough' (38), but he is triply wrong. She is a sentimental schoolgirl who believes in life. McDonagh gives Girleen the key and perhaps the only life-affirming speech in *The Lonesome West* when she explains why she's not afraid of cemeteries:

> [E]ven if you're sad or something, or lonely or something, you're still better off than them lost in the ground or in the lake, because . . . at least you've got the *chance* of being happy, and even if it's a real little chance, it's more than them dead ones have. And it's not that you're saying 'Hah, I'm better than ye', no, because in the long run it might end up that you have a worse life than ever they had and you'd've been better off as dead as them, there and then. (38–9)

Both *The Pillowman*, specifically Katurian's story by the same name which considers the merits of sparing a child a life of misery, and Ken's argument against Ray's despair in *In Bruges*, echo Girleen's sentiment.

A comparable inversion of stereotypes is at work in McDonagh's representation of maternal figures: rather than giving us the stereotypical nurturing, self-sacrificing mothers, he confronts us instead with the consummately selfish Mag, the alcoholic Mammy Dougal, and the vindictive and avaricious Maryjohnny Rafferty. Two of those three women express their desire to see their children dead. And in *Cripple*, not only was Billy's mother 'awful ugly . . . she'd scare a pig' (69), but she made every effort to kill her son.

Throughout the twentieth century, the representation onstage of Irish women, especially ones from the west of Ireland, was a flashpoint. Harris argues that 'controversies about representations of "Irish life" . . . consistently focused on gender and sexuality' (12). Disturbances over Synge's *Playboy* and O'Casey's *Plough and the* Stars, for instance, both focused on representations of gender. Arthur Griffith, founder of Sinn Fein and first president of Dáil Éireann, attacked Synge's *In the Shadow of the Glen* (1903) for defaming Irish women, whom he saw as 'the most virtuous . . . in the world' (*United Irishman,* 1903: 2). Later, Griffith denounced *Playboy* on the same grounds. Analogous attacks on O'Casey's play asserted that depiction of Rosie Redmond was a vicious slur on Irish womanhood because there were no prostitutes in Ireland. Adrian Frazier writes that 'it is not at all ridiculous that some should claim Irish women were chaste; it may, however, be questionable whether they should be proud of the claim, Irish Jansenism amounting to something like a mass neurosis' (Frazier, 1990: 81).

Questions of gender are intimately connected to family relationships in McDonagh's Irish plays, in which the nuclear family is a principal source of identity. Characters are routinely located and locate themselves in relation to their parents, siblings and children. Perhaps conspicuously, the only complete nuclear families (with two parents and at least one child) are found outside Ireland, in *The Pillowman* and *In Bruges.* Geography does not, however, alter the fact that Katurian kills both his parents. Only *In Bruges* is without parricide.

Throughout the twentieth century and into the twenty-first, the birth rate in Ireland was the highest in Europe. Between the founding of the Irish Free State in 1922 and 1983 the birth rate per thousand was consistently between 19 and 23.2 births per 1,000. In the mid-1980s, the birth rate dropped back to the mid-teens, and by 2008 and 2009 stood at 16.7. Yet readers of McDonagh's Irish plays might wonder how any Irish children were conceived.

In the Irish plays chastity seems far less one of the heavenly virtues of the Catholic faith than an unfortunate circumstance or an enforced condition. As Shaun Richards's comparison of McDonagh and Synge observes: 'Matching the violence and madness of the plays is the pervasive sense of bodily functions, sexual desire, blasphemy, and general degeneracy' (Richards, 2003: 204). What some audiences might expect from an Irish play (or at least what American cinema has made of gender construction within an Irish family) surfaces in Scene Seven of *Cripple,* Billy's Hollywood screen test:

'Farewell Father and Mother too, and sister Mary I have none but you. And for my brother, he's alone, He's pointing

> pikes on the grinding stone' . . .What's that, Mammy? Me
> prayers? I know. Sure, would I be forgetting, as well as you
> taught them to me? (*Blesses himself.*) (53)

In lines lifted directly from the patriotic ballad 'The Croppy Boy' and
invoking the clichéd image of the nurturing Irish mother, Billy
laments that he is far from the land and his beloved nuclear family.

Gender issues are greatly complicated because there are few heterosexual relationships, even fewer marriages. None of the Irish characters
of childbearing age, male or female, finds a sense of self as a spouse or
parent. Despite this present-day reality, there were marriages for several
of McDonagh's characters. Both Mick in *A Skull* and Babbybobby in
The Cripple fondly remember their wives' culinary deficiencies. Like
them, Ken in *In Bruges* is a widower; his service to Harry originates in
seeking revenge for the murder of his wife some thirty years earlier.
The parent–child relationships are not as happy. Billy's parents tried
to drown him. The Connors brothers' father died over 'a jibe about
Coleman's hairstyle' (29). Padraic has his pistol at his father's head
when he is interrupted by his fellow hard men. Maureen's murder of
her mother, horrific as it is, is understood in light of her desperation.
As in Katurian's murder of his parents, the parents' cruelty to the child
allows an audience to see the murderer with something beyond
abomination.

The plays in *The Leenane Trilogy* bring only a dozen characters on
stage, four in each play. Of that dozen, none is sexually active, but
three were once married, all of whom are widows or widowers by the
time they appear on stage. Mag Folan and Maryjohnny Rafferty, now
in their seventies, have both had children. Mick's relation with his
dead wife seems no less engrossing and complex since her death seven
years ago. Of the remaining characters, most are in their forties, so
marriage or some sexual relationship while remaining a possibility, is
one that appears to be quickly fading.

Although none of McDonagh's protagonists enjoys a healthy or
even adequate sex life, heterosexual romances appear with regularity:
Helen and Billy; Girleen and Father Welsh; Maureen and Pato; Mairead
and Padraic; Chloe and Ray. All are unfulfilled. In *The Cripple*, Helen

kisses Billy just before he and the audience sees that he has tuberculosis and is unlikely to live long. Seeing Girleen's grief over Father Welsh's suicide, Valene offers a sinister prospect for her: 'It's the mental they'll be putting Girleen in before long if she carries on' (54). The most demonstrative scene of sexual desire is Mairead's and Padraic's *pas de deux* of lust and violence in *The Lieutenant*:

> **Padraic** *and* **Mairead** *seem to almost glide across the room,*
> *their eyes locked on each other.* **Padraic** *caresses her hair and*
> *cheek, impressed beyond words at her abilities with a gun . . .*
> *The gunmen shoot towards the right.* **Padraic** *and* **Mairead**
> *step over to where the two handguns lie on the table and*
> **Padraic** *picks them up. They move up behind* **Brendan** *and,*
> *with* **Mairead** *caressing the muscles in his back and shoulders,*
> **Padraic** *puts both guns up to* **Brendan***'s head and fires, killing*
> *him instantly . . .* **Padraic** *and* **Mairead** *move slowly towards*
> **Joey***, their eyes still locked in love.* (52)

As Patrick Lonergan points out elsewhere in this book, the scene shows that terrorist violence is portrayed as not impeding but facilitating sexual expression.

In *In Bruges* and *The Beauty Queen* romance does lead to a physical encounter, but in both instances the text makes clear that there was no completion. In the former, Eirik's arrival interrupts Ray and Chloe and if the viewer might wonder about their sexual relationship, Ray explains to Ken exactly what did not transpire. Pato's letter apologises to Maureen for his inability to perform sexually (a consequence he says of excessive drink), but proposes that she travel with him to America.

The Beauty Queen offers the fullest exploration of the debilitating constraints on an unmarried woman rural Ireland. So rigid are those strictures that Mag can respond to her forty-year-old daughter's admission that she has only kissed two men by calling her a whore (15), and five scenes later comment: 'You still do have the look of a virgin about you you always have had. (*Without malice.*) You always will' (47). Like Girleen and Helen, Maureen flaunts her imaginary sexual activities, waving a shortbread finger 'phallically' (45) and proclaiming herself 'the king of the experts' in all matters sexual. The inability of Maureen and Pato to succeed in the physical act leaves their relationship in doubt, facilitates the continuing miscommunication between them, and precipitates the double tragedy of Mag's death and Maureen's madness.

Wildly exaggerated or purely imaginary claims conceal the lack of sexual opportunity, let alone experience, and not just for McDonagh's colleens. Coleman, for instance, taunts Valene about Girleen's sexual favours:

> **Coleman** I said let me have a bottle on tick and I'll be giving you a big kiss, now. She said 'If you let me be touching you below, sure you can have a bottle for nothing.' . . .
> **Valene** Girleen wouldn't touch you below if you bought her a pony, let alone giving poteen away on top of it. (17)

Improbably, Coleman did have some romantic opportunities. Valene confesses that Maureen Folan once, long ago, wanted to date Coleman:

> Maureen Folan did once ask me to ask you if you wanted to see a film at the Claddagh Palace with her, and she'd've driven ye and paid for dinner too, and from the tone of her voice it sounded like you'd've been on a promise after, but I never passed the message onto ya, out of nothing but pure spite. (57)

Coleman, moreover, tells Father Welsh that he was once in love: 'At tech this was. Alison O'Hoolihan. This gorgeous red hair on her' (3). Alison had a pencil lodged in her tonsil and ended up marrying the doctor who treated her. Valene in the last of his apologies to Coleman admits: 'That was me nudged that pencil, and it wasn't an accident at all. Pure jealous I was' (59). Coleman's opportunities for a sexually fulfilled life are now in the distant past.

Of the brothers, Valene is feminised by his compulsive 'checking' (to make sure Coleman hasn't stolen his poteen or Taytos), purchasing women's magazines and obsessively collecting, first of plastic then of ceramic religious figurines. Valene celebrates his skills in displaying the statues: 'I'm a great one for shelf arranging I am' (43). Coleman and Valene are bound to each other in an infantile cycle of what Father Welsh describes as 'the daily grudges and faults and moans and baby-crimes against each other' (42). Valene has spent decades stoking their love–hate relations to assure that Coleman does not stray. Valene's motive is nearly identical to Mag's: both cling to the last remaining relative for fear of being alone: 'Well, I could've let you go to jail but I didn't want you going to jail and it wasn't out of miserliness that I stopped you going to jail. It was more out of I didn't want all on me own to be left here. I'd've missed ya' (56). Like Mag, the Connor brothers are only seen in a domestic sphere, often return- ing from funerals.

So impoverished is the experience of sexuality in McDonagh's Irish plays that Johnny in *The Cripple*, who specialises in gossip reporting the scandalous and grotesque, fails to recognise what might be his most sensational piece of news: 'A child seen them [the rivals Jack Ellery and Pat Brennan, both men], just this morning there, kissing the faces off each other in a haybarn. I can't make it out for the life of me. Two fellas kissing, and two fellas who don't even like each other' (72).

In reviewing *The Leenane Trilogy* Fintan O'Toole wroye that 'the Ireland of these plays is one in which all authority has collapsed' (O'Toole, 1997: 179). Yet isolated as they are within closed groups, McDonagh's characters share a sense of the normative that is particu- larly relevant to the treatment of gender. In his study *Masculinities and the Contemporary Irish Theatre*, Brian Singleton writes that 'the patriarchal authority of the cultural construction of Irishness render[s] dominant a singular hegemonic masculinity' (2011: 13), one that imbricates heterosexuality, patriotism and bravery. McDonagh evokes and subverts that Irish singular hegemonic masculinity in *The Cripple*, as for instance when Johnny threatens to blackmail Babbybobby for 'kissing green-teeth-girls in Antrim' (27), and refuses to keep quiet about it: 'You'll never get me to make such a promise. I can withstand any torture. Like Kevin Barry I am' (28). Evoking the memory of the martyred republican who refused to inform under torture, in his next line Johnny vows never to repeat this gossip. As in the interpolation by

McDonagh of patriotic ballads, 'The Croppy Boy' and 'The Patriot Game' in *The Lieutenant,* here the pieties of Irish republicans are as meaningless as those of the Catholic faith.

McDonagh's characters freely offer ludicrous observations of variance from prescribed gender norms. When asked what America was like, Billy in *The Cripple* says 'It's just the same as Ireland really. Full of fat women with beards' (64). Garda Tim Hanlon confesses, 'I like a good fight between women, although I couldn't say that while on duty, like' (28). And as shown above, in *The Lieutenant* such gender transgressions abound. However much gender-bending is suggested by Davey, Mairead and Padraic in *The Lieutenant of Inishmore,* there are very plain, old-fashioned gender norms in circulation. Just before Padraic first kisses Mairead, he offers her this advice:

> It's for your own good I'm saying this, Mairead. Be staying home, now, and marry some nice fella. Let your hair grow out a tadeen and some fella's bound to be looking twice at you some day, and if you learn how to cook and sew too, sure, that's double your chances. Maybe treble. (36)

By the time Mairead kills Padraic, she is wearing a pretty dress.

One of the most dependable features of McDonagh's Hiberno-English in the Irish plays is the puerile euphemisms that relate to gender and sexuality, the most memorable of which appear in *The Lieutenant of Inishmore* and *The Lonesome West.* When Coleman and Valene return from Father Welsh's funeral, Valene comments on how lovely the young nuns were and Coleman fantasises about 'touch[ing] them nuns both upstairs and downstairs' (55). So infantile is their view of sexuality, even sexual desire, that a physical let alone emotional relationship seems highly unlikely.

McDonagh's characters routinely insult one another and the most popular of insults impugn the ability to attain heterosexual fulfilment. Coleman and Valene structure their lives around such insults: Coleman taunts Valene, saying 'Valene the Virgin that V stands for' (21), and Valene calls Coleman 'a virgin fecking gayboy [who] couldn't pay a drunk monkey to go interfering with him' (23). Similarly, when

Padraic initially deflects Mairead's advances, she asks if he prefers boys. He responds unequivocally: 'I do not prefer boys! There's no boy-preferers involved in Irish terrorism, I'll tell you that! They stipulate when you join' (33). Mairead's beloved cat, Sir Roger is, of course, named after one of the most celebrated boy-preferer in Irish nationalism.

One of the shared, normative assumptions is that men do not cry. Toby's situation at the beginning of *Behanding in Spokane* is similar to James Hanley's in Scene Two of *The Lieutenant* on several counts. Both are defenceless captives held by a gun-toting obsessed man whose sanity is in question. Both dissolve into tears while pleading for their release. And the captors mock them for effeminate tears. Padraic describes James, who is suspended upside down, as 'off bawling like some fool of a girl' (10). In *A Behanding*, when Toby cries in response to what must seem like a mock execution, Carmichael sees it as proof that he is a 'fag', only one of many insults that Toby endures. Once Marilyn has dragged the terrified Toby out of the closet, Carmichael taunts him: 'What a fag . . . See? *Crying.* Fag' (7).

Like Padraic, Carmichael offers a brutal, simplistic equation: if a man cries, he must be a fag; QED. Both seek to extend their control over their captive by humiliating as well as torturing him. McDonagh exposes the absurdity of the logic that equates crying and being a 'fag' as both Carmichael and Padraic shed tears. In recounting the loss of his hand, a story that grows more dubious as the play unfolds, Carmichael recalls what happened after his hand was severed: 'Well, the boy stopped crying, quite quickly, *he* wasn't a fag' (10). Padraic will himself dissolve in tears, '*Crying heavily*' (14), when he learns that his beloved cat Wee Thomas may be ill, or perhaps just off his food. Padraic's mawkish attachment to Wee Thomas, in fact, provides James with the opportunity to extricate himself by telling Padraic about his own cat Dominic. Padraic not only releases James, but then gives his fellow cat-lover money for the bus trip to the hospital. Moreover, Carmichael's solicitous phone calls to and from his mother suggest a parallel to Padraic's attachment to his cat.

Especially in the plays premiered since 2000, McDonagh's men routinely cry. In *The Pillowman*, Michal (37, 39), Katurian (21, 31,

39, *et passim*), Ariel (51) and even the Pillowman (32) all do so. In *Six Shooter*, the Kid calls the man whose son has just died a 'cry baby'; later, Donnelly weeps over his wife's death. In guilt and grief, Ray breaks down early in *In Bruges* and several more times in the course of the film; Ken does as well – and even more often in the script than in the film as released.

McDonagh's gravitation toward the closed world of men is equally evident in his more recent works. The bond between Ken and Harry is a debt of honour, due because Harry took revenge on the man who killed Ken's wife. In defying Harry, Ken explains his motivations in a way that disarms Harry, at least figuratively: 'Harry. I am totally in your debt. The things that's gone between us in the past, I love you unreservedly for all that. For your integrity, for your honour. I love you' (73). Harry accuses Ken of 'coming over all Gandhi on me' because this, too, violates the macho code under which they have operated for decades. In their gangster world, Harry, Ken and Ray abide by a code as rigid as that of any Western hero and its stricture against killing a child is absolute. Harry orders Ken to kill Ray, although not before Ray has the opportunity to experience what Harry enjoyed as a child. His code enables Harry to think of himself as a 'nice man' and 'a normal person'. It also demands his suicide.

The transgression of gender expectations is, of course, part of a much more pervasive pattern of inversion, intrinsic to the creation of suspense and comedy, in McDonagh's work. Likewise, it is fundamental to the description of his work as postmodern. Gender construction remains one of the rare sources of identity over which McDonagh's characters still hold some power.

CONCLUSION

A fashionably downbeat ending

The first time I saw a play by Martin McDonagh was when the National Theatre production of *The Cripple of Inishmaan* toured to Dublin in the summer of 1997. Like almost everyone else present, I was aware of McDonagh's sudden celebrity and his unprecedented success; like at least some of those present, I was also aware that he'd attracted some media criticism, and that there was a growing fear that he was exploiting anti-Irish stereotypes for the delight of London audiences. As I took my seat I had the sense of pleasurable anticipation that one experiences before seeing work by any exciting young writer for the first time. But I also wondered if there might be trouble: I found myself wondering what might happen if the Dublin audience found itself unable to tolerate the presentation of stereotypically thick Irish characters by the British National Theatre.

At it happened, there was one walk-out during the action, but not for the reasons I had anticipated.

In the play's final scene, Billy is having his head bandaged by the town doctor, who takes the opportunity to discourage his patient from insulting his aunts. 'You shouldn't talk to them like that, now, Billy,' says the doctor:

Billy   Ah, they keep going on and on.
Doctor   I know they do, but they're women. (*CI*, 78)

The audience laughed at this casually sexist remark. But then I became aware of a disturbance: two people who had been seated in the middle of a row obviously considered the comment too much to take, and they loudly and angrily stormed out of the theatre. I couldn't catch much of what they were saying, but the word 'disgraceful' was clearly audible.

It's difficult to account for that reaction. My temptation at the time was to react dismissively. As I've illustrated already, *Cripple* takes a gleeful swipe at several much-loved Irish figures (such as Kevin Barry and Michael Collins), it describes Hitler as a 'nice enough fella' and it presents the Irish in ways that are less than flattering. Why would one sexist remark by one character in a work of fiction seem so intolerable when compared with everything that had come before it? It might be that the people concerned had been seething for the entire production, and that the doctor's remarks were the final outrage. Or it might be that the remark itself was considered sufficiently offensive to justify a walkout. Either way, it seemed strange to me that people could be insulted by the expression of such views by characters in a play. I never thought that McDonagh wanted us to share the doctor's opinion that women talk too much, or Helen's view that Jesus was full of himself, or Billy's conviction that Ireland is just like America because it's 'full of fat women with beards'. Nor did I assume that those views must be held by McDonagh himself. I couldn't understand the need to storm out angrily.

As I mentioned in the Introduction, these kinds of strong personal reactions to McDonagh's plays and films are actually quite common (at least in my own experience). Just as the audience members who walked out in Dublin in 1997 found the play intolerably sexist, so would there later be people who would judge *The Leenane Trilogy* or *The Lieutenant of Inishmore* to be pandering to anti-Irish sentiment, and would find *A Behanding in Spokane* to be racist.

It has often seemed to me that those negative responses are not caused by the sentiments expressed in the plays, but by the laughter that comes from the audience in response. What is upsetting is not the sexism of the characters, but the audience's willingness to laugh at that sexism – or apparent racism or apparent anti-Irish sentiment. This is a fine example of how McDonagh's plays force us to laugh at things that shouldn't be funny. I've been to dozens of productions of the plays, and I almost always overhear people saying as they leave the theatre that they cannot believe that they were laughing at such awful occurrences, such outrageous utterances, such despicable acts of violence. To an extent, it is understandable that some audiences might worry that by laughing at someone or something they are trivialising or, even worse, expressing contempt for the object of the joke. There's always a fear that a theatre audience can find itself transformed into a mob: our collective act of laughter can seem cruel and even vindictive because a large group represented by 'us' is laughing at a minority, either on the stage or in the auditorium. That explains the discomfort that some Irish people report when watching McDonagh's plays in England – and indeed it also explains the discomfort that some English people report in the same context (as exemplified by Mary Luckhurst's article on that topic which I mentioned in the Introduction). So as I look back to that production of *Cripple* in 1997, I find myself wondering if the couple who stormed out of the theatre did so in protest at McDonagh's joke or in disgust at the audience's willingness to laugh so complacently at it.

That difficulty of distinguishing between the author's actions and an audience's reactions dominates the critical reception of McDonagh's work – and, as I've attempted to argue in this book, it is one of the key features of that work. McDonagh's plays and films are deliberately ambiguous; their indeterminacy of meaning is what gives them their power. But that indeterminacy also explains why they are sometimes misinterpreted – and it explains too why people are sometimes offended by them.

In the preceding chapters that observation has repeatedly returned us to the issue of responsibility. Without wishing to over-simplify what is undoubtedly a complex series of interactions between author, theatre-makers and audience (and the mediation of those interactions by journalists, marketers, publishers, academics and so on), it seems to me that the key responsibility for interpretation lies with the audience. To ask oneself the question that dominates the reception of McDonagh's work – 'why am I laughing at this?' – can and (I would suggest) ought to initiate a creative process; it ought to encourage us to face our own complacencies and assumptions. I suggested when discussing *A Behanding in Spokane* that in some ways Marilyn is more racist than Carmichael, that the difference between them is that he *knows* he's racist, but that her constant attempt to use politically correct rhetoric has the impact of emphasising Toby's difference from her – just as her desire to protect him implies that she actually feels superior to him. McDonagh's use of humour in the play thus allows the audience the space to explore a taboo subject – namely, the continuing impact of racism on daily life in America. But it's up to the audience to make use of that imaginative space and to question why they're laughing at something which in most other contexts would horrify them. Some audience members ask such questions when they leave McDonagh's plays or films. But many others don't.

Nevertheless, I hope to have made clear that McDonagh's *oeuvre* in its entirety is deeply engaged with the issue of interpretation. The three major themes that I've explored are family, religion and narrative – which have in common the responsibilities that are imposed upon us when we choose to interpret something. Many of McDonagh's characters suffer because they feel that their lives have in some ways been preordained by their families or their environment. Maureen cannot escape from either Mag or Ireland in *Beauty Queen*; if Mick in *Skull* is innocent of murdering his wife, the attitude of his fellow villagers is so negative that he may as well be guilty; and while in *The Pillowman* Katurian's parents successfully torture Michal, it's never fully clear whether they succeeded in their experiment of creating a great writer. Religion, similarly, is seen not as offering solace but as imposing duties upon people in ways that may be oppressive – from Ray's sense of guilt in *In Bruges* to Father Welsh's horrendous suicide in *The Lonesome West*. Finally, all of the plays and films show a suspicion of narratives that are handed down to us: the mythology of Irish republicanism as presented in *The Lieutenant*, the myth-making of *Man of Aran* and indeed of *The Cripple of Inishmaan* itself, the stories told by Kid in *Six Shooter*.

These themes are presented differently, but all three might also be considered together as examples of *inheritance*. Each of them comes together to allow us to ask what it means to inherit something – what we should do when we are given something from the past and told that it can determine our actions in the present or future. And in every case the same response arises: we cannot passively accept what we've been given but must instead make it new. The tragedy for Maureen in *Beauty Queen* is that she shows an ability to be an individual, but instead becomes just like her mother. Less tragic but no less regrettable is Mairead's inability in *The Lieutenant of Inishmore* to reject the myths of Irish Republicanism and to forge her own sense of national politics (or, for that matter, her own sense of morality). Religion in many of the works appears only to produce unhappiness or to justify amorality; the most admirable characters are those who are self-legislating rather than subservient to inherited rules and customs. Similarly, the happiness of Billy at the end of *Cripple* is caused (in part) by his ability to choose self-determination over the narratives imposed upon him by Hollywood and his fellow islanders. For all McDonagh's characters, then, a major distinction is between those who *create* their own lives and those who instead merely reproduce the inherited narratives of family, religion, national tradition, politics, geography, gender and so on. Storytelling thus becomes an ethical choice: to be creative is the only way of acting morally in the world – even if storytelling can sometimes be a vehicle for immorality too.

That discussion of theme leads us back to the problem of reception. The plays and films suggest that happiness is possible only through a willingness to interpret reality and then act accordingly – so it seems reasonable to suggest that the same principle should also govern the reception of the work itself. Part of the enjoyment of any McDonagh work lies in a willingness to embrace its ambiguity, to see our uncertainty not as a frustrating shutting down of meaning, but as the initiation of our own contribution to the creative process. But there is also a need to move beyond creativity, and to consider how our interpretation of the plays allows us to re-read ourselves. If we find ourselves laughing at violence, political murder, terrorism, the bullying and marginalising of the weak and vulnerable – if we find ourselves undisturbed by the apparent mockery of things that are normally treated as sacred or sacrosanct – then there are (at least) two possible responses. One is to become angry: to criticise the author, to leave the theatre, to complain in print or in person about being forced to endure an unpleasant experience. And another is to ask a question: why am I reacting like this?

I don't wish to seem dismissive of those who have reacted angrily to or been upset or offended by McDonagh's work. But I do wish to propose that one purpose – and one major value – of that work is that it allows audiences to subject their responses to closer scrutiny than is possible in almost any other cultural context.

I would also suggest that this openness to interpretation is the major reason for McDonagh's global success. In the interview in this book, Garry Hynes suggests that the plays in *The Leenane Trilogy* will make sense in any country that has experience of a peasant culture, whether it's Ireland, Russia, parts of the United States, or elsewhere. I don't disagree with that suggestion, but mention it simply to allude to what we might term the 'universal' qualities of the work: what Hynes is referring to are those features of the plays that will be received in the same way by audiences in different countries. There is evidence that some features of the plays and films are seen as having universal value (leaving aside the problems that humanities scholars tend to have with the term 'universal'). The plight of Maureen in *Beauty Queen* tends to be interpreted in much the same way wherever the play is performed; similarly, audiences at *Cripple* tend to engage emotionally with Billy without there being much evidence of variation of response from one place to another. In both plays, audiences seem able to identify with the plight of sensitive individuals who are surrounded by an indifferent, unsympathetic and occasionally hostile mass of others. To a certain extent, then, we might assume that McDonagh's ability to create such sympathetic characters might account for the success of his work in so many different countries.

Yet what is fascinating about McDonagh is that most of the evidence suggests that his work is actually received very differently from one country to another. As I explained when discussing *The Lieutenant of Inishmore*, the interpretation of that play has been strongly determined by the experience (or lack of experience) of a local culture with global terrorism since 11 September 2001. The treatment of family in many of the plays has fed into countless local concerns – so that, for example, *The Beauty Queen* has occasioned debates about the care of the elderly in Washington DC, about respect for senior citizens in Japan, about emigration in Ireland, and so on. Similarly, the evidence suggests that most international productions of *The Cripple of Inishmaan* have encouraged audiences not to reconsider what they know about Ireland, but instead to think about how their own locality is represented on the global stage – whether that locality is New Zealand or Los Angeles or elsewhere.

In my book *Theatre and Globalization* I described this feature of McDonagh's work as an example of reflexivity: my argument was that his global success arises because, when audiences watch his plays, they do not *receive* a meaning that is being conveyed from the author to themselves – rather, they find their own concerns and preoccupations being reflected back to them. So, again, I'm proposing the conclusion that the value of McDonagh's plays and films is not that they tell us something about Ireland or England or McDonagh himself, but that they can show us something of ourselves – perhaps something that we value, perhaps something that we hadn't been aware of, perhaps something that makes us very uncomfortable or angry.

That assertion in turn raises again the issue of national traditions, of how we categorise McDonagh. As I've discussed, he has usually resisted being described as either Irish or English, and, as Garry Hynes points out, elements of both cultures can be found in his work. I hope to have made clear that to describe McDonagh simply as an Irish writer would be to limit severely our understanding of his achievements and significance. Among other things, the tendency to focus on McDonagh as an Irish writer has obscured his indebtedness to Pinter, which is one of the more interesting features of his work. Perhaps, then, it is most accurate to see McDonagh as a second-generation Irish writer, and thus to consider his work in the context of (among others) the Pogues. That group's anarchism, their reinvention of tradition, their belonging in both Ireland and England without being fully at home in either place, all seem to offer useful ways of thinking about McDonagh, as he himself has acknowledged. Yet to use that model would involve overlooking or ignoring the many different responses to McDonagh in countries outside Ireland and the UK.

It might then be tempting to see him as an international writer, given that his work is so widely produced around the world. But the word 'international' tends to be used to describe communication from one national culture to another, and I have sought to suggest that one of the major features of McDonagh's drama is that it's not trying to communicate any one meaning to anyone. For that reason, I have described McDonagh as a global playwright – perhaps *the* major global playwright of his generation: he succeeds around the world because his work can be adapted to each locality that it appears in, and can be reinterpreted from one place to another, and from one time to another. For that reason, I would argue that to debate endlessly the issues of Irishness in McDonagh's work is a distraction – and a rather parochial one at that – from the wealth of possible responses to his writing around the world. Audiences and theatre-makers have found so many different ways of bringing the plays to life on stage that it seems a shame to prioritise Ireland to the exclusion of anywhere else, even if that country is the setting of most of the work – and even if Irish people are the ones being represented in the work. There are many interesting ways of seeing McDonagh and we should be alert to the variety.

This openness to interpretation may explain the controversies that have attended McDonagh's career to date, but I hope to have shown how it is also what makes him an interesting and valuable writer. I'm aware of course that there is a risk in reaching this conclusion: that my declaration that there is no single meaning in McDonagh's work may itself be interpreted as an *imposition* of a single meaning upon that work. It is certainly possible to misinterpret McDonagh – both the man and his drama – and it is my conviction that he has suffered more from such misinterpretation than most other writers ever do. My intention, nevertheless, is not to narrow down the interpretation of McDonagh's work, but rather to call for an opening out – for a broadening of discussion of how audiences have received the work, for a greater understanding of how he is received differently from one place to another, for a more considered analysis of the ethical consequences of his treatment of difference. And, perhaps most importantly, I hope to have established something that has not been given sufficient attention in the past: the fact that McDonagh is a great storyteller – not because of the truths that he conveys to us, but because of his willingness to allow us to uncover such truths for and about ourselves.

RESOURCES

CHRONOLOGY

1970

On 26 March, Martin McDonagh is born in south-east London. His father, John, is originally from Connemara, while his mother Mary McDonagh (*née* Harte) is originally from Sligo. With his elder brother John Michael, McDonagh will spend many summer holidays during his childhood returning to the west of Ireland to visit his parents' families.

1984

McDonagh's first visit to the theatre, to see Al Pacino playing Donny in David Mamet's *American Buffalo*, at the Duke of York's Theatre, London. During the next thirteen years, McDonagh only goes to the theatre occasionally: he states in 1997 that he has seen 'maybe twenty plays'.

1986–1993

McDonagh quits school at the age of sixteen. He works in a variety of jobs during this period, stocking shelves at a supermarket and doing clerical work at the Department of Trade and Industry. He also spends some time on the dole, receiving social welfare payments. He begins writing during the early 1990s. His parents return to Ireland, while he and his brother remain in London, both spending most of their time writing.

1994

Realising that his style is too obviously influenced by the work of Mamet and Harold Pinter, McDonagh decides to start writing in an exaggerated version of the speech he had heard during summer visits to Ireland. This inspires a burst of creativity, and he drafts seven plays in quick succession: *The Beauty Queen of Leenane, A Skull in Connemara* and *The Lonesome West* (collectively known as *The Leenane Trilogy*); *The Cripple of Inishmaan, The Lieutenant of Inishmore* and *The Banshees of Inisheer* (collectively known as *The Aran Islands Trilogy*);

and *The Pillowman*. Six of these plays will be produced between 1996 and 2003; the seventh, *The Banshees of Inisheer*, remains unproduced.

1995

Garry Hynes, who has recently returned to Galway's Druid Theatre after working as Artistic Director of the Abbey Theatre in Dublin, decides to read through the company's recent batch of unsolicited submissions. She finds McDonagh's scripts, and immediately buys the rights to stage *The Leenane Trilogy*.

1996

Druid Theatre premieres *The Beauty Queen of Leenane* at the Town Hall Theatre on 1 February. Garry Hynes directs. After a brief Irish tour, it transfers to the Royal Court Theatre Upstairs, opening on 29 February. In November, the play opens at the Duke of York's Theatre in London's West End. As the year concludes, McDonagh is named 'Most Promising Newcomer' at the George Devine Awards. A confrontation with Sean Connery at the awards ceremony is widely reported in the British tabloid press.

1997

The Cripple of Inishmaan opens at the National Theatre, London, in January, where it is directed by Nicholas Hytner. In April, a rehearsed reading of *The Pillowman* is staged in Galway as part of the Cúirt International Festival of Literature. In June, *A Skull in Connemara* and *The Lonesome West* premiere in Galway, where they play in repertory with *The Beauty Queen* as *The Leenane Trilogy*, which is again directed by Hynes. The *Trilogy* transfers to the Royal Court in London in July.

1998

The Leenane Trilogy tours in January to the Sydney Festival, where the Australian media quiz McDonagh about his interest in Australian soap opera. In April, *The Beauty Queen* opens at the Walter Kerr Theatre in New York. It is nominated for six Tony Awards, winning four of them. Hynes becomes the first woman to win a Tony for direction, while during his acceptance speech the actor Tom Murphy becomes the first person to say the word 'feck' on prime-time American television.

1999

On 27 April, *The Lonesome West* opens at the Lyceum Theatre in Broadway, where it is nominated for four Tonys. McDonagh's attempts to produce *The Lieutenant of Inishmore* are unsuccessful; he states publicly that he will not produce any more plays until *The Lieutenant* appears.

2000

Druid's production of *The Beauty Queen* receives an extended run in Dublin for the first time, appearing at the Gaiety Theatre for almost three months. While the play is a commercial success, Dublin critics are generally critical of what they see as the production's 'stage Irish' qualities.

2001

The Lieutenant of Inishmore is premiered by the Royal Shakespeare Company at The Other Place, Stratford-upon-Avon, on 11 May. It is directed by Wilson Milam. It transfers to the Barbican in London later that year. *The Lonesome West* receives its first extended run in Dublin, playing from 2 August to 29 September.

2002

The Lieutenant of Inishmore plays at the Garrick Theatre in London's West End. It is awarded an Olivier Award for Best New Comedy.

2003

In November, John Crowley directs the premiere of *The Pillowman* at the National Theatre, London.

2004

The Pillowman wins an Olivier Award for Best New Play.

2005

McDonagh writes and directs a short film, *Six Shooter*. The National Theatre's production of *The Pillowman* visits Ireland, playing for five nights in Cork in March. The following month, *The Pillowman* opens at the Booth Theater on Broadway, in a production directed by John Crowley and starring Jeff Goldblum and Billy Crudup. It is nominated for four Tonys, winning two (for set and lighting design).

2006

McDonagh wins an Oscar for best short film for *Six Shooter*. Wilson Milam's production of *The Lieutenant of Inishmore* opens at New York's Atlantic Theater in February. It transfers to Broadway in May, where it is nominated for five Tonys.

2008

McDonagh writes and directs *In Bruges*, his first feature film. Starring Colin Farrell, Brendan Gleeson and Ralph Fiennes, the film is a critical and commercial success. In September, Druid Theatre presents the first professional Irish production of *The Cripple of Inishmaan*, which transfers to New York's Atlantic Theater in December.

2009

McDonagh receives his second Oscar nomination, for Best Original Screenplay for *In Bruges*. Colin Farrell is awarded a Golden Globe for his performance in that film.

2010

McDonagh's seventh play, *A Behanding in Spokane*, premieres on Broadway on 8 March. Directed by John Crowley and starring Christopher Walken, it is the first of McDonagh's plays to be set entirely in America.

2011

The Guard, a film written and directed by John Michael McDonagh, opens. McDonagh is executive producer. As the year draws to a close, McDonagh's second feature film, *Seven Psychopaths*, enters into pre-production.

A NOTE ON LANGUAGE

Reviews of McDonagh's Irish plays often call attention to the accent and idiom of the characters. His use of Irish speech is sometimes seen as positive, in that it renders the plays somewhat more exotic for audiences (especially when they are performed outside Ireland and Britain). Yet at other times, the dialogue is seen as an impediment to the appreciation, understanding and performance of the work. Central to such criticisms is the notion that McDonagh is portraying an authentic form of Irish speech, and hence that actors must be able to perform an 'accurate' Irish accent, which audiences must in turn be able to decipher. Such approaches are slightly misguided. It is true that McDonagh draws on words and syntactical constructions that can be heard in Ireland, but the speech he creates is largely invented. It's therefore probably fair to say that there is no one 'correct' way of delivering his characters' lines.

McDonagh has spoken occasionally about his use of Irish speech, and has always seemed keen to emphasise its artificiality. As Eamonn Jordan mentions in his essay earlier in this book, McDonagh had originally decided to use a version of Irish speech as a way of escaping the influence of Pinter and Mamet. 'I wanted to develop some kind of dialogue style as strange and heightened as [Mamet and Pinter's],' he told Fintan O'Toole shortly before the premiere of *The Leenane Trilogy*. But that style needed to be '*twisted* in some way so the influence wasn't as obvious . . . And then I sort of remembered the way my uncles spoke back in Galway, the structure of their sentences. I didn't think of it as structure, just as a kind of rhythm in the speech. And that seemed an interesting way to go, to try to do something with that language that wouldn't be English or American' (1997: 1).

Eleven years later, while he was promoting *In Bruges* at the Sundance Festival, McDonagh spoke again about his use of Irish speech:

'I think it's because Gaelic was so prevalent in the west [of Ireland],' he explained . . . 'Gaelic was my dad's first language and there are a lot of words in Gaelic that don't have any English equivalent and when they speak in English, the syntax is sort of back-to-front. When I started to write in the Irish vernacular, it freed things up for me, story-wise and dialogue-wise. The way I write in Irish is not the way anyone actually speaks. It's a strange idiom, but I felt it was my own.' (Lacey, 2008)

This statement is very useful, since it helps us to identify the major ways in which McDonagh uses Irish speech: he draws on words that cannot be expressed in Standard English and also reproduces the 'back-to-front' syntax of Irish-English speech. And crucially, he states unambiguously that his version of Irish speech is 'not the way anyone actually speaks'.

We can see very quickly how McDonagh's description applies to the Irish plays. For instance, he uses many Irish slang words that don't have an exact English equivalent: words like 'feck', 'biteen', 'lube', 'skitter', 'gob' and so on all have English synonyms but none that captures the fine nuances of meaning implied by those words. He also uses an unfamiliar syntax, organising his sentences according to the rules of the Irish language, even though the words being used are English. For example, when Valene tells Welsh that 'A great parish it is you run' in the first scene of *Lonesome West* (*LW*, 8), he is breaking the rules of English syntax by placing *you run* at the end of the sentence. Similarly, in *Lieutenant* we find the following sentences: 'Poor Wee Thomas's head, a bicycle wouldn't do damage that decent. Damage that decent you'd have to go out of your way to do' (*LI*, 5). This skewed composition attempts to capture the strange syntax of Hiberno-English, which often orders sentences as if the speaker is thinking in Irish but using English words.

McDonagh also reproduces the verb tenses of Hiberno-English. The Irish language has a more complex version of the present tense than English does, and can therefore express a state called the 'habitual present', which can be used to describe the actions of a person who is doing something in the present moment that is part of a longer process of repetition. This construction appears constantly in the plays, as for instance when Coleman tells Welsh in *Lonesome West* that he can 'be doing what you like' or when Welsh in response says 'Don't be swearing today of all days' (*LW*, 4).

Related to that use of the word 'be' is the constructive of the imperative (that is, an order from one person to another), which is sometimes formed by using the word 'be' followed by the present participle of a verb. 'Be stopping!' means the same thing as 'Stop!', though there is a slight difference in emphasis: 'be stopping' might be construed as a demand to come to a gradual conclusion, whereas 'stop' implies an immediate conclusion.

A particularly common feature of McDonagh's characters' Irish speech is the use of the suffix '-een' at the end of the words, as sometimes used as a diminutive in Hiberno-English speech. This means that it can be used to suggest that something is small; hence, 'biteen' would mean something like 'a little bit', while 'Girleen' means 'little girl'. But it is also sometimes used to express affection (as in 'loveen') or condescension ('ladeen'). The nuances are usually evident from the context, but some uses of the suffix have been glossed in the section following.

McDonagh's Irish speech can be considered an example of literary Hiberno-English. The term 'Hiberno-English', while somewhat controversial, is generally used to describe English as it is spoken in Ireland, especially when that speech displays traces of the Irish language. Many dramatists have made use of a poeticised form of Hiberno-English speech in their plays, and while such work is often praised for its beauty, it also tends to attract criticism for being inauthentic. That mixture of praise and criticism has also dominated the reception of the work of J.M. Synge and Sean O'Casey, among many others.

It is important to emphasise that there are several different dialects of Hiberno-English, with notable variations in accent and vocabulary due to social class and/or geographical location. McDonagh's Hiberno-English is in contrast quite homogeneous: we don't notice many differences between the speech of doctors, priests, builders or shopkeepers; nor are there obvious differences based on the characters' age. Similarly, the speech of the characters from Northern Ireland in *Lieutenant* is largely indistinguishable from the speech of everyone else in the play. Indeed, in most productions of *The Lieutenant*, no attempt is made to perform the roles of Christy, Brendan and Joey in Northern Irish accents. Likewise, McDonagh's two Dublin crooks in *In Bruges* rarely use accents that would mark them out specifically as being from Ireland's capital city. In fact, McDonagh has stated that the script as originally written envisaged the two hitmen as being Londoners; the decision to make them Irish only happened after Gleeson and Farrell signed on to the movie – yet the change required McDonagh to alter only about a dozen words, he claims.

For McDonagh, this use of Irish speech arises for aesthetic reasons, and not from a desire to be authentic. While all of the Hiberno-English used by McDonagh is derived from actual usage, no one in Ireland ever speaks like a character in a McDonagh play – any more than an Elizabethan Londoner would have spoken like a character in a Shakespeare play. The dialect that he uses is based on the form of speech used in rural Galway and Mayo, especially in those parts that still use the Irish language. But none of the plays depends for its success on that accent being re-created correctly.

There are several excellent studies of Hiberno-English in print. The classic, which is still very useful, is P.W. Joyce's *English as We Speak it in Ireland* (1911). Also immensely valuable is T.P. Dolan's *Dictionary of Hiberno-English* (2007), which was frequently consulted when the glossary below was being prepared, as was the *Oxford English Dictionary*, which provides very useful glosses on some Hiberno-English slang words. An excellent and accessible introduction to the field is Bernard Shine's *Slanguage* (2008).

The glossary below is presented in alphabetical order. The plays or films in which the word originally appears are mentioned in parentheses, using the abbreviations set out at the start of this book. The glossary features words that are part of ordinary Hiberno-English (that is, words that are universally used in Ireland), words which are considered slang and non-Irish words which may not be widely understood. It also includes some Standard English words whose unusual spelling is due to their non-standard pronunciation.

GLOSSARY

Agin The word 'against' is sometimes pronounced 'agin' (to rhyme with 'a bin') in Hiberno-English speech. [*SC, LW*]

Ar A shortened form of the word 'arrah', still widely used in the west of Ireland in informal speech, to mean something like 'Oh come on now' or 'For goodness' sake'. It's also sometimes used to express indifference. It may originate from an expression meaning something like 'Oh God'. [*SC, LW, CI, SS*]

Arging A mispronunciation of the word 'arguing'. [*LW*]

Arsed The slang expression 'I can't be arsed' means that the speaker cannot be bothered to do something. [*SS*]

Arsing To 'arse around' means to waste time by doing something foolish or trivial. [*BQ*]

Aye 'Yes'. While this word is frequently used by characters in McDonagh's plays, it is not very commonly used in the west of Ireland. [*BQ, SC, LW, SS*]

Babby Baby. The word is occasionally pronounced in this way (rhyming with 'shabby') in Ireland. [*BQ, SC, LI*]

Bandying To bandy something about means to use it in a reckless or disrespectful manner. [*SC, CI*]

Bawling Crying. In Ireland, the word 'bawl' is not used to refer to the act of shouting, but instead to an act of uncontrollable weeping. [*LI, SS*]

Beag As used in *Skull*, 'beag' is the Irish word for 'little'. Hence, 'Mary Beag' means 'Little Mary'. The word is pronounced 'byug' [*SC*]

Bitcheen A little bitch. Here the diminutive is used to worsen the original insult. [*LI*]

Biteen   A little bit. [*SC, LW, CI, LI*]

Blackguard   Dolan glosses this word as a 'ruffian, rogue or scoun-drel'. It is also often used as a verb to refer to the act of lying or insulting someone. This word became archaic in English in the nine-teenth century, but is still occasionally used in the west of Ireland today. [*SC*]

Bob   The word 'bob' formerly meant 'shilling', but now refers to any small amount of money, and here probably means 'a few pounds'. [*CI, LW*]

Boxeen   A little box. [*CI*]

Brookeen   A little brook. [*LW*]

Brutal   The word 'brutal' is often used by critics to describe char-acters in McDonagh's plays. In an Irish context, however, the word 'brutal' does not always mean 'fiercely violent' but something closer to 'terrible'. Thus to, describe a play as 'brutal' would mean that it is very bad, and not that its characters are very violent. In *Six Shooter*, the phrase 'brutal-looking baby' means that the child looks very ugly. [*SS*]

Cadging   To beg from someone, usually money. [*SC*]

Ceilidh   Pronounced 'kay-*lee*', this word refers to a traditional Irish dance. [*BQ*]

Chipping in   This slang expression means to interject into a conver-sation, perhaps in an unwelcome or obtrusive fashion. [*SC*]

Codding   Lying, joking, or teasing. This Hiberno-English word is of uncertain origin according to Dolan, but is still widely used. [*LI, SS*]

Colleen   Anglicisation of the Irish word *cailín*, meaning 'a girl'. [*CI*]

Danceen   A little dance. [*SC*]

Decent   The word 'decent' is often used in McDonagh's plays to mean 'admirable' – but not in the sense of 'upright' or 'morally praiseworthy', as we find in *Lieutenant* with the reference to 'damage that decent'. [*LW, LI*]

Diddled   To 'diddle out of' is to swindle or cheat someone. [*LW*]

Differ (*noun*)   Means the same thing as the word 'difference', often in the phrase 'same differ'. Used occasionally in Hiberno-English. [*BQ, CI, LI*]

Doolally   A slang word, taken from India according to the OED, to refer to a person whose actions are 'characterised by an unbalanced state of mind'. [*BQ*]

Eej / Eejit   Sometimes shortened to 'eej' the word 'eejit' is probably derived from the English 'idiot', though as Dolan points out it is often used less pejoratively than that English word; indeed, it can sometimes be used almost as a term of endearment. [*BQ, SC*]

Feasteen   This means something like 'a lovely little feast'. [*LW*]

Feck   A slang word, used mainly in Ireland, roughly equivalent to 'fuck' in vulgar English. But while it is often assumed that the word 'feck' is an Irish mispronunciation of 'fuck', it probably comes from the Elizabethan English 'fecks', meaning 'in faith' (as in Shakespeare's *The Winter's Tale*, I, ii, 171: 'I' fecks!'). Characters in McDonagh's plays are called 'fecks' and 'feckers', are told to 'feck off', worry about being 'fecked up' by their enemies and use the word 'fecking' to describe any object that they dislike. In all such cases, the word 'fuck' would have the same meaning. Note, however, that the word 'feck' is never used to refer to sexual intercourse, and that 'feck' is not thought to be as crude a word as 'fuck'. [*BQ, SC, LW, CI, LI*]

Flogging   In some contexts, 'to flog' can mean 'to sell' something. The word has a slightly negative connotation: to 'flog' something means that the object being sold is considered almost valueless, or that the vendor is largely indifferent to the price it fetches. [*LW*]

Gallivanting   Travelling carelessly to many different places. [*BQ, LI*]

Gangerman   London slang for a foreman on a building site. [*BQ*]

Gasurs   The word 'gasur' is an Hiberno-English word meaning 'boy'. It is possibly derived from the French *garçon*. The word is spelled GOSAWER in McDonagh's Aran Islands plays. [*BQ, SC, LW, LI*]

Gets Means roughly the same thing (and conveys the same kind of insult) as the word 'bastard'. This slang word came to Ireland from England, and remains in use in parts of both countries. [*CI*]

Gipping 'To gip' means to cheat or to swindle. The word is not widely used in Ireland. [*LI*]

Gob 'Gob' usually means 'mouth', though it can also be used to refer to spit. Gob is a loan word from Irish. [*BQ, LW, LI*]

Gobshites The word 'gobshite' is an insulting term in Hiberno-English, combining the word 'gob', meaning 'mouth' or 'spit', with the regionalised pronunciation of the word 'shit'. A rough English equivalent would be something like 'stupid bastard'. [*SC, LW*]

Goob From the Irish *gobán*, the word 'goob' is usually used to refer to a person who pretends to know more than he does. It is not widely used in Ireland. [*LI*]

Gosawer [*CI*]   See GASURS.

Hairing Rushing. An Irish slang word, not widely used. [*LI*]

Hogging To 'hog' means to keep something greedily to oneself. [*CI*]

Huffy Slang. To be 'huffy' means to be in a bad temper; usually the word is used dismissively by one person about another's mood. [*SS*]

Humping The word 'humping' is used in *Lonesome West* to mean 'carrying' as in 'humping a dead policeman'. [*LW*]

Jeebies A euphemistic pronunciation of 'Jesus', used rather like the word 'Jeepers' in American-English. It is not widely used in Ireland. [*SC, CI*]

Ladeen A little lad. Used in this way, the suffix -een makes the word a term of endearment: 'ladeen' is mostly used in a complimentary fashion, though it can also be used as a form of condescension. [*SC*]

Listeen Another use of -een as a diminutive, here meaning simply a short list. [*LW*]

Loopy A Standard English slang word, which according to the *OED* emerged in the early twentieth century. It means 'mad' and is mildly pejorative. [*BQ*]

Loveen A term of endearment, literally meaning 'my little love'. [*LI*]

Lube Perhaps an Anglicisation of the Gaelic word *lúbaire*, meaning a 'rogue', or the word *lúbán*, meaning 'a mistake'. The word 'lube' is not widely used in Ireland. [*LW, LI*]

Lugging In Standard English, the word 'lug' would usually mean 'to pull from', but in Hiberno-English it generally is used to refer to carrying something heavy from one place to another. [*SS*]

Lummox Described by the *OED* as a dialect word, it means 'A large, heavy, or clumsy person; an ungainly or stupid lout'. [*SC*]

Minge Slang for a woman's pubic hair. [*LI*]

Mongo A highly offensive term of abuse, derived from the word 'mongolism', which was originally used to describe people with Down's Syndrome. [*LI*]

Noteen A little note. [*CI*]

Pegging 'To peg' is an Irish colloquialism, meaning 'to throw'. [*BQ, SC, LW, CI, LI*]

Peneen Another use of -een: 'the little pen'. As used in *Lonesome West*, the diminutive is being used sarcastically – Coleman is trying to provoke his brother. [*LW*]

Picking me up When Girleen asks that people would not 'pick her up' on something, she means 'don't correct me'. [*LW*]

Pissed In Hiberno-English slang, the word 'pissed' is an impolite term for 'drunk'. Someone who is 'pissed to the gills' is being described as drinking 'like a fish' – that is, they consume alcohol at an alarming rate. [*LW*]

Polis The police. This pronunciation was common in Ireland and parts of England. [*BQ, CI*]

Poteen   An Irish alcoholic drink. It is usually distilled from potatoes, and is extremely potent. Until the late 1990s it was illegal to sell or brew poteen in Ireland. The fact that many of the characters in McDonagh's drink it shows the extent to which their community does not take certain laws very seriously. [SC, LW, CI, LI]

Praitie   Potatoes. This is a loan-word from the Irish *práta*. [BQ, SC, CI]

Rake   A slang word, to mean an abundance of something. Hence, 'a rake of rakes' is 'an abundance of rakes'. [SC, CI]

Scould   A mispronunciation of 'scald'. [BQ]

Shebang   American-English slang word. The expression 'the whole shebang' would suggest 'including everything under discussion'. [SC]

Shenanigans   Unruly behaviour. A colloquial term, possibly derived from Irish. [SC, LI]

Shillelagh   An Irish blackthorn stick, usually used for the purposes of battle. (CI)

Skitter (noun), **skittering** (verb)   The word 'skitter' is a colloquialism for excrement. Hence, the word 'skitter' means much the same as 'shit'. When Father Welsh tells Girleen not to be 'skittering' her money away, he means that she is throwing her money away as if it's nothing more than shit. The word is also used as a personal insult in *Skull* – to call someone 'skitter' is the same as calling him or her 'a shit' in Standard English. [BQ, SC, LW, CI, LI]

Skivvy   A colloquialism in Standard English for a maidservant, usually implying a slur on her status. [BQ]

Slapeen   'Slapeen' involves another use of the suffix -een, here meaning 'a little slap'. Its use in *Lonesome West* is a softening of the word, which implies that Girleen is being flirtatious. [LW]

Smatter   A fragment or small piece of something. [LI]

Smutterings   Obscure word, possibly referring to the action of muttering obscenities under one's breath. [BQ]

Spa   A highly insulting term, short for 'spastic'. [*SS*]

Tadeen   'A little bit'. [*SC, LI*]

Taking a pop   To 'take a pop' at someone usually means to attempt to hit them, but it can be used in a more general sense to refer to any attempt to do something that is unlikely to succeed. [*LW*]

Terror   The word 'terror' is sometimes used in Hiberno-English speech to mean something like 'very bad' though it may occasionally include a hint of grudging admiration too. In *Lonesome West*, the phrase 'terror for the drink' is used by Coleman to mean that Father Welsh drinks far too much – though it's not clear whether Coleman sees this as a particularly bad thing. [*LW*]

Tinkering   As used by Girleen in *Lonesome West*, 'to tinker' means to investigate something in a carefree or possibly even careless manner. [*LW*]

Trippeen   A little trip, a short journey. [*CI*]

Wee   Small. [*SC*]

Weedy   A slang word, often used to refer to someone who is physically weak and (perhaps) cowardly. [*LW*]

Wittering   Mindless chattering. [*SC*]

Yokes   As Joyce states, a yoke is 'any article, contrivance, or apparatus, for use in some work'. 'That's a *quare* yoke Bill,' says a countryman when he first saw a motor car.' [*SS*]

GUIDE TO ALLUSIONS

Listed below are definitions for the various allusions in McDonagh's plays and films. I have only listed explicit references; there are many more vague allusions or 'nods of the head' (to borrow a phrase from *In Bruges*). Terms that appear elsewhere in the glossary are given in SMALL CAPS. The abbreviations given at the start of the book are used to identify where the allusion originally appears. Hence the abbreviation '*LI*' in the entry for 'Ace of Spades' indicates that this song was mentioned in *Lieutenant of Inishmore*.

'Ace of Spades'   A song by the British heavy metal group Motorhead (1980). [*LI*]

'All Kinds of Everything'   The winning song at the 1970 Eurovision Song Contest. It was performed by DANA, who represented Ireland in that year's competition. Its chorus involves the repetition of the phrase 'all kinds of everything remind me of you'. Its inclusion in *Skull*, during a scene in which body parts are being smashed to pieces, gives new meaning to that phrase. [*SC*]

Andrews, Eamonn   An Irish-born TV and radio presenter who found fame in Britain from the 1960s onwards, mainly as the host of *This Is Your Life*. His inclusion in *The Leenane Trilogy* is one of many references to Irish people who emigrated to Britain. [*SC*]

Banshee   A female spirit in Irish mythology, usually seen as a harbinger of death. When Billy hears 'the wail of the banshee', he is saying that his death is imminent. [*CI*]

Barry, Kevin (1902–1920)   A member of the IRA who fought in the Irish War of Independence from Britain (1919–1921). He was executed at the age of eighteen after his involvement in an attack on the British army which resulted in the death of three soldiers. He is seen within Irish Republican culture as a martyr. [*CI*]

Behan, Brendan and **Dominic** The Behans, as Padraic calls them in *Lieutenant*, were a family famous both as nationalists and as writers. The best known member was the playwright Brendan Behan (1923–64), who was a member of the IRA before he turned to writing. The song 'THE PATRIOT GAME' was written by his folk-singing brother Dominic (1928–89). [*LI*]

Bella A UK-based women's magazine. [*LW*]

Biggles Goes to Borneo One of a series of books about a British fighter pilot, written by W.E. Johns. The book *Biggles in Borneo* appeared in 1943, so its appearance in *Cripple* is anachronistic. The story involves Biggles' interactions with a group of natives who are presented as subhuman savages – creating an interesting parallel with the representation of the Aran Islands by Robert Flaherty. [*CI*]

Birmingham Six A group of six Irishmen who were wrongfully convicted of the IRA's pub bombings in Birmingham. They spent sixteen years in prison. In the context of *The Leenane Trilogy*, they can be seen as another example of the status of the Irish in Britain. [*BQ*]

Black Panthers An African-American counter-cultural and revolutionary movement, most active in the 1960s and 1970s. [*BS*]

Bloody Sunday There have been many 'Bloody Sundays' in Irish history, but the one referred to in *Lieutenant* occurred on 30 January 1972 – a notorious incident during the Troubles in which the British Army opened fire on a Catholic civil rights march in Derry, killing thirteen unarmed civilians and wounding many others. [*LI*]

'The Body of an American' A song by the Pogues, written by Shane McGowan. It is sung by Pato at the beginning of Scene Three of *Beauty Queen*. In keeping with the play's themes, the song concerns emigration from Ireland. [*BQ*]

Bosco An Irish children's television programme, broadcast in the late 1970s and 1980s. The title character was a hand puppet with distinctive red hair. He generally interacted with adult presenters, such as 'the lass . . . had brown eyes' whom Ray mentions. [*BQ*]

Bronski Beat   A British pop band, active in the mid-1980s. In *Six Shooter*, the Kid is probably referring to lead-singer Jimmy Sommerville as 'the gay one', but in fact all members of the group were openly gay. [*SS*]

Bugs Bunny   A wisecracking cartoon character, who appeared in the Warner Brothers 'Looney Tunes' series. He was often chased around by Elmer Fudd. [*BQ*]

Casement, Roger   Mairead's cat Sir Roger takes its name from Sir Roger Casement (1864–1916), the Irish diplomat and patriot. He achieved fame for his reports on human rights abuses in the Congo. In 1916, he attempted to smuggle arms into Ireland from Germany for use in the Easter Rising against British rule. He was captured by the British army, tried for treason and executed. There has been a great deal of controversy about Casement's homosexuality since his death, something that McDonagh possibly is alluding to when Padraic suggests that there are no 'boy-preferers' in Irish terrorism. Also notable is that, despite Mairead's Republicanism, she retains the British title 'Sir' in her cat's name. [*LI*]

Casey, Eamon   The Bishop of Galway from 1976 until he was forced to resign in 1992, when it was revealed that he had fathered a child with an American woman in 1974. He is presumably the target of Mag's comment that 'There was a priest the news Wednesday had a babby with a Yank!' [*BQ*]

The Chieftains   A highly respected traditional Irish group, which has achieved worldwide fame since it was established in the 1960s. [*BQ*]

Claddagh Palace   A cinema in Galway city centre (approximately 65 kilometres from Leenane), demolished in the early 1990s. [*LW*]

Collins, Michael   The leader of the IRA during the War of Independence against Britain. Collins negotiated the 1921 treaty that gave Ireland partial independence, and which resulted in the partition of the island into the Irish Free State and Northern Ireland. He was assassinated in 1922 during the Irish Civil War. [*CI*]

Complan   A powdered food, originally designed for use in hospitals. It is mixed with water and provides essential nutrients in an easily digestible form – once, of course, it is fully dissolved. [*BQ*]

A Country Practice   Australian soap opera about a medical practice in a rural town in New South Wales. Its representation of rural life contrasts starkly with McDonagh's. The show was broadcast on Irish and British television in the late 1980s and throughout the 1990s. [*BQ*]

Cranham and Blakely   The pseudonyms used by Ken and Ray in *In Bruges* are taken from the surnames of Kenneth Cranham and Colin Blakely, actors who appeared in the BBC TV version of Harold Pinter's *The Dumb Waiter*. [*IB*]

Cromwell, Oliver (1599–1658)   Lord Protector of Britain during the republican Commonwealth. He is seen within Ireland as one of the villains of the country's history, mainly due to his involvement in massacres of Irish Catholics in Drogheda and Wexford. As McDonagh implies in *Lieutenant*, his name is a byword for English tyranny within Ireland. [*LI*]

'The Croppy Boy'   A traditional Irish ballad about a young 'croppy' – a member of a group of Irish rebels who fought against the British in 1798. [*CI*]

Curtis, Tony (1925–2010)   American film actor, probably best known for his role in *Some Like It Hot* (1959), which co-starred Jack Lemmon and Marilyn Monroe. [*SS*]

Dana   'Dana' Rosemary Scallon won the 1970 Eurovision Song Contest with her song 'ALL KINDS OF EVERYTHING'. That song is mentioned in *Skull* as a relic from Ireland's distant past but, in fact, Scallon became a candidate for Ireland's presidency in 1997, the year in which *The Leenane Trilogy* premiered. In 1999, she was elected an MEP (Member of the European Parliament) for Ireland-West, a constituency that includes both Leenane and the Aran Islands. She has often spoken about her strong fidelity to Catholicism, a characteristic which also had an impact on her political views. She continues to release music and is a minor celebrity on Irish television. In 2011, she again became a nominee for the Presidency of Ireland. [*SC*]

De Gierigaard en de Dood ['The Miser and Death'] A painting by the Dutch artist Jan Provoost, on display at the Groeningemuseum, Bruges. The picture shows a skeletal Death coming to take a mortal to the underworld. [*IB*]

de Valera, Eamon (1882–1975) The dominant figure of twentieth-century Irish politics, he was centrally involved in the Irish War of Independence, and was Taoiseach of the country for most of the period 1932–1959, before becoming President from 1959 to 1973. His reputation has declined severely in Ireland in recent years, due to his economic isolationism, commitment to neutrality in the Second World War and promotion of conservative Catholic values. [*SC*]

Don't Look Now A 1973 film by Nicolas Roeg about a couple who go to Venice after the tragic death of their daughter. The film's presentation of the ghostly figure of the daughter (who wears a red coat) has often been imitated. The movie is also well known for an unusually intimate sex-scene between its stars, Donald Sutherland and Julie Christie. [*IB*]

'The Dying Rebel' An Irish 'rebel' song, in which a parent proudly celebrates the death of her son in the Easter 1916 Rising in Dublin. [*LI*]

European Championships A football tournament, held every four years in various countries around Europe. Because it is mentioned in *The Beauty Queen* as happening 'next year', we can date that play to 1995: the tournament being referred to was the 1996 championship, which was held in England. [*BQ*]

The Famine Although there were numerous famines in Ireland, right up to the end of the nineteenth century, the phrase 'famine times' in *Lonesome West* refers to the Great Famine of 1845 to (approximately) 1849. In that famine, roughly one million Irish people died of starvation, while another million emigrated, mostly to Britain and north America. The famine was caused (in part) by over-dependence on the potato crop, which failed due to blight over several years. There is a strong sense in which Irish culture has subsequently been 'haunted' by the famine. [*SC, LW*]

Fantasy Island   An American television show, which aired in the late 1970s and early 1980s, in which people could travel to a mysterious Pacific island to live out their fantasies, usually for a price. [*IB*]

Flaherty, Robert (1884–1951)   An American filmmaker who pioneered the development of the documentary form in films such as *Nanook of the North* (1922) and *Man of Aran* (1934). [*CI*]

Freeman's Catalogue   Freeman's is a UK-based company that sold clothes and jewellery by mail order. Customers would choose their products from a catalogue, which was also usually distributed by post. Given Leenane's isolation, this is one of easiest ways for Girleen to 'buy a few nice things' in *Lonesome West*. [*LW*]

Freud, Sigmund (1856–1939)   Austrian founder of psychoanalysis. [*SS*]

Frosties   A breakfast cereal produced by Kellogg's. [*LI*]

Gandhi, Mohandas Karamchand (1869–1948)   The leader of the Indian movement for independence from Britain. Due to his commitment to non-violent civil disobedience, his name is a byword for peaceful activism, and is used as such in *In Bruges*. [*IB*]

Gaye, Marvin (1939–1984)   American soul singer, whose best-known album is probably *What's Going On* (1971). He was shot dead by his father (also called Marvin) in 1984 in a domestic altercation. [*SS*]

The Guildford Four   This quartet, wrongfully convicted of terrorist activities and membership of the IRA, spent fourteen years in British prisons before they were exonerated. Their story was recounted in Jim Sheridan's *In the Name of the Father* (1993). See also the BIRMINGHAM SIX. [*LI*]

Guinness   A famous Irish stout. [*LW*]

Hello!   A magazine that features photo-essays about the domestic lives and weddings of celebrities and (in its English edition) members of the British royal family. [*IB*]

Hendrix, Jimi (1942–70)   American musician, and possibly the greatest electric guitarist who ever lived. It was stated after his death that he had asphyxiated on his own vomit, but that autopsy ruling was later thrown into some doubt. [*SC*]

Hill Street Blues An American television drama about a fictitious police precinct. It aired during the 1980s, and can be seen as a precursor of the grittier and more realistic police dramas that emerged from the late 1990s onwards, such as HBO's *The Wire*. [*SC, LW*]

Honey Nut Loops A breakfast cereal, produced by Kellogg's. Since 2008, they have been known only as 'Honey Loops'. [*LW*]

House of Elliot A BBC television series broadcast during the early 1990s. [*LI*]

INLA The Irish National Liberation Army, a small Republican paramilitary group established in 1975. Like the IRA, their aim was to force the British Army to leave Northern Ireland, and to reunify the island. The group was responsible for many brutal murders, including the killing of AIREY NEAVE. It was also noted for having had a number of internal feuds that led members to kill each other (hence McDonagh's frequent jokes about splinter groups in *Lieutenant*). [*LI*]

IRA The Irish Republican Army. The main Republican paramilitary group during the Northern Irish Troubles, their aim was to force the British army to withdraw from Ulster. They were responsible for many shootings and bombings, not just in Northern Ireland but also in Britain and mainland Europe. Central to their activities was the use of military language to explain and justify their actions. Hence, they referred to their terrorist campaign as an 'armed struggle' and stated that many of their victims were 'valid targets'. Since the Good Friday Agreement of 1998, the IRA has been largely (but not entirely) inactive. During the Troubles, the IRA was responsible for the deaths of almost 1,800 people. [*LI*]

The Judgement of Cambyses A painting by Gerard David, still on display in Bruges. It depicts the flaying alive of a man who accepted a bribe. [*IB*]

Kennedy, John F. (Jack) (1917–63) The thirty-fifth President of the United States, infamously assassinated in 1963. He had strong ancestral ties to Ireland, where he was regarded as a hero. He visited Ireland a few months before his death. He was reputed to have had many affairs during his married life, which may explain why Maureen in *Beauty Queen* praises his brother Bobby (below) for being kinder to women. [*BQ, SC*]

Kennedy, Robert (1925–68)   Brother of JFK, he was assassinated in 1968 while seeking the Democratic Party's nomination for President. [*BQ, SC*]

Ker-Plunk   A children's board game. Players pull straws from a plastic container, upon which a number of marbles rest. Each time a straw is removed, there is a possibility that one of the marbles may fall (creating the 'ker-plunk' noise). The winner is the player who lets the fewest marbles fall. [*LW*]

Kimberley biscuits   An Irish biscuit, manufactured by Jacobs. [*BQ*]

King, Colman 'Tiger'   The 'actor' who played 'Man of Aran' in ROBERT FLAHERTY's documentary of the same name. He is described in *Cripple* as ugly, but in fact was admired for his good looks by many fans of Flaherty's film. [*CI*]

Leaving Certificate   Final exam for post-primary students in Ireland, usually taken when students are aged seventeen or eighteen. [*SC*]

Lennon, John (1940–80)   A member of the Beatles, he was assassinated outside his New York home in 1980 (hence Ray's decision to blame American tourists for Lennon's death). [*IB*]

Majors, Lee   An American actor, born in 1939, probably best known for his starring roles in the US TV shows *The Six Million Dollar Man* (from the mid-1970s) and *The Fall Guy* (from the early 1980s). [*BS*]

Manchester United   One of the world's most famous football clubs, known informally as 'Man Utd'. Their 'away shirt' was the strip they used to play in matches away from home. Assuming that *Skull* is set in 1995, the away strip would probably have been a black jersey with gold trimming, with the word 'Sharp Viewcam' written across the chest (promoting the club's sponsors at that time). [*SC*]

Marx, Karl (1818–83)   Author of *Capital* and co-author of *The Communist Manifesto*. Some strands of Irish Republicanism are sympathetic to Marxist ideals. [*LI*]

McCartney, Paul (1942–)   One of the four Beatles. As is alluded to in *Lieutenant*, he was arrested in Japan for drug possession in 1980. [*LI*]

McMillan and Wife   An American crime drama, broadcast in the early 1970s. It featured Rock Hudson and Susan Saint James as a married couple who solved crimes together. [*SC*]

Mikado biscuits   Another Irish brand of biscuits, manufactured by Jacobs. [*SC*]

Milligan, Spike (1918–2002)   Comedian, author and broadcaster. He became an Irish citizen in 1962, but lived and worked in the UK for most of his life. He suffered from bipolar disorder, and was hospitalised on many occasions for depression and nervous breakdown. [*BQ*]

Murphy, Delia (1902–71)   A singer who collected and recorded many Irish folk songs, including 'THE SPINNING WHEEL'. [*BQ*]

Neave, Airey   Killed by an INLA car-bomb at Westminster in March 1979, Neave was Margaret Thatcher's Shadow Secretary of State for Northern Ireland at the time of his death. [*LI*]

O'Hara, Maureen   Irish film actress, born in 1920, and probably best known for starring alongside JOHN WAYNE in John Ford's 1952 movie THE QUIET MAN. [*SC*]

Omniplex   A cinema in Galway. [*LI*]

Paella   A Spanish food dish with chicken, seafood, rice and vegetables. The fact that Johnnypateenmike can afford such ingredients suggests that he is not quite as badly off as he makes out. [*CI*]

'Patriot Game'   An Irish rebel song, composed by DOMINIC BEHAN. Like 'THE DYING REBEL', the song concerns a young man who dies as a member of the IRA. [*LI*]

Petrocelli   An American legal drama, broadcast in the mid-1970s. [*SC*]

The Pied Piper of Hamelin   A German folk legend, collected by the Brothers Grimm, among others. The story goes that the Piper went to Hamelin, promising to rid the town of a plague of rats in return for a fee. The piper lured the rats away from Hamelin by playing music, and leading them to a nearby river where they all drowned. Afterwards, the people of Hamelin refused to pay him, so he lured their children away in revenge, again using his pipe. There are different versions of the end of the story, but in some, a lame boy is left behind because he is unable to follow the other children. [*PM*]

Powell, Robert   An English actor, probably best known for playing the title role in the 1977 TV serial *Jesus of Nazareth*. [*IB*]

Pringles   A brand of crisps, usually sold in a tall cylindrical tube. As the Kid implies in *Six Shooter*, they would be regarded as 'fancy crisps', at least when compared with TAYTOS. [*SS*]

The Quiet Man   A 1952 John Ford film, starring JOHN WAYNE and MAUREEN O'HARA. It involves the return to Ireland of an American (Wayne) who falls in love with a feisty Irish colleen. Their courtship and marriage can be seen as a variation on *The Taming of the Shrew*. The film has often been criticised for its stereotyping of the Irish, but it remains a popular feature of the west of Ireland tourist trade [*SC*]

Quincy   American crime drama about a medical investigator. It ran in the US during the late 1970s and early 1980s. [*SC*]

R2D2   A robot that featured in the STAR WARS films. The robot was operated by the dwarf actor Kenny Baker. [*IB*]

Ripples   Another brand of crisp, with ridged edges. [*SS*]

Sheba   A cat food. [*LI*]

Sons and Daughters   An Australian soap opera. Given its appearance in *Beauty Queen*, there is another obvious contrast between the idealised Australian presentation of the relationship between children and parents and McDonagh's version of the same theme. [*BQ*]

Spiderman   A superhero whose adventures are serialised by Marvel Comics. One of his most dangerous enemies is Doctor Octopus, an evil scientist who moves around on four metallic legs that resemble the tentacles of an octopus. [*LW*]

'The Spinning Wheel'   A traditional Irish song, recorded by DELIA MURPHY, in which a young girl living in rural Ireland seeks to deceive her grandmother so that she can be with her lover. [*BQ*]

St Martin   In *Lonesome West*, Valene refers to St Martin de Porres, a sixteenth-century Peruvian saint who is often represented in statues as being black. Valene has chosen the saint not for what he did but because having two 'darkie' saints on either end of his collection 'balances out symmetrical'. St Martin was famed for his work with and on behalf of the poor. Among the miracles attributed to him was the power of levitation – something that places the brothers' discussion about 'levitating darkies' in an interesting context. [*LW*]

Star Wars   A series of movies directed by George Lucas. The first *Star Wars* trilogy (1977–83) featured the characters Han Solo, Luke Skywalker, Chewie (also known as Chewbacca) and Princess Leia, all of whom are mentioned in *Skull in Connemara*. See also YODA and R2-D2. [*SC*]

Starsky and Hutch   American TV show about two cops. Among the show's most distinctive features was the pair's bright red car, which featured a white speed line down its side. [*SC*]

Steiger, Rod (1925–2002)   An American actor, well known for such films as *On the Waterfront* (1954), *Doctor Zhivago* (1965) and *In the Heat of the Night* (1967). He won an Academy Award for his performance in the last of these. [*SS*]

The Sullivans   Probably more of a drama than a soap opera, *The Sullivans* was yet another Australian import to British and Irish television. It focused on the life of a family during the Second World War, its treatment of domestic relationships at a time of crisis acting as another contrast with the situation of *Beauty Queen*. [*BQ*]

Swingball   A game in which a tennis ball is tied to a long pole by an elastic string. One player hits the ball to another using a racket, and the ball should 'swing' back to the original player on the elastic string. [*BQ*]

Take a Break   A women's magazine, imported into Ireland from the UK. It is rather similar in content to WOMAN'S OWN, though it occasionally adopts a somewhat lighter tone. [*LW*]

Tayto crisps   A popular and inexpensive Irish brand of crisps. [*BQ, LW, SS*]

Tech   Short for 'technical college'. Traditionally, these were post-primary schools that prepared students for a trade rather than a profession or university, though the distinction no longer applies. [*LI, LW*]

Time Bandits   A 1981 movie directed by Terry Gilliam, about a young boy who travels through time with a group of dwarves. [*IB*]

Tinkers   Now considered a derogatory term for Irish travellers. The travellers are a nomadic people who live in Ireland. [*SC*]

Top of the Pops   A weekly BBC television series, broadcast until 2006. It involved a countdown of the best-selling pop singles – a slightly different kind of 'hit-list' to the one that Padraic and Mairead have in mind in *Lieutenant*. The irony here is that the two characters are referring to a programme that is British rather than Irish. [*LI*]

Tottenham   Tottenham Hotspur – a British football team, based in London. As Ray implies in *In Bruges*, they have tended to be only moderately successful in recent years. In the 2007/8 season (when *In Bruges* was released) they finished eleventh out of twenty teams in the English Premier League – not shit, but 'not all that great either' as Ray puts it. [*IB*]

Villechaize, Hervé (1943–93)   Actor who was a dwarf. As Ray states, he starred in FANTASY ISLAND, and is also well known for playing the role of Nick Nack in several James Bond films. He committed suicide in 1993. [*IB*]

Vol-au-vent   A small pie, made with a pastry casing and a hollow centre that is usually filled with meat or fish. The term is taken from the French, and literally means 'flight in the wind'. Because of their small size, vol-au-vents are often used as appetisers or snacks on semi-formal occasions. [*LW*]

Waco   A city in Texas, notorious due to a stand-off between the FBI and members of the Branch Davidian sect in 1993. Seventy-four people died when the group's compound was set on fire. [*BS*]

Wagon Wheels   A chunky chocolate biscuit. [*BQ*]

Wayne, John (1907–79)   American actor, famous for having appeared in numerous Westerns, and probably best known in Ireland for his role in THE QUIET MAN [*SC*]

West, Fred and Rosemary   An English couple who abused and murdered at least a dozen young girls (including one of their own daughters) from the period 1967 until their arrest in 1994. [*SS*]

Wine gums   Soft, jelly-like sweets. [*BQ*]

Woman's Own   A British women's magazine. [*LW*]

X-Men   A comic book published by Marvel Comics since 1963, focusing on a band of super-powered teenagers who are rejected by their society for being 'mutants'. [*LI*]

Yoda   A character in the STAR WARS franchise of movies, Yoda is short, green and approximately 900 years old. Despite his appearance, he is a formidable warrior. [*BS*]

FURTHER READING

The list below is divided into various categories, starting with original scripts by McDonagh himself. I have included sections for the individual plays (where there have been articles specifically dedicated to them), but the bulk of scholarship about McDonagh tends to focus on his entire *oeuvre*. There are also references to newspaper articles and interviews, many of which are still available online. Any other texts mentioned in this book are listed in the 'texts cited' section at the end. Some of the information provided below is taken from the *MLA International Bibliography*; I have also made some use of the Lexis-Nexis database for publication details of newspaper articles.

Plays and scripts by Martin McDonagh

The Beauty Queen of Leenane (London: Methuen Drama, 1996).
A Skull in Connemara (London: Methuen Drama, 1997).
The Lonesome West (London: Methuen Drama, 1997).
The Cripple of Inishmaan (London: Methuen Drama, 1997).
Martin McDonagh Plays: One (London: Methuen Drama, 1999).
The Lieutenant of Inishmore (London: Methuen Drama, 2001).
The Pillowman (London: Faber, 2003).
In Bruges (London: Faber, 2007).
A Behanding in Spokane (New York: Dramatists Play Service, 2011).

McDonagh: general profiles and criticism

Cadden, Michael, 'Violence, Storytelling, and Irish Aesthetics: A Theatergoer's Guide to Martin McDonagh', *Princeton University Library Chronicle*, 68 (Autumn 2006): 1–2 (Winter 2007): 671–83.
Chambers, Lilian, and Eamonn Jordan (eds), *A World of Savage Stories: The Theatre of Martin McDonagh* (Dublin: Carysfort Press, 2006).
Dean, Joan FitzPatrick, 'Martin McDonagh's Stagecraft', in Richard Rankin Russell (ed.), *Martin McDonagh: A Casebook* (London: Routledge, 2007): 25–40.

Doyle, Maria, 'Breaking Bodies: The Presence of Violence on Martin McDonagh's Stage', in Richard Rankin Russell (ed.), *Martin McDonagh: A Casebook* (London: Routledge, 2007): 92–110.

Eldred, Laura, 'Martin McDonagh and the Contemporary Gothic', in Richard Rankin Russell (ed.), *Martin McDonagh: A Casebook* (London: Routledge, 2007).

Feeney, Joseph, 'Martin McDonagh: Dramatist of the West', *Studies: An Irish Quarterly Review*, 87, 345 (Spring 1998): 24–32.

Grene, Nicholas, 'Black Pastoral: 1990s Images of Ireland', in Martin Procházka (ed.), *After History* (Prague: Litteraria Pragensia, 2006): 243–55.

Jordan, Eamonn, 'The Native Quarter:The Hyphenated-Real: The Drama of Martin McDonagh', in Ciarin Ross (ed.), *Sub-Versions: Trans-National Readings of Modern Irish Literature* (Amsterdam, Netherlands: Rodopi, 2010): 219–42.

Lanters, José, 'The Identity Politics of Martin McDonagh', in Richard Rankin Russell (ed.), *Martin McDonagh: A Casebook* (London: Routledge, 2007): 9–24.

Lonergan, Patrick. '"The Laughter Will Come of Itself. The Tears Are Inevitable": Martin McDonagh, Globalization, and Irish Theatre Criticism', *Modern Drama*, 47, 4 (Winter 2004): 636–58.

Lyons, Paddy, 'The Montage of Semblance: Martin McDonagh's Dramaturgy', in Paddy Lyons and Alison O'Malley-Younger (eds), *No Country for Old Men: Fresh Perspectives on Irish Literature* (Oxford: Peter Lang, 2009).

Merriman, Vic, 'Staging Contemporary Ireland: Heartsickness and Hopes Deferred', in Shaun Richards (ed.), *The Cambridge Companion to Twentieth-Century Irish Drama* (Cambridge University Press, 2004): 244–257.

Merriman, Victor, 'Theatre of Tiger Trash', *Irish University Review*, 29, 2 (1999): 305–17.

Mikami, Hiroko, 'Not Lost in Translation: Martin McDonagh in Japan', *Waseda University Research Papers*, http://dspace.wul.waseda.ac.jp/dspace/bitstream/2065/26868/1/003.pdf.

Peters, Susanne, 'The Anglo-Irish Playwright Martin McDonagh: Postmodernist Zeitgeist as Cliché and a (Re)Turn to the Voice of Common Sense', in Klaus Stierstorfer (ed.), *Beyond Postmodernism: Reassessments in Literature, Theory, and Culture* (Berlin: de Gruyter, 2003): 291–302.

Pilný, Ondrej, 'Martin McDonagh: Parody? Satire? Complacency?', *Irish Studies Review*, 12, 2 (August 2004): 225–32.

Rees, Catherine, 'How to Stage Globalisation? Martin McDonagh: An Irishman on TV', *Contemporary Theatre Review: An International Journal*, 16, 1 (February 2006): 114–22.

Rennhak, Katharina, 'Moving Beyond Irish (Post)Colonialism by Commodifying (Post)Colonial Stage Irishness: Martin McDonagh's Plays as Global Commodities', in Rainer Emig et al. (eds), *Commodifying (Post)Colonialism: Othering, Reification, Commodification and the New Literatures and Cultures in English* (Amsterdam, Netherlands: Rodopi, 2010): 161–76.

Russell, Richard Rankin, (ed.), *Martin McDonagh: A Casebook* (London: Routledge, 2007).

Sierz, Aleks, 'Martin McDonagh', www.inyerface-theatre.com

Sierz, Aleks, *In-Yer-Face Theatre: British Drama Today* (London: Faber, 2001).

Wall, Eamonn. 'A Wild West Show: The Plays of Martin McDonagh', in *Writing the Irish West: Ecologies and Traditions* (Notre Dame, IN: University of Notre Dame Press, 2011): 113–38.

Wallace, Clare, 'Pastiche Soup, Bad Taste, Biting Irony and Martin McDonagh', *Litteraria Pragensia: Studies in Literature and Culture*, 15, 29 (2005): 3–38.

The Beauty Queen of Leenane

Boles, William C., 'Violence at the Royal Court: Martin McDonagh's *The Beauty Queen of Leenane* and Mark Ravenhill's *Shopping and Fucking*', *Theatre Symposium: A Journal of the Southeastern Theatre Conference*, 7 (1999): 125–35.

Castleberry, Marion, 'Comedy and Violence in *The Beauty Queen of Leenane*', in Richard Rankin Russell (ed.), *Martin McDonagh: A Casebook* (London: Routledge, 2007): 41–59.

Diehl, Heath A., 'Classic Realism, Irish Nationalism and a New Breed of Angry Young Man in Martin McDonagh's *The Beauty Queen of Leenane*', *Journal of the Midwest Modern Language Association*, 34, 2 (Spring 2001): 98–117.

Husband, Andrew, 'The Environment of the Moment: Non-Places in Martin McDonagh's *The Beauty Queen of Leenane*', *Texas Theatre Journal*, 6, 1 (January 2010): 1–13.

Klein, Hildegard, 'Matricide-Violating the Sacred Mother–Daughter Bond in *The Beauty Queen of Leenane*', *Gender Studies*, 1, 8 (2008): 139–49.

Morrison, Christopher S., 'Bread and Butter to Boiling Oil: From Wilde's Afternoon Tea to *The Beauty Queen of Leenane*', *New Hibernia Review/Iris Éireannach Nua: A Quarterly Record of Irish Studies*, 14, 3 (Autumn 2010): 106–20.

The Leenane Trilogy

Andrews, Charles, 'National Tragedy as Religion in Martin McDonagh's *Leenane Trilogy*'. *Journal of Religion and Theatre*, 5, 2 (Fall 2006): 136–43.

Lachman, Michal, 'From Both Sides of the Irish Sea': The Grotesque, Parody, and Satire in Martin McDonagh's *The Leenane Trilogy*'. *Hungarian Journal of English and American Studies*, 10: 1–2 (Spring–Fall 2004): 61–73.

Pocock, Stephanie, '"The 'Ineffectual Father Welsh/Walsh"?, Anti-Catholicism and Catholicism in Martin McDonagh's *The Leenane Trilogy*', in Richard Rankin Russell (ed.), *Martin McDonagh: A Casebook* (London: Routledge, 2007).

Vandevelde, Karen, 'Postmodern Theatricality in the Dutch/Flemish Adaptation of Martin McDonagh's *The Leenane Trilogy*', in Richard Rankin Russell (ed.), *Martin McDonagh: A Casebook* (London: Routledge, 2007): 77–91.

The Cripple of Inishmaan

Connor, David J., 'He Swaggers: Reflections on the Title Character in *The Cripple of Inishmaan*', *Disability Studies Quarterly*, 29, 1 (Winter 2009).

McGonigle, Lisa, 'Keeping It Reel: Hollywood and Authenticity in Two Recent Irish Plays', in Shane Alcobia-Murphy (ed.), *What Rough Beasts?: Irish and Scottish Studies in the New Millennium* (Newcastle upon Tyne: Cambridge Scholars, 2008): 153–66.

Meszaros, M. Beth, 'Enlightened by Our Afflictions: Portrayals of Disability in the Comic Theatre of Beth Henley and Martin McDonagh', *Disability Studies Quarterly*, 23 (Summer–Fall 2003): 3–4.

O'Brien, Karen, ' "Ireland Mustn't Be Such a Bad Place So": Mapping the "Real" Terrain of the Aran Islands', *Journal of Dramatic Theory and Criticism*, 20, 2 (Spring 2006): 169–83.

Roberts, Robin, 'Gendered Media Rivalry: Irish Drama and American Film', *Australasian Drama Studies*, 43 (October 2003): 108–27.

The Lieutenant of Inishmore

Jordan, Eamonn, 'Martin McDonagh's *The Lieutenant of Inishmore*: Commemoration and Dismemberment through Farce', *Hungarian Journal of English and American Studies*, 15, 2 (Fall 2009): 369–86.

Lonergan, Patrick, 'Too Dangerous to Be Done? Martin McDonagh's *Lieutenant of Inishmore*', *Irish Studies Review*, 13, 1 (February, 2005): 65–78.

Luckhurst, Mary, 'Martin McDonagh's *Lieutenant of Inishmore*: Selling (-Out) to the English', *Contemporary Theatre Review: An International Journal*, 14, 4 (November 2004): 34–41.

Molloy, Frank, 'Cats and Comedy: *The Lieutenant of Inishmore* Comes to Sydney', *ABEI Journal: The Brazilian Journal of Irish Studies*, 7 (June 2005): 75–82.

Rees, Catherine, 'The Good, the Bad, and the Ugly: The Politics of Morality in Martin McDonagh's *The Lieutenant of Inishmore*', *New Theatre Quarterly*, 21, 1 (February 2005): 28–33.

Wilcock, Mike, 'Put to Silence': Murder, Madness, and "Moral Neutrality" in Shakespeare's *Titus Andronicus* and Martin McDonagh's *The Lieutenant of Inishmore*', *Irish University Review: A Journal of Irish Studies*, 38, 2 (Autumn–Winter 2008): 325–69.

The Pillowman

Cliff, Brian, '*The Pillowman*: A New Story to Tell', in Richard Rankin Russell (ed.), *Martin McDonagh: A Casebook* (London: Routledge, 2007): 131–48.

Huber, Werner, 'From Leenane to Kamenice: The De-Hibernicising of Martin McDonagh?', in Christopher Houswitsch (ed.), *Literary Views on Post-Wall Europe: Essays in Honour of Uwe Boker* (Trier: WVT): 283–94.

Jordan, Eamonn, 'The Fallacies of Cultural Narratives, Re-Enactment, Legacy, and Agency in Arthur Miller's *Death of a Salesman* and Martin McDonagh's *The Pillowman*', *Hungarian Journal of English and American Studies*, 11, 2 (Fall 2005): 45–62.

Worthen, Hana, and W.B. Worthen, '*The Pillowman* and the Ethics of Allegory', *Modern Drama*, 49, 2 (Summer 2006): 155–73.

In Bruges

Dean, Joan F., 'Review of *In Bruges*', *Estudios Irlandeses*, 4 (2009): 166–9.

Norman, Lance, '"It Is a Bit Over-Elaborate"; or Dumb Waiters, Dead Children and Martinizing the Pinteresque', in Craig N. Owens (ed.), *Pinter Et Cetera* (Newcastle upon Tyne: Cambridge Scholars, 2009): 139–58.

Newspaper profiles, reviews and interviews

Als, Hilton, 'Underhanded: Martin McDonagh's Slap in the Face', *New Yorker* (5 March 2010).

Barth, Diana, 'Maeliosa's Malevolent Turn', *Irish Voice* (11 May 1999): 26.

Billington, Michael, 'Excessive Talent for Plundering Irish Past', *Guardian* (10 August 1997): 26.

Caesar, Ed, 'Hard Acts to Follow', *Sunday Times* (6 April 2008): *Culture*, 8.

Clapp, Susannah, 'Pack Up Your Troubles', *Observer* (30 November 2003), www.guardian.co.uk/stage/2003/nov/30/theatre.turkey.

Crawley, Peter, 'Thicker than Water', *Irish Times* (25 September 2003): *The Ticket*, 2–3.

Danaher, Patricia, 'Bored to Death', *Sunday Times* (10 February 2008): *Culture*, 4.

Dening, Penelope, 'The Scribe of Kilburn', *Irish Times* (18 April 2001): 12.

Dening, Penelope, 'The Wordsmith of Camberwell', *Irish Times* (8 July 1997): 12.

Hoggard, Liz, 'Playboy of the West End World', *Independent* (15 June 2002).

Hopkin, Philip, 'The Queen of Broadway is Back!', *Irish Voice* (4 May 1999).

Lacey, Liam, 'He Didn't Want to Make a "Playwright's Movie"', *Globe and Mail* (8 February 2008).

Lahr, John. 'Blood Simple', *New Yorker* (13 March 2006): 92–4.

Lawson, Mark, 'Sick-buckets Needed in the Stalls', *Guardian* (28 April 2001).

Mac Dubhghaill, Uinsionn, 'Drama Sails to Seven Islands', *Irish Times* (27 November 1996).

McBride, Charlie, 'Martin McDonagh: Back to Where it All Started,' *Galway Advertiser* (11 September 2008).

NBC News Transcripts, 'Playwright Martin McDonagh Takes Broadway by Storm', *Today Show* (16 April 1998).

O'Hagan, Sean, 'The Wild West', *Guardian* (24 March 2001).

O'Toole, Fintan, 'A Mind in Connemara: The Savage World of Martin McDonagh', *New Yorker* (6 March 2006): 40–7.

O'Toole, Fintan, 'Martin McDonagh is Famous for Telling Sean Connery to F*** Off. He Also Happens to be a Brilliant Playwright', *Guardian* (2 December 1996): T11.

O'Toole, Fintan, 'Nowhere Man', *Irish Times* (26 April 1997): *Weekend*, 1–2.

Rosenthal, Daniel, 'How to Slay 'Em in the Isles', *Independent* (11 April 2001).

Ross, Michael, 'Hynes Means Business', *Sunday Times* (18 May 2003).

Ross, Michael, 'Dawn Bradfield is Rising Once Again as the Star of *Jane Eyre*', *Sunday Times* (23 November 2003).

Spencer, Charles, 'Devastating Masterpiece of Black Comedy', *Daily Telegraph* (28 June 2002): 13.

Taylor, Paul, 'Review: *The Pillowman* at the Cottesloe Theatre, NT, London', *Independent* (17 November, 2003): *Features*, 16.

Ward, David, 'RSC Fires off Warning Shot to Patrons', *Guardian* (7 April 2001).

McDonagh and Irish drama/Irish dramatists

Grene, Nicholas, 'Ireland in Two Minds: Martin McDonagh and Conor McPherson', *Yearbook of English Studies*, 35 (2005): 298-311.

Harris, Peter James, 'Sex and Violence: The Shift from Synge to McDonagh', *Hungarian Journal of English and American Studies*, 10:1–2 (Spring–Fall 2004): 51–9.

Kryzaniak, Dagmara, 'A Disrupted Family in a Troubled Country: A Sociolinguistic Insight into the Domestic/National Crises in the Works of Two Irish Playwrights: Sean O'Casey and Martin McDonagh', in Liliana Sikorska (ed.), *Ironies of Art/ Tragedies of Life* (Frankfurt: Peter Lang, 2005): 195–212.

Lanters, José, 'Playwrights of the Western World: Synge, Murphy, McDonagh', in Stephen Watt et al. (eds), *A Century of Irish Drama: Widening the Stage* (Bloomington, IN: Indiana University Press, 2000): 204–22.

Richards, Shaun, 'The Outpouring of a Morbid, Unhealthy Mind: The Critical Condition of Synge and McDonagh', *Irish University Review: A Journal of Irish Studies*, 33, 1 (Spring–Summer 2003): 201–14.

Roche, Anthony, 'Re-working the Workhouse Ward: McDonagh, Beckett, and Gregory', *Irish University Review: A Journal of Irish Studies*, 34, 1 (Spring–Summer 2004): 171–84.

General studies of contemporary Irish drama

Grene, Nicholas, *The Politics of Irish Drama* (Cambridge: Cambridge University Press, 1999).

Hynes, Jerome (ed.), *Druid: The First Ten Years* (Galway: Druid Performing Arts and the Galway Arts Festival, 1985).

Lonergan, Patrick, *Theatre and Globalization: Irish Drama in the Celtic Tiger Era* (Basingstoke: Palgrave, 2009).

Maguire, Tom, *Making Theatre in Northern Ireland: Through and Beyond the Troubles* (Exeter: University of Exeter Press, 2006).

Morash, Christopher, *A History of Irish Theatre* (Cambridge: Cambridge University Press, 2001).

Pilkington, Lionel, *Theatre and Ireland* (Basingstoke: Palgrave, 2010).

Pilkington, Lionel, *Theatre and the State in Twentieth-Century Ireland* (London: Routledge, 2001).

Richards, Shaun, *The Cambridge Companion to Modern Irish Drama* (Cambridge: Cambridge University Press, 2004).

Roche, Anthony, *Contemporary Irish Drama* (Basingstoke: Palgrave, 2009).

Singleton, Brian, *Masculinities and the Contemporary Irish Theatre* (London: Palgrave Macmillan, 2011).

Useful websites

A Hiberno-English Archive: www.hiberno-english.com

CAIN Web Service: Conflict and Politics in Northern Ireland since 1968: http://cain.ulst.ac.uk

Druid Theatre (includes information about original productions of *The Leenane Trilogy*): www.druid.ie

The Irish Playography (production details of every Irish play produced since 2004): www.irishplayography.com

Books about Hiberno-English

Dolan, T.P., *A Dictionary of Hiberno-English* (Dublin: Gill and Macmillan, 2006).

Joyce, P.W., *English as We Speak It in Ireland* (1911).

Share, Bernard, *Slanguage: A Dictionary of Irish Slang and Colloquial English in Ireland*, third edn (Dublin: Gill and Macmillan, 2008).

Other texts cited

Baudrillard, Jean, *Simulacra and Simulation*, trans. Sheila Faria Glaser (Ann Arbor: University of Michigan, 1994).

Beckett, Samuel, *Complete Dramatic Works* (London: Faber, 2006).

Bradley, Anthony, and Maryann Gialanella Valiulis (eds), *Gender and Sexuality in Modern Ireland* (Amherst: University of Massachusetts Press, 1997).

Buell, Lawrence, *The Environmental Imagination: Thoreau, Nature Writing, and the Formation of American Culture* (Cambridge, MA: Belknap Press of Harvard University Press, 1995).

Buell, Lawrence, *The Future of Environmental Criticism: Environmental Crisis and Literary Imagination* (Malden, MA, and Oxford: Blackwell, 2005).

Chaudhuri, Una, '"There Must Be a Lot of Fish in that Lake": Toward an Ecological Theater', *Theatre*, 25, 1 (Spring/Summer 1994): 23–31.

Clark, Timothy, *The Cambridge Introduction to Literature and the Environment* (Cambridge: Cambridge University Press, 2011).

Cless, Downing, *Ecology and Environment in European Drama* (New York: Routledge, 2010).

Constable, Catherine, 'Postmodernism and Film', in *The Cambridge Companion to Postmodernism*, ed. Stephen Connor (Cambridge: Cambridge University Press, 2004): 43–61.

Deane, Seamus, *Civilians and Barbarians: Field Day Pamphlet*, no. 3. reprinted in *Ireland's Field Day* (Derry: Field Day Theatre, 1985).

English, Richard, *Armed Struggle: The History of the IRA* (Basingstoke: Macmillan, 2003).

Frazier, Adrian, *Behind the Scenes: Yeats, Horniman, and the Struggle for the Abbey Theatre* (Berkeley: University of California Press, 1990).

Garrard, Greg, *Ecocriticism* (London: Routledge, 2004).

Gibson, Andrew, 'Afterword' in Sean Kennedy (ed.), *Beckett and Ireland* (Cambridge: Cambridge University Press, 2010).

Glotfelty, Cheryl, 'Introduction: Literary Studies in an Age of Environmental Crisis', *The Ecocriticism Reader: Landmarks in Literary Ecology*, eds Cheryl Glotfelty and Harold Fromm (Athens: University of Georgia Press, 1996): xv–xxxvii.

Harris, Susan Cannon, *Gender in Modern Irish Drama* (Bloomington: Indiana University Press, 2002).

Hassan, Ihab, *The Postmodern Turn: Essays in Postmodern Theory and Culture* (Columbus: Ohio State University Press, 1987).

Heinlein, Kurt, *Green Theatre: Promoting Ecological Preservation and Advancing the Sustainability of Humanity and Nature* (Saarbrücken: VDM Verlag Dr. Mueller E.K., 2007).

Hewes, Henry, 'Probing Pinter's Play', *Saturday Review* (8 April 1967): 56.

Hutcheon, Linda, 'Irony, Nostalgia, and the Postmodern', University of Toronto English Library (19 January, 1998): 12 (www.library.utoronto.ca/utel/criticism/hutchinp.html).

Jameson, Fredric, 'Foreword', in Lyotard, *The Postmodern Condition*: vii–xxi.

Keohane, Kieran, and Carmen Kuhling, *Collision Culture: Transformations in Everyday Life in Ireland* (Dublin: Liffey Press, 2004).

Kershaw, Baz, *The Radical in Performance: Between Brecht and Baudrillard* (London: Routledge, 1999).

Kershaw, Baz, 'Eco-activitst Performance: The Environment as Partner in Protest', *TDR* 46, 1 (Spring 2002): 118–30.

Kiberd, Declan, *Inventing Ireland: The Literature of the Modern Nation* (London: Vintage, 1997).

Kilian, Monika, *Modern and Postmodern Strategies. Gaming and the Question of Morality: Adorno, Rorty, Lyotard, and Enzensberger* (New York: Peter Lang, 1998).

Lyotard, Jean-François. *The Postmodern Condition: A Report on Knowledge*, trans. Geoff Bennington and Brian Massumi (Minneapolis: University of Minnesota Press, 1984).

Magee, Patrick, *Gangsters or Guerillas? Representations of Irish Republicans in 'Troubles Fiction'* (Belfast: Beyond the Pale, 2001).

Maloney, Ed, *The Secret History of the IRA* (London: Allen Lane, 2002).

May, Theresa J., 'Beyond Bambi: Toward a Dangerous Ecocriticsm in Theatre Studies', *Theatre Topics*, 17, 2 (September 2007): 95–110.

McKelly, James C., 'The Double Truth, Ruth: *Do the Right Thing* and the Culture of Ambiguity', *African American Review*, 32, 2 (1998): 215–27.

Mullen, Pat, *The Man of Aran* (Cambridge, MA: MIT Press, 1935).

Murphy, Patrick, *Further Afield in the Study of Nature-Oriented Literature* (Charlottesville: University of Virginia Press, 2000).

Negra, Diane (ed.), *The Irish in Us: Irishness, Performativity, and Popular Culture* (Durham, NC: Duke University Press, 2006).

O'Brien, Harvey, *The Real Ireland* (Manchester, Manchester University Press, 2004).

O'Connor, Barbara, 'Colleens and Comely Maidens: Representing and Performing Irish Femininity in the Nineteenth and Twentieth Centuries', *Ireland in Focus: Film, Photography and Popular Culture*, eds Eóin Flannery and Michael J. Griffin (Syracuse, NY: Syracuse University Press, 2009).

Pinter, Harold, *Plays, 1* (London: Faber, 1996).

Pinter, Harold, *Plays, 4* (London: Faber, 1998).

Rafter, Kevin, *Sinn Féin 1905–2005: In the Shadow of Gunmen* (Dublin: Gill and Macmillan, 2005).

Smyth, Gerry, 'Hippies, Liberals, and the Ecocritical Sublime', *Key Words: A Journal of Cultural Materialism*, 2 (1999): 94–110.

Synge, J.M., *Plays 2* (Gerrards Cross: Colin Smythe, 1982).

INDEX

Major discussions of topics are indicated in **bold type**. Plays and films are listed under the names of their authors or directors, except for McDonagh's, which are entered under their titles.

NOTES ON CONTRIBUTORS

Joan FitzPatrick Dean is Curators' Teaching Professor of English at the University of Missouri–Kansas City where she teaches dramatic literature and film. Her study of the film and play of Brian Friel's *Dancing at Lughnasa* was published by Cork University Press and the Irish Institute for Film in 2003, and her *Riot and Great Anger: Stage Censorship in Twentieth-Century Ireland* appeared in 2004. Recent publications have appeared in *New Hibernia Review, Irish University Review* and *Theatre Journal.*

Eamonn Jordan is Lecturer in Drama Studies at the School of English, Drama and Film, University College Dublin. His book *The Feast of Famine: The Plays of Frank McGuinness* (1997) is the first full-length study on McGuinness's work. In 2000, he edited *Theatre Stuff: Critical Essays on Contemporary Irish Theatre* and in 2006 co-edited with Lilian Chambers *The Theatre of Martin McDonagh: A World of Savage Stories* (2006). His *Dissident Dramaturgies: Contemporary Irish Theatre* was published in 2010.

José Lanters is Professor of English and Co-director of the Center for Celtic Studies at the University of Wisconsin–Milwaukee. From 2007 to 2009 she served as president of the American Conference for Irish Studies. She has published extensively on Irish drama and fiction, her most recent book being *The 'Tinkers' in Irish Literature: Unsettled Subjects and the Construction of Difference* (Irish Academic Press, 2008). Her current project deals with the theatre of Thomas Kilroy.

Karen O'Brien is David G. Frey Fellow Assistant Professor of Dramatic Art at University of North Carolina, Chapel Hill. Her publications include articles and reviews on Irish literature and theatre in '*Out of the Earth': Ecocritical Readings of Irish Texts, Journal of Dramatic Theory and Criticism, Theatre Research International* and *Theatre Journal.* She is currently working on a manuscript on the plays of Marina Carr and Conor McPherson.